"*The Incarnation of God* is a theological jugg.... dichotomous thinking about the person and work of Jesus Christ. Reclaiming grossly neglected biblical, patristic, and reformational teaching, Clark and Johnson reestablish the incarnation as the proper center and ground for all evangelical theology, and demonstrate with profundity and potency the tectonic implications of our Lord's assumption of human flesh."

> **Joel Scandrett**, Assistant Professor of Historical Theology and Director of the Robert E. Webber Center, Trinity School for Ministry

"Clark and Johnson clearly and eloquently lay out the significance of the incarnation as the centerpiece of Christian theology. Their fascinating reflections on the relation of the incarnation to other aspects of Christian faith introduce us to depths of truth that most Christians have never dreamed of, let alone explored. Their exposition grows out of the rich tradition of Christian reflection on the incarnation, and it is a joy to see my hero Athanasius and my late mentor T. F. Torrance figure so prominently in these pages. It is a pleasure to recommend this book."

> **Donald M. Fairbairn Jr.**, Robert E. Cooley Professor of Early Christianity, Gordon-Conwell Theological Seminary; author, *Life in the Trinity* and *Grace and Christology in the Early Church*

"Remedying a major deficiency in evangelical literature, this fine book on the incarnation informs readers of how the central apostolic confession—in Jesus of Nazareth, God has come among us as man—governs our understanding of every aspect of the Christian faith, informs every feature of our discipleship, and grounds pastoral comfort in the heart of God. The authors of this profound study highlight why the incarnation guarantees our salvation, acquaints us with the only Savior we can ever have, allows us to know God, enlivens our obedience, renders the church the bride of Christ, and, not least, informs Christians concerning the logic of God's intention for human sexuality."

> **Victor A. Shepherd**, Professor of Theology, Tyndale University College and Seminary; author, *Interpreting Martin Luther* and *The Nature and Function of Faith in the Theology of John Calvin*

"*The Incarnation of God* is an engrossing and stunningly well-conceived book. The theological significance of the great central miracle of Christian faith is laid forth with clarity and conviction. Reflecting an impressive range of research and timely apologetic concern, this is a book for thoughtful reading. I endorse it with enthusiasm."

> **Andrew Purves**, Jean and Nancy Davis Professor of Historical Theology, Pittsburgh Theological Seminary; author, *Reconstructing Pastoral Theology* and *The Crucifixion of Ministry*

"This tightly argued and comprehensive theology centered in the incarnation makes a fitting textbook for introductory theology courses. Clark and Johnson's incisive claims reflect the decisive importance of Jesus's incarnation for the Christian faith and life. The student not only will come away with a better grasp of the incarnation's significance, but also will be grasped more profoundly in holistic worship by the incarnate Lord through this compelling read."

Paul Louis Metzger, Professor of Christian Theology & Theology of Culture, Multnomah Biblical Seminary; coauthor, *Exploring Ecclesiology*; editor, *Trinitarian Soundings in Systematic Theology*

"Recent attention to the theme of the believer's union with Christ has stimulated renewed interest in the person of the Christ with whom Christians are united. In dialogue with the best of the Christian tradition and recent theology, Clark and Johnson explore the incarnation in ways that both academics and pastors will find helpful."

William B. Evans, Younts Professor of Bible and Religion, Erskine College; author, *Imputation and Impartation* and *What Is the Incarnation?*

THE INCARNATION *of* GOD

THE
INCARNATION
of GOD

✣

THE MYSTERY *of*
THE GOSPEL AS THE FOUNDATION
of EVANGELICAL THEOLOGY

✣

JOHN C. CLARK *AND*
MARCUS PETER JOHNSON

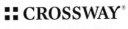
WHEATON, ILLINOIS

The Incarnation of God: The Mystery of the Gospel as the Foundation of Evangelical Theology

Copyright © 2015 by John C. Clark and Marcus Peter Johnson

Published by Crossway
    1300 Crescent Street
    Wheaton, Illinois 60187

Cover design: Studio Gearbox

Cover image: *"Flight into Egypt, Virgin Mary with Baby Jesus, and Joseph,"*
    supplied by Photos.com/Thinkstock
    "Antwerp-Deposition of the Cross by Josef Janssens,"
    supplied by Sedmak/Thinkstock

First printing 2015

Printed in the United States of America

Unless otherwise indicated, all Scripture quotations are from the ESV® Bible (The Holy Bible, English Standard Version®), copyright © 2001 by Crossway, a publishing ministry of Good News Publishers. 2011 Text Edition. Used by permission. All rights reserved.

Scripture references marked NIV are taken from The Holy Bible, New International Version®, NIV®. Copyright © 1973, 1978, 1984, 2011 by Biblica, Inc.™ Used by permission. All rights reserved worldwide.

All emphases in Scripture quotations have been added by the authors.

Trade paperback ISBN: 978-1-4335-4187-2
ePub ISBN: 978-1-4335-4190-2
PDF ISBN: 978-1-4335-4188-9
Mobipocket ISBN: 978-1-4335-4189-6

Library of Congress Cataloging-in-Publication Data
Clark, John C., 1970-
The incarnation of God : the mystery of the Gospel as the
foundation of Evangelical theology / John C. Clark and Marcus
Peter Johnson.
    pages cm
  Includes bibliographical references and index.
  ISBN 978-1-4335-4187-2 (tp)
1. Incarnation. 2. Incarnation—History of doctrines.
3. Evangelicalism. I. Johnson, Marcus Peter, 1971-   II. Title.
BT220.C585   2015
232'.1—dc23   2014027304

Crossway is a publishing ministry of Good News Publishers.

To our wives and children,
with immense affection
and gratitude

Contents

Preface

C. S. Lewis observed in 1941 that modern Christians are too easily pleased, that our desires, far from being too strong, are, in fact, too weak. "We are half-hearted creatures," he said. But do we not tend to be a restless and weary people, an aspiring and ambitious people, those who long for, and often lust after, a great many things? Yes! This illustrates Lewis's point, for he contended that our preoccupation with relative trivialities "when infinite joy is offered us" only punctuates our halfheartedness, showing us to be "like an ignorant child who wants to go on making mud pies in a slum because he cannot imagine what is meant by the offer of a holiday at the sea."[1] If this described Christians of Lewis's day, then all the more does it describe those of our own, when our sense of reality is skewed by media manipulation and our scope of vision is stunted by technological inundation. To Lewis's astute appraisal we thus add: the church's awareness of mystery and sense of wonder are presently in short supply.

This situation prompts another question, more basic and searching than the one above. What might prompt the church, Jesus Christ's holy bride, to do anything less than sing with full heart, full throat, and abiding, abounding wonder to him who is her infinite joy, to him who alone can both fortify and satisfy her desires? This book was born of the conviction that, at bottom, the modern church does not sufficiently see and savor the astounding mystery—the supreme mystery—at the very heart of our Christian confession: God the Son, without ceasing to be fully God, has become fully human. The eternal Word became flesh, entering our existence, the deepest ground of our being, to forevermore live his divine

---

[1] C. S. Lewis, *The Weight of Glory* (1949; repr., New York: HarperCollins, 2001), 26.

life in our human nature. This our Lord did to grant us a life-giving, life-transforming share in his communion with the Father through the Spirit, the glorious firstfruits of his reconciling all things in heaven and earth in himself (Eph. 1:10; Col. 1:20). The nineteenth-century Reformed church-man John Williamson Nevin thus exclaims:

> *"The Word became flesh!"* In this simple, but sublime enunciation, we have the whole gospel comprehended in a word. . . . The incarnation is the key that unlocks the sense of all God's revelations. It is the key that unlocks the sense of all God's works, and brings to light the true meaning of the universe. . . . The incarnation forms thus the great central fact of the world.[2]

Nevin's assessment is spot-on. God entered the world in and as the man Jesus Christ, such that the meaning of God, man, and the world—the meaning of the Creator, the human creature, and all creation—is given full and final, concrete and definitive, expression in him. Scripture testifies that the fullness of deity dwells bodily in the man Jesus Christ; that he is the visible image of the invisible God; that all things were created by, through, and for him; and that in him all things hold together, so that in everything he might be preeminent (Col. 1:15–18; 2:9). The incarnation of God, therefore, is the supreme mystery at the center of our Christian confession, and no less at the center of all reality. Consequently, *all* conceptions of reality that fail to see and savor that all things hold together in Christ, and that he is preeminent in all things, can never be anything but abstract conceptions of virtual realities—that is, invariably hollow and ultimately vacuous concepts *pulled away from reality.*

Because the incarnation of God lies at the heart of all reality, all books about the incarnation are necessarily noncomprehensive and nonexhaustive. This book is positively no exception to that rule. Its aim is to explore the relation of the incarnation to other major facets of the Christian faith, demonstrating that Christ holds together, and should indeed be preeminent in, the whole of our Christian confession. We, the authors, long to see the great central fact of the incarnation deeply penetrate and captivate the hearts and minds of modern Christians, to the end that the modern church

---

[2] John Williamson Nevin, *The Mystical Presence: A Vindication of the Reformed or Calvinistic Doctrine of the Holy Eucharist* (Philadelphia: J. B. Lippencott, 1846), 199.

might more robustly delight in Jesus Christ, who is altogether worthy of nothing less.

The proper context of theology is the worshiping community, which means authentic theology is done *by* and *for* the church to cultivate her fidelity and vitality. Given that theology is done *by* the church, this book reflects the utter seriousness with which we, the authors, take the great tradition of the historic Christian faith. Orthodoxy is a sacred trust to be prized, protected, and passed along; thus, it is our privilege to stand on the shoulders of giants—predecessors and contemporaries alike. We value theological creativity, but not theological novelty; so if anything here initially suggests the latter, we submit that what is old, when long neglected or forgotten, sometimes seems new. Given that theology is done *for* the church, moreover, this book is intended to be read with benefit by those burdened to advance the work and witness of the worshiping community—including undergraduate and graduate theology students, pastors, and informed lay Christians.

As professors of theology, we wish to thank our students at Moody Bible Institute. The eagerness and earnestness of your engagement with us is immensely encouraging and instructive. Special gratitude goes to Chesney Crouch, Caleb and Lynnae Douglas, Kate Kuntzman, Fred Morelli, Jenna Perrine, and Liz Slinger, whose generous input has directly influenced this book. Of course, whatever shortcomings that remain are attributable only to us. We are by no means unaware that theology—both our writing and your reading—is done east of Eden. As such, this book is offered with humility, in the hope that it shall be received in kind.

Finally, this book is dedicated to our wives and children. How might one adequately express love and gratitude to the bride who is bone of his bone and flesh of his flesh? Kate and Stacie, our living unions with you have helped us grasp the glorious reality of being in living union with Jesus Christ, and what it means that male and female are together the image of God. Two becoming one has not always been easy, but you have pressed into this holy calling with such gentle strength, and done it so well. And now to you, William, Gwyneth, and Peter—living images of the gospel, so bright and beautiful. You have shown us how sweet it is to be dads and, in turn, helped us marvel at how sweet it is to be children of the Father. May the three of you, now and forever, taste and see with us that our Lord is good. Drink deeply the life and love lavished upon you by the Father in and through his incarnate Son, for he has come in your flesh to be your ever-faithful, never-failing Savior.

John C. Clark and Marcus Peter Johnson
Chicago, Illinois
September 2014
Sixteenth Sunday after Pentecost

Abbreviations

1

The Supreme Mystery at the Center of the Christian Confession

THE INCARNATION OF GOD

"Truth must necessarily be stranger than fiction; for fiction is the creation of the human mind and therefore congenial to it."[1] With characteristic playfulness, G. K. Chesterton makes an observation about which he is deadly serious, a profound point that none of us can afford to miss. All forms of fiction, no matter how skillfully, creatively, and compellingly crafted, are shaped by and limited to the confines of our imaginations. It simply cannot be otherwise, given that fiction is, at bottom, the product of human ingenuity. Truth, on the other hand, shares neither the origin nor the inherent limitations of fiction. It does not follow, of course, that the two are innately adverse. On the contrary, truth and fiction can sometimes coexist in harmonious and complimentary ways, as long as no illusions are cherished as to which is which. But whenever fiction is accepted as truth, whenever nonreality is confused with reality, dangers and difficulties inevitably ensue.

Due to the inclinations of our hearts and the prevailing convictions of

---

[1] *Chesterton Day by Day: The Wit and Wisdom of G. K. Chesterton*, ed. Michael W. Perry (Seattle: Inkling Books, 2002), 99.

our cultural milieus, it is all too easy for us to live under the influence of deeply seated and rarely challenged assumptions. Among the most basic and common assumptions of contemporary culture is that the nature, meaning, and goal of human existence is self-explanatory, that one's self-understanding is the proper starting point and controlling principle for understanding all of reality. Thus, as J. I. Packer notes in his modern Christian classic *Knowing God*, "It is no wonder that thoughtful people find the gospel of Jesus Christ hard to believe, for the realities with which it deals pass our understanding."[2] Such "thoughtful people" pose manifold questions: How could Jesus of Nazareth have performed the numerous miracles recorded in Scripture? How could the sufferings of this man, culminating in his death between two criminals on a Roman gibbet, result in God's forgiveness of sinners? How could the same pierced, pummeled, and ruined body that was lowered from the cross and placed in a tomb have been raised to incorruptible life? How could this man have ascended into heaven, reconciling the redeemed to the God from whom they were alienated? Questions of this sort could certainly be multiplied.

Packer observes, however, that such questions arise when difficulties are found in the wrong places, when we fail to identify and apprehend "the supreme mystery" of the gospel. That mystery is not found in the Good Friday event of Christ's crucifixion or even in the Easter Sunday event of his resurrection. Rather, the Christmas event of Christ's birth is where "the profoundest and most unfathomable depths of the Christian revelation lie. . . . Nothing in fiction is so fantastic as is this truth of the Incarnation."[3] This same point is stressed by C. S. Lewis, who remarks:

> The Central Miracle asserted by Christians is the Incarnation. . . . Every other miracle prepares for this, or exhibits this, or results from this. . . . The fitness, and therefore credibility, of the particular miracles depends on their relation to the Grand Miracle; all discussion of them in isolation from it is futile.[4]

These observations by Packer and Lewis are neither new nor novel. They merely echo a conviction deeply rooted in the consciousness of the Christian church from her inception. Martin Luther, the sixteenth-century

---

[2] J. I. Packer, *Knowing God*, 20th anniversary ed. (Downers Grove, IL: IVP, 1993), 52.
[3] Ibid., 52–53.
[4] C. S. Lewis, *Miracles* (1947; repr., New York: Touchstone, 1996), 143.

Reformer, notes that the "church fathers took particular delight" in the apostolic testimony that the Word became flesh and dwelt among us. Luther himself wholeheartedly shared the early church's delight in the incarnation, exulting:

> He [Jesus Christ] condescends to assume my flesh and blood, my body and soul. He does not become an angel or another magnificent creature; He becomes man. This is a token of God's mercy to wretched human beings; the human heart cannot grasp or understand, let alone express it.[5]

Yet while Packer and Lewis show considerable continuity with their Christian predecessors, they seem somewhat out of step with many of their Christian contemporaries. In 1937, Dorothy Sayers laments, "The Incarnation is the most dramatic thing about Christianity, and indeed, the most dramatic thing that ever entered into the mind of man; but if you tell people so, they stare at you in bewilderment."[6] Bewilderment would be understandable, even expected, if Sayers were describing only the reactions of non-Christians or if by "bewilderment" she meant something akin to the sense of wonder Luther exhibits. Regrettably, this is not the case. Moreover, the situation Sayers describes has not shown signs of widespread improvement since she wrote. The supreme mystery that the Word became flesh, that God, in the person of Jesus Christ, participates unreservedly in the same human nature that we ourselves possess, is at the very center of the Christian faith. All too often, however, modern Christians view the incarnation with something closer to consternation than wonder, and as a result, they tend to push this grandest of realities from the center to the periphery of their confession.

Our contemporary situation notwithstanding, the incarnation must ever remain what John Webster calls "the primary affirmation of the church," for Jesus Christ can never be other than "the incomparably comprehensive context of all creaturely being, knowing and acting, because in and as him God is with humankind in free, creative, and saving love."[7] This is an as-

---

[5] "Sermon on the Gospel of St. John 6:47," in *Luther's Works*, 55 vols., ed. Jaroslav Pelikan and Helmut T. Lehmann (St. Louis: Concordia; Philadelphia: Fortress, 1955–), 22:102–3 (hereafter *LW*).

[6] Dorothy Sayers to Father Kelly, October 4, 1937, *The Letters of Dorothy L. Sayers*, vol. 2, ed. Barbara Reynolds (Cambridge: Dorothy L. Sayers Society, 1997), 43.

[7] John Webster, "Incarnation," in *The Blackwell Companion to Modern Theology*, ed. Gareth Jones (Oxford: Blackwell, 2004), 204 (hereafter *BCMT*).

toundingly bold declaration in that it situates the knowledge of all things in the context of our knowing Jesus Christ as the divine self-exposition of God and man, identifying the incarnation as the watershed between truth and fiction. The apostle Paul says nothing less when he announces that in Jesus Christ "all things hold together . . . that in everything he might be preeminent" (Col. 1:17–18).

This book is a sustained yet necessarily nonexhaustive exploration of the incarnation, a subject as rich and unfathomable as the incarnate God himself. The aim of this chapter is to give this exploration some needed background and vocabulary, contours and context, a broad and sturdy skeletal structure to be filled in by the chapters that follow. We shall pursue this aim by discussing: (1) the nature and function of doctrine; (2) Trinitarian and christological developments regarding the incarnation in the early centuries of the church; and (3) several core convictions that characterize our approach to this supreme mystery of the gospel.

THE PERIL AND EXCITEMENT OF CHRISTIAN ORTHODOXY

It is not the case, of course, that modern Christians are in the habit of explicitly denying or overtly repudiating the incarnation. Rather, it is that modern Christians routinely find themselves in a subtle state of malaise regarding the enfleshment of God in the person of Jesus Christ, in that their ongoing affirmation of this essential feature of Christian orthodoxy is coupled with an ever-increasing vagueness as to its significance and implications. Among the most salient reasons for this malaise is the perception among many modern Christians of the doctrines that constitute Christian orthodoxy. In their assessment, doctrine in particular, and orthodoxy in general, suggest something petty, pedantic, outmoded, and irrelevant. Matters of doctrinal orthodoxy, including a doctrinally orthodox understanding of Jesus Christ, are thus met with exasperation, irritation, or, worse still, that most subtle and chilling form of contempt, indifference.

To be sure, such perceptions and responses are not completely lacking in warrant, given that the doctrinal expositions of some theologians possess all the winsomeness, clarity, and pastoral warmth of an electrical diagram for a nuclear submarine. It is altogether good and wise to be repelled by that which distorts and perverts, and caricatures of orthodoxy are certainly no exception to this rule. Yet it appears that modern Christians need to exercise a greater degree of discernment when experiencing such repulsion, because in rejecting caricatures of orthodoxy, many have come to undervalue and overlook the very nature and function of doctrine itself.

Chesterton makes an apt observation when he quips, "People have fallen into a foolish habit of speaking of orthodoxy as something heavy, humdrum, and safe." More insightful still is his retort to this tired and ultimately unfounded sentiment: "There never was anything so perilous or so exciting as orthodoxy."[8] In other words, anything but tedious and benign, orthodoxy enriches, sustains, and heals precisely because its doctrinal substance enshrines the triune God of the gospel—singing to Jesus Christ and drawing the church ever more deeply into the inexhaustible wonders and innumerable implications of new life in him.

Yet what exactly is orthodoxy? In the sense it is used here, orthodoxy refers to a set of key doctrines articulated by the early church and, from that time forward, embraced by all major expressions of Christianity—Eastern Orthodoxy, Roman Catholicism, and Protestantism. Though all doctrines are considered important, these particular doctrines are deemed to be so essential to the integrity of the church's confession that to deny them is tantamount to denying the triune God of the gospel, and thus to departing from the Christian faith. Significantly, the term *orthodoxy* is a combination of two Greek words, *orthos*, which means "right" or "true," and *doxa*, which means "belief" or "worship." Thus, the etymological structure and meaning of the term *orthodoxy* indicates that right belief and true worship are inextricably and symbiotically related, so that whenever one falls down, the other is certain to follow. In other words, because the church is first and foremost a worshiping community, she can exist with authenticity and vitality only when her worship is informed and impelled by sound doctrine. It is for this reason that whenever the church has been most robust throughout history, she has been marked by a passion for doctrine, not an aversion to it. For this same reason, the diminished and confused sense of worship all too common to the modern church is invariably attended by a failure to appreciate the importance of doctrine.[9]

Lest we make an idol of doctrine, however, we must clearly grasp that

---

[8] G. K. Chesterton, *Orthodoxy* (1908; repr., Colorado Springs, CO: Harold Shaw Publishers, 2001), 148–49.
[9] Gerald L. Bray, *Creeds, Councils and Christ: Did the Early Christians Misrepresent Jesus?* (Fearn, Ross-shire, U.K.: Mentor, 1997), 8–9.

doctrine is not an end in itself, but rather a means to an infinitely greater and grander end. Doctrine is neither a substitute for God nor a set of preconceived notions about God, as doctrine does not possess an abstract reality and truth independent of the God to whom it refers.[10] Because the Christian faith is not a theory about God, it never has been, nor ever could be, merely a matter of formulating the right combination of words about him. The Christian faith is about the living Word. Thus, the substance and sum of the Christian faith is not a well-ordered series of factually true propositions, but a person who is himself the embodied Truth of both God and man, the Truth who is God *as man*. This person gives rise to doctrine the moment we begin to wrestle with the questions of who he is and what it means to be encountered, claimed, and redeemed by him.[11]

Clearly, then, it is crucial to discern the nature of the relationship between the person who is the embodied Truth (John 1:14; 14:6) and doctrinal truths about the Truth. On the one hand, we acknowledge that there is a categorical, qualitative distinction between the living person of Jesus Christ and the propositional pronouncements the church makes about him; the two must never be confused or conflated. On the other hand, we recognize and embrace the living person of Jesus Christ as the Truth only as he comes to us clothed in his gospel, only as the propositional pronouncements of the church accurately describe the living Word for us and commend him to us. These truths about the Truth, these words about the Word, constitute the God-given, Spirit-vivified vehicle in and through which Jesus Christ gives himself to us and forges himself within us; thus, the two must never be sundered, severed, or set against one another. Doctrine, rightly understood, concerns both the propositional and the personal. That is because factually true propositions, apart from the living person of Christ, become dry, doctrinaire, and dead, just as the living person of Christ, apart from biblically sourced and normed propositions about him, becomes ambiguous, malleable, and unintelligible. As such, Christian orthodoxy sets itself sharply against arid rationalism and idiosyncratic subjectivism by the settled conviction that the Truth is always both living person and living Word.[12]

---

[10] Andrew Purves, *Reconstructing Pastoral Theology: A Christological Foundation* (Louisville, KY: Westminster John Knox Press, 2004), 13.

[11] Alister E. McGrath, *Understanding Doctrine: What It Is—and Why It Matters* (Grand Rapids: Zondervan, 1990), viii, 2–3.

[12] Thomas F. Torrance, *The School of Faith: The Catechisms of the Reformed Church* (New York: Harper and Brothers Publishers, 1959), xxxii.

Consequently, the peril of orthodoxy is determined by nothing less or other than the service these doctrinal truths render to the Truth; disregard for them is, quite simply, disregard for him. Yet the excitement of orthodoxy lies in the reality that the living Truth claims and masters us precisely as we continue to immerse ourselves in the truths by which he enhances our knowledge of him, intensifies our affections for him, quickens our trust in him, and enlivens our obedience to him.[13]

WHO DO MY PEOPLE SAY THAT I AM?

As Jesus traveled with his disciples to a district of Galilee called Caesarea Philippi, he posed a monumental question regarding his identity and significance: "Who do people say that the Son of Man is?" Then, as now, there was no shortage of speculation on this matter. Thus, the disciples answered, "Some say John the Baptist, others say Elijah, and others Jeremiah or one of the prophets." Pressing the matter further, Jesus replied, "But who do *you* say that I am?" Speaking for his fellow disciples, and setting apostolic precedent for the church ever since, Peter proclaimed, "You are the Christ, the Son of the living God" (Matt. 16:13–16).

Looking more broadly at the New Testament, we find two apostolic exclamations that affirm and develop Peter's statement. Together they constitute not only the earliest recorded witness of the Christian faith, but also the doctrinally orthodox understanding of Jesus Christ that has been integral to the Christian faith from its inception.

The first exclamation is that Jesus is Lord (Rom. 10:9; 1 Cor. 12:3; 2 Cor. 4:5; Phil. 2:11). This earliest and most basic element of the church's confession speaks to Jesus's lordly claim upon his people and, in turn, to their fitting commitment to and worship of him. Further, this exclamation speaks to the nature of Jesus's relationship to God, in that the apostles seized upon the title *kyrios*, or "Lord," a title employed to translate the sacred name of God from Old Testament Hebrew into New Testament Greek, and used that title regularly throughout their writings to refer to Jesus (Rom. 1:7; 5:1; 1 Cor. 1:10; Eph. 1:2–3; Phil. 3:8; Col. 2:6; 1 Thess. 5:9; James 2:1; Rev. 1:8).[14]

The second exclamation is not so much a confession as a doxology, for

---

[13] Victor A. Shepherd, *Our Evangelical Faith* (Toronto, ON: Clements Publishing, 2006), 11–12.

[14] McGrath, *Understanding Doctrine*, 123; Webster, "Incarnation," 208.

unlike the first, it is not a proclamation of faith directed primarily to men, but a cry of praise addressed to God. That cry is "Abba! Father!" In the epistle to the Romans, we find that, after believers receive the Spirit, who bears inner witness to them that they are children of God, they cry to God as their Abba, or Father (Rom. 8:15–17). Or, as Paul writes elsewhere, "And because you are sons, God has sent the Spirit of his Son into our hearts, crying, 'Abba! Father!'" (Gal. 4:6). Paul's words signal the coming to fruition of Jesus's promise that his Father would grant his disciples the Spirit, whose ministry would acquaint them with Jesus in an even more profound and intimate manner. The soon-to-ascend Jesus consoled his disciples by telling them that when he came to them in the indwelling Spirit, they would "know that I am in my Father, and you in me, and I in you" (John 14:16–20).

The apostolic confession that Jesus is Lord indicates that from the outset Christians equated Jesus—the man from Nazareth, the son of Mary, born in Bethlehem—with God, the Maker of heaven and earth, the One who revealed himself to the Hebrew patriarchs as Yahweh. At the same time, we must not miss the implicitly Trinitarian context and meaning of the cry "Abba! Father!" This form of address is not a product of the church's own choosing or making. This address is distinctive to Jesus, who alone spoke of God in this fashion. To utter this cry after Jesus—or, better, in, through, and with Jesus—is to acknowledge that Christians learned to do so from Jesus himself through the indwelling ministry of the Spirit, who grants us the benefits that first belonged exclusively to the utterly unique and eternal Son of the Father.[15]

When the apostles confessed Jesus to be the Christ, the Son of the living God, the Lord, the One who teaches us to call his Father our Father, they were by no means publicizing a series of novel speculations about God. On the contrary, they were describing an experience that they believed they already shared with their fellow Christians: the experience of God opening his inner life to them through the revealing and reconciling ministrations of the Son and the Spirit. In the apostolic confession of Jesus Christ, we see how that experience reshaped human thought and language into a vehicle capable of articulating a mystery that unaided reason was, is, and forever shall be unable to fathom. From the beginning, Christian knowledge of God in Christ was first experiential and then doctrinal.

---

[15] Thomas A. Smail, *The Forgotten Father* (Grand Rapids: Eerdmans, 1981), 30–31.

Let us be altogether clear on this point: to affirm the primacy of experiential knowledge of God in this sense is not to suggest that the apostolic confession of Jesus Christ is a theoretical construct that is the product of the apostles' reflection upon themselves and their intuitions about God. True knowledge of God is neither unmediated nor intuitive; this knowledge is not the product of independent self-analysis, and thus cannot be obtained by self-generated efforts to probe one's inner thoughts or feelings. We are affirming, therefore, that the apostolic confession of Jesus Christ is the Spirit-generated, Spirit-superintended witness of the church's experience of the saving incursion and ongoing presence of God in Jesus Christ. Knowledge of God in Christ is first experiential and then doctrinal because it is revelatory and relational knowledge rather than neutral and detached knowledge—the kind of knowledge that neither is nor can be generated by logical syllogisms. Doctrine is absolutely indispensable in that it interprets and informs this experience, articulating what it means and entails to know God in Christ.

The order of the relationship between experience and doctrine is anything but arbitrary, in that it constitutes an order of knowledge that has always marked authentic Christian understanding and confession.[16] In fact, whenever this order of knowledge has been inverted, so that theory gains the pride of place over experience, the apostolic confession of Christ has been terribly distorted and sometimes altogether denatured.[17]

No Shortage of Speculation: The Post-Apostolic Church and Heresy

The Trinitarian and christological controversies that attended the early centuries of the post-apostolic church were prompted by such inversions of this apostolically established order of knowledge. The byproducts of these inversions are known as heresies. To be sure, the very word *heresy* has become so unfashionable of late as to be something of an embarrassment, finding precious little place in modern Christian discourse. But lest

---

[16] For instance, John Calvin excoriates "the cold exhortations of the philosophers" by cautioning that true knowledge of God in Christ "is not apprehended by the understanding and memory alone, as other disciplines are, but it is received only when it possesses the whole soul, and finds a seat and resting place in the inmost affection of the heart." *Institutes of the Christian Religion*, 2 vols., ed. John T. McNeill, trans. Ford Lewis Battles, Library of Christian Classics (Philadelphia: Westminster Press, 1960), 3.6.4 (hereafter *Inst.*). Here Calvin enlarges upon Luther's pithier observation that "experience alone makes the theologian." "Table Talk Recorded by Veit Dietrick, 1535," in *LW*, 54:7.

[17] Gerald L. Bray, "Out of the Box: The Christian Experience of God in Trinity," in *God the Holy Trinity: Reflections on Christian Faith and Practice*, ed. Timothy George (Grand Rapids: Baker Academic, 2006), 39.

we too quickly and facilely attribute this phenomenon to our generosity and largeheartedness, we would be wise to consider how this phenomenon might also betray a confusion and dullness—a failure of faith and nerve—that would rightly vex our Christian predecessors. The word *heresy*, which comes from the Greek *hairesis*, was not a description used by our Christian predecessors to identify or assess forms of self-consciously non-Christian belief. Consequently, we must avoid the common misconception that heresies are the byproducts of challenges posed to the church from *outside*, attacks on the church's confession by those who overtly oppose the Christian faith. On the contrary, heresies are the byproducts of challenges posed to the church from *inside*. In other words, heresies arise when ostensibly well-intentioned interpretations of key elements of the Christian faith prove to be so inadequate and erroneous that espousing and propagating them forfeits core Christian affirmations about the triune God of the gospel.[18]

Understandably, then, Christians through the centuries have viewed heresy as dangerous and, if left unchecked, positively destructive. Ironically, however, heresy has also proved to be quite valuable to the church, for when confronted by interpretations of the faith that seemed problematic, the church has been prompted time and again to reexamine: (1) Scripture, the apostolic source and norm of her faith, life, and worship; (2) the connections between doctrines, so as to assess the cogency and coherency of her confession; and (3) the connection between right doctrine and right worship—between the faith and faithful living—as these are as inseparable as two sides of a coin. Inadequate and erroneous interpretations of the Christian faith have thus been used by God to sanctify the church's thinking as she seeks to faithfully articulate the apostolic confession of Jesus Christ, the doctrinal orthodoxy that has been integral to the Christian faith from its inception.

Amidst such challenges, the early church sought to examine and evaluate not only those challenges but also her teaching, preaching, worship, witness, and mission in light of those challenges. Assessing where and why there was adequacy or deficiency, the early church purposed to take the doctrinal orthodoxy of the apostolic confession of Jesus Christ and render the substance of that orthodoxy more pointed, explicit, and amplified as the demands of each situation warranted. Of course, proponents of all such

---

[18] McGrath, *Understanding Doctrine*, 112–16.

challenges claimed biblical support and championed those challenges in the thought and language forms of their time and culture. To magnify the true meaning of the biblical witness, therefore, the early church found herself having to move beyond the mere recitation of biblical proof texts in order to give accurate expression to God's identity and acts in a biblically coherent manner. Fidelity to Jesus Christ required the early church to be theologically critical and constructive, to be theologically creative without succumbing to theological novelty, and to adapt to the thought and language forms of the context without adopting its ideologies.

A recurring theme quickly emerged, and it constitutes a major and momentous difference between Christian orthodoxy and heresy. Christian orthodoxy is characterized by a commitment to articulating doctrine in a manner that safeguards the mystery and wonder that must always retain a place in the church's thinking and speaking about the triune God of the gospel. Heresy, on the other hand, does not seek to safeguard this mystery. Instead, heresy attempts to solve it. As Chesterton hints in his remark cited at the beginning of this chapter, heresy is characterized by a deep reticence, even a dogged refusal, to be appropriately unsettled when faced with the inherent strangeness of truth; in an effort to domesticate that strangeness, to remove its scandal, heresy creates a fiction more readily congenial to the human mind.

Nowhere is this more evident than in the Trinitarian and christological controversies that precipitated the First Council of Nicaea (325) and the Council of Chalcedon (451). The pronouncements of these two councils are among the most significant theological statements in the entirety of post-apostolic church history, and both are inestimably important for our exploration of the incarnation. Here we have Christian orthodoxy's definitive response to the all-important question that Jesus poses to his church, namely, "Who do *you* say that I am?" (Matt. 16:15).

Who Is the Incarnate Christ in Relation to God?

The First Council of Nicaea came about as a direct result of the first major doctrinal challenge faced by the post-apostolic church. This challenge concerned Trinitarian controversies that arose within the church regarding the deity of Jesus Christ, or more to the point, regarding the nature of the relationship between the man Jesus from Nazareth and Yahweh, the God and Maker of heaven and earth. These controversies came in various forms, including the heresies of modalism and adoptionism.[19]

Modalism—sometimes called Sabellianism after a third-century Roman named Sabellius, who championed this view—maintained that God is not three persons, but rather one person who projects himself in three different "modes," doing so in three successive stages as Father, Son, and Spirit. Defending monotheism against what appeared to some as tritheism—the belief in and worship of three gods—modalism "solved" the mystery of God's three-in-oneness by denying the personal distinctiveness of the Father, Son, and Spirit. Thus, according to modalism, the nature of the relationship between Jesus and Yahweh is that they are not only one God, but also only one person.

Adoptionism, on the other hand, maintained that the man Jesus from Nazareth was not God in any essential, substantial sense, only a mere man, but he was adopted by God due to his extraordinary piety, thereby becoming the Son of God. In an effort to explain how Jesus could be divine and God could still be one, adoptionism "solved" the mystery of God's three-in-oneness by denying the Son's pretemporal equality with the Father. Thus, in the view of adoptionism, the nature of the relationship between Jesus and Yahweh is that of distinct divine persons, but not distinct persons who are both inherently God.

Yet the most significant of the pre-Nicene controversies came in the form of Arianism, a movement that derived its name from Arius, a prominent minister in Alexandria, Egypt, during the early fourth century. Arius insisted that the Father, Son, and Spirit are not coeternal and essentially, substantially coequal persons. He used the term *uncaused* or *unoriginate* as the most basic definition of what God is like. But only the Father is eternally existent, he said, as the Father alone is inherently God. The Son is but a creature, created from nothing like all other creatures. By Arius's definition,

---

[19] The aim of this book is to expound upon the incarnation in accord with the Trinitarian and christological theology of Nicaea and Chalcedon, not to trace with great depth or breadth the historical and doctrinal developments that precipitated Nicaea and Chalcedon. Much fine research is available on the latter. In addition to the pertinent material in the multivolume overviews of the history of doctrinal development by Justo L. González, *A History of Christian Thought*, 2nd rev. ed., 3 vols. (Nashville, TN: Abingdon, 1987), and Jaroslav Pelikan, *The Christian Tradition: A History of the Development of Doctrine*, 5 vols. (Chicago: University of Chicago Press, 1975–1991), see J. N. D. Kelly, *Early Christian Doctrines* (London: Adam & Charles Black, 1958); Edmund J. Fortman, *The Triune God: A Historical Study of the Doctrine of the Trinity* (Philadelphia: Westminster Press, 1972); Frances M. Young, *From Nicaea to Chalcedon: A Guide to the Literature and Its Background* (Philadelphia: Fortress, 1983); and R. P. C. Hanson, *The Search for the Christian Doctrine of God: The Arian Controversy, 318–381* (London: T&T Clark, 1988).

then, the Son, by virtue of his very sonship, cannot truly be God. However, the Arians were quick to add that the creatureliness of the Son is unique, since he was created before all other things and took part with his Father in the creation of all things brought into existence after him. As such, the relationship between Jesus and Yahweh is indeed singular and exceptional, as Jesus is the only Son that Yahweh made in this particular sense. Nonetheless, while Jesus can be called the Son of God as a title of honor, he is not God the Son, as his nature is not that of God the Father. Thus, by imposing the alien logic of the classical Greek philosophical tradition upon the Christian faith, Arius "solved" the mystery of God's three-in-oneness by dissolving the triune God of the gospel into a hierarchy of beings, reducing the Son and the Spirit to creatures ontologically inferior to the Father.[20]

The brilliant and indefatigable Athanasius was stunned by the presumption and naiveté of his older Alexandrian contemporary. He asked: Can there be knowledge of an uninvolved God absent from human history? Is it not the case that God can be known only when and where he discloses himself to us? How, then, could we speak about knowledge of God, in terms of God's *self*-disclosure, if such knowledge were to come from created things—even from a created Son? Are not all created things, by very definition, categorically and qualitatively different from God, and thus not God? Is it not then the case that we truly know the meaning of God as Creator only as a result of knowing God as Father, not the other way around? And if so, is it not the case that God is known as Father only as God is known in the Son? Let us turn to Athanasius himself:

> And they [Arians], when they call Him Unoriginate, name Him only from His works, and know not the Son any more than the Greeks; but he who calls God Father, names Him from the Word [Jesus Christ]; and knowing the Word, he acknowledges Him to be Framer of all, and understands that through Him all things have been made. Therefore it is more pious and more accurate to signify God from the Son and call Him Father, than to name Him from his works and call Him Unoriginate. . . . And "Unoriginate" is a word of the Greeks, who know not the Son; but "Father" has been acknowledged and vouchsafed by our Lord. For He, knowing Himself whose Son He was, said, "I am in the Father, and the Father is in Me;" and, "He that hath seen Me, hath seen the Father," and

---

[20] Bray, "Out of the Box," 39; McGrath, *Understanding Doctrine*, 117.

"I and the Father are One;" but nowhere is He found to call the Father Unoriginate. . . . A vain thing then is their argument about the term "Unoriginate," as is now proved, and nothing more than a fantasy.[21]

Athanasius maintained, with unmistakable clarity and conviction, that the Arians started their thinking about God in the wrong place, and did so with profoundly detrimental results, because faithful and theologically accurate thinking about God must begin with Jesus Christ.[22] "Christian faith starts with the knowledge of God in Jesus Christ," concurs T. F. Torrance.[23] And John Leith echoes this sentiment with irreducible concision, declaring, "God, for Christians, is defined by Jesus Christ."[24]

Beginning his prolific career in the early 1870s, church historian Adolf von Harnack popularized the notion that the early centuries of the post-apostolic church featured an acute Hellenization of the Christian faith.[25] Athanasius's words, representative of his own prodigiously influential career as a churchman and theologian, strongly suggest otherwise. To be sure, Athanasius and his fellow shapers of early Christian orthodoxy adapted to their context by appropriating Greek thought and language. Yet far from adopting the ideological substance of classical Hellenism, the early church altered the basic assumptions of that worldview so as to espouse and propagate a distinctively Christian Trinitarian and christological confession. For the early church, terms such as *word, image, form, being, act, substance*, and the like took on meanings very different from those in Platonic, Aristotelian, or Stoic thought—meanings that were distinctly "un-Greek." Rather than building an acutely Hellenized Christian faith, in fact, the early church transformed familiar Greek thought and language into vehicles capable of giving faithful and theologically accurate expression to the identity and acts of the triune God of the gospel.[26]

In response to challenges posed by the likes of modalism, adoptionism, and Arianism, the church affirmed her faith in one God who exists eternally

---

[21] Athanasius, *Against the Arians*, 1.33–34, in *Nicene and Post-Nicene Fathers*, 2nd series, ed. Philip Schaff and Henry Wace (1890; repr., Peabody, MA: Hendrickson Publishers, 1995), 4:326 (hereafter *NPNF*).

[22] Michael Reeves, *Delighting in the Trinity: An Introduction to the Christian Faith* (Downers Grove, IL: IVP Academic, 2012), 21–22.

[23] Thomas F. Torrance, *Incarnation: The Person and Life of Christ*, ed. Robert T. Walker (Downers Grove, IL: IVP Academic, 2008), 37.

[24] John H. Leith, *Basic Christian Doctrine* (Louisville, KY: Westminster John Knox Press, 1993), 45.

[25] Adolf von Harnack, *History of Dogma*, trans. Neil Buchanan (London: Williams & Norgate, 1894), 1:47ff., and elsewhere throughout von Harnack's published works.

[26] Thomas F. Torrance, *The Trinitarian Faith: The Evangelical Theology of the Ancient Catholic Church* (London: T&T Clark, 1991), 68–75.

as three distinct, coequally divine persons: God the Father, God the Son, and God the Spirit. Reflecting the sentiments we just observed in Athanasius, the first confession in the Nicene Creed regarding the first person of the Trinity is that he is "Father," and *subsequently*, that he is "creator of all things visible and invisible."[27] The order of this confession is intentional and crucial, as there is precisely nothing robustly or even distinctively Christian in the mere confession that God is Creator. This is readily and routinely affirmed by non-Christians of many sorts, and always has been. In itself, this affirmation requires or suggests no knowledge of God as Father and no particular conviction regarding Jesus Christ. By identifying the first person of the Trinity as Father and *then* Creator, therefore, the Nicene Creed indicates that the meaning of God as Creator is truly known only as a result of knowing God as Father; and God is truly known as Father only as he is known in the Son—by, through, and for whom all things were created, and in whom all things hold together (John 1:3; Col. 1:16–17; Heb. 1:1–3).

With respect to Jesus Christ, the Nicene Creed confesses his deity without qualification or condition, affirming the church's belief that the man Jesus is not only the Son of God, but also God the Son. On the nature of the relationship between the Son and the Father, the Creed states:

> We believe . . . in one Lord Jesus Christ, the Son of God, begotten of the Father as only begotten, that is, from the essence [reality] of the Father . . . God from God, Light from Light, true God from true God, begotten not created . . . of the same essence [reality] as the Father . . . through whom all things came into being, both in heaven and in earth.[28]

The Nicene confession of God's three-in-oneness means the term *Trinity* is not merely a way of thinking and speaking about God, an intellectual construct that gives us a tidy handle on him. On the contrary, Christian orthodoxy maintains that God is actually and intrinsically triune, as opposed to God's triunity being some sort of nonessential appendage that may be added to or removed from him at whim. Because God is triune, he cannot be rightly thought or spoken of except as triune. Thus, any and every confession of God not freighted with Trinitarian content is the confession of

---

[27] "The Creed of Nicaea (325)," in *Creeds of the Churches: A Reader in Christian Doctrine from the Bible to the Present*, 3rd ed., ed. John H. Leith (Louisville, KY: John Knox Press, 1982), 30 (hereafter *CC*).
[28] Ibid., 30–31.

a necessarily non-Christian deity, a "god" intrinsically different from and alien to the God of Scripture.

What is more, the Nicene affirmation that Jesus Christ is of the same essence as the Father means that Christ participates unreservedly in the Father's divine nature and majesty. If the Son is only like the Father, then the Son is ultimately different from the Father, given that no *quantity* of similitude, no matter how great, constitutes the *quality* of sameness. With respect to his deity, whatever we say about the Son can and must be said about the Father, except "Son." Likewise, whatever we say about the Father can and must be said about the Son, except "Father."

That Jesus Christ is identical in essence with the Father is inexhaustibly rich in gospel significance. It means that who the triune God has been eternally in his inner life he now is and forever shall be toward us in Jesus Christ through the Spirit, the personal agent of Christ's presence and power (John 14:16–20, 25–26; 15:26; 16:4–15). Jesus Christ really and truly is Immanuel, God with us (Matt. 1:23). John's Gospel tells us that Jesus Christ makes the Father known, that the Son exegetes, or interprets, the Father for us in the intimate and loving manner that previously only the eternal Son, in the eternal communion of the Spirit, has known him (John 1:18; 17:25–26). There being no true knowledge of God as Father independent of or remote from God the Son, Christ causes us to participate with him in his own relationship with the Father; thus, Jesus insists that no one knows the Father except the Son and anyone to whom the Son graciously chooses to reveal the Father (Matt. 11:27; Luke 10:22).

To see, hear, and receive Jesus Christ, then, is to see, hear, and receive the Father, just as to deny and reject Jesus Christ is to deny and reject the Father (Luke 10:16; John 14:9–10). In other words, there is no search to be undertaken or appeal to be made to God over the head or behind the back of Jesus Christ. On the contrary, the fact that Christ is identical in essence with the Father means the Father's sending of the Son is nothing less, different, or other than the self-giving of God as God has forever been in himself. To say otherwise would render the gospel bleak news indeed, as it would mean there is no ontological, and thus no epistemological, connection between the gifts of God—love, truth, righteousness, holiness, life, and so forth—and the Giver of those gifts. Those gifts would be but created mediums—dissoluble, detachable, and with no inherent relation to God himself. For instance, we could confess that God is love (1 John 4:8) and that God so loved the world that he gave his only begotten Son to needy sinners (John 3:16). Tragically, however, we would be forced to conclude that the love God is in himself is not the love we know and possess in our reception of Jesus Christ.[29]

Who Is the Incarnate Christ in Relation to Humanity?

Working knowledge of the First Council of Nicaea is indispensable for exploring the meaning and implications of the incarnation. Yet Nicaea does not provide the whole of the necessary background. No sooner did this council pronounce on the deity of Jesus Christ than the church was faced with a second major doctrinal challenge, one directly related to the first. This challenge consisted of christological controversies that arose within the church regarding Jesus's humanity and its relation to his deity, or, more to the point, regarding the nature of the relationship between God the Son and humankind.

Much like the Trinitarian controversies that precipitated the formulation of the Nicene Creed, these christological controversies came in various forms. The first of note was Apollinarianism, named after Apollinarius, the fourth-century bishop of Laodicea. An energetic advocate of Nicene orthodoxy, Apollinarius maintained that while God the Son did assume a true and full human body at the incarnation, the same could not be said about a true and full human mind. The human mind is the seat of sin, reasoned Apollinarius, so Jesus's mind cannot be truly and fully human; that would diminish the dignity of God the Son and subject our Savior to the very condition from which fallen humanity needs saving. Consequently, while Apollinarius affirmed the true and full deity of Jesus Christ, he "solved" the mystery of the incarnation of God by denying that Christ is truly and fully human.

Gregory of Nazianzus, the fourth-century archbishop of Constantinople, was profoundly troubled by the claims of Apollinarius. Even if it were plausible to so neatly dichotomize the human body from the human mind, he asked, what benefit would an Apollinarian view of the incarnation be with regard to addressing and healing the corrupted state of fallen humanity? If the human body is not what needs redeeming, why did God the

---

[29] Torrance, *The Trinitarian Faith*, 132–45.

Son assume such a body? On the other hand, if the human mind is indeed the seat of sin, then is not the mind what needs to be addressed and healed by an encounter with God in Christ? Is it not then all the more important that God the Son would assume such a mind? When Apollinarius speaks of the incarnation, does he not speak of an abstract and hypothetical "humanity" that is not actually *our* humanity? Does Apollinarius then not speak of an incarnation that fails to address and heal what actually ails fallen humans, leaving them in their corruption? Moreover, is it not that corruption affects the totality of our fallen humanity, making it imperative that God the Son would assume every aspect of that humanity? Gregory writes:

> If anyone has put his trust in Him [Jesus Christ] as a Man without a human mind, he is really bereft of mind, and quite unworthy of salvation. For that which He has not assumed He has not healed; but that which is united to His Godhead is also saved. If only half Adam fell, then that which Christ assumes and saves may be half also; but if the whole of his nature fell, it must be united to the whole nature of Him that was begotten, and so be saved as a whole. Let them not, then, begrudge us our complete salvation, or clothe the Saviour only with bones and nerves and the portraiture of humanity.[30]

Following Apollinarianism in the fifth century were Nestorianism and Eutychianism. The former emerged when Nestorius, an archbishop of Constantinople subsequent to Gregory, took exception to the church's long-established confession that Mary, the mother of Jesus, was *theotokos*, a Greek term meaning "God-bearer." How could Mary, being finite and temporal, really and truly give birth to God the Son, who is infinite and eternal? The second person of the Trinity was surely joined to a true and full human nature in Mary's womb, thought Nestorius, yet all the human attributes and experiences of Jesus Christ should be ascribed to a humanity that remains a personal subject *distinct* from God the Son. Nestorians were accused of maintaining that while Jesus Christ is truly and fully divine and human, there is no intrinsic union between his divine and human natures. Whereas Nestorians affirmed the true and full reality of both the deity and humanity of Jesus Christ, then, they "solved" the mystery of the incarnation of God by denying

---

[30] Gregory of Nazianzus, "To Cledonius the Priest against Apollinarius," *Letters on the Apollinarian Controversy*, no. 101, in *NPNF*, 7:440.

that Christ's deity and humanity are truly and fully united in one personal subject. Does this suggest that Jesus's two natures are related in an extrinsic and abstract manner? Might this imply that his deity and humanity may be turned on and off, as it were, by being exhibited and exercised intermittently? Would espousing Nestorian notions cause the church to think and speak of her Lord as if he were two persons, or as if he had a split personality?

Eutyches was a contemporary of Nestorius and a fellow churchman in Constantinople. He deemed Nestorian claims immensely erroneous, and in countering those claims, championed a position known as Eutychianism. Sometimes called Monophysitism, a compound Greek term derived from *monos*, which means "single," and *physis*, which means "nature," Eutychianism maintained that a person must possess one nature, not two. God the Son assumed a true and full human nature in Mary's womb, contended Eutyches. But that human nature was taken up into God the Son's divine nature and absorbed like a raindrop in the ocean, with the result that the incarnate Christ has only a single nature. Therefore, while Eutychians affirmed that Jesus is one personal subject, they "solved" the mystery of the incarnation of God by denying the true and full reality of both Christ's deity and humanity; rather, they saw his two natures intermingling in such a way as to render him a *tertium quid*—that is, a "third something"!

Responding to the challenges of Apollinarianism, Nestorianism, and Eutychianism, the church affirmed her faith in the incarnate One, Jesus Christ, who is truly and fully God, truly and fully man, and whose deity and humanity are truly and fully united in his one person. The Council of Chalcedon's pronouncement, known as "the Definition of Chalcedon," reads:

> Following, then, the holy fathers, we . . . confess the one and only Son, our Lord Jesus Christ. This selfsame one is perfect . . . both in deity . . . and also in human-ness; this selfsame one is also actually . . . God and actually man, with a rational soul . . . and a body. He is of the same reality as God [*homoousion tō patri*] as far as his deity is concerned and of the same reality as we are ourselves [*homoousion hēmin*] as far as his human-ness is concerned; thus like us in all respects, sin only excepted. . . . For us and on behalf of our salvation, this selfsame one was born of Mary the virgin, who is God-bearer [*theotokos*] in respect to his human-ness. . . . We apprehend . . . this one and only Christ—Son, Lord, only-begotten—in two natures . . . ; [and we do this] without confusing

the two natures . . . , without transmuting one nature into the other
. . . , without dividing them into two separate categories . . . , without
contrasting them according to area or function. . . . The distinctiveness
of each nature is not nullified by the union. Instead, the "properties"
. . . of each nature are conserved and both natures concur . . . in one
"person" . . . and in one *hypostasis*. They are not divided or cut into two
prosōpa [persons], but are together the one and only and only-begotten
Logos of God, the Lord Jesus Christ.[31]

Christian orthodoxy confesses that Jesus Christ possesses two natures,
a perfect divine nature and a perfect human nature, the former being the
same as that of God the Father and God the Spirit, the latter being the
same as ours, his fellow humans. Inextricably united in Mary's womb, these
two natures shall remain forever united in one person, the person of Jesus
Christ. In other words, Christ's divine and human natures are joined in *hypostatic*, or personal, union—an intrinsic and concrete union, as opposed
to an extrinsic and abstract union, one that is merely metaphorical, moral,
volitional, legal, or ideational. Moreover, the integrity of each nature is
upheld in this personal union, not undermined or overturned. As stated in
what are often called the Definition of Chalcedon's "four fences," which
are meant to safeguard rather than solve the mystery of the incarnation
of God, deity and humanity subsist in Jesus Christ without: (1) confusion,
(2) transmutation, (3) division, or (4) contradistinction.

The all-important question Jesus poses to his church is, "Who do *you*
say that I am?" (Matt. 16:15). When the church dares to respond according to the apostolic witness of Scripture and the benchmarks of Christian
orthodoxy derived from Scripture—including the Nicene Creed and the
Definition of Chalcedon—the answer is staggering: Jesus Christ is the very
content and meaning of reality. The incarnation teaches us that just as
there is no true knowledge of God the Father to be had independently of
or remotely from God the Son, there is no true knowledge of humanity
to be had independently of or remotely from the God who comes to us
in and as the man Jesus. Blaise Pascal touches on this point when musing:
"Not only do we only know God through Jesus Christ, but we only know
ourselves through Jesus Christ; we only know life and death through Jesus

---

[31] "The Definition of Chalcedon (451)," in *CC*, 35–36.

Christ. Apart from Jesus Christ we cannot know the meaning of our life or our death, of God or of ourselves."[32] Fashioning notions about God and humanity, then projecting those notions on God and humanity independently of or remotely from him who truly, fully, perfectly embodies God and humanity, is but an exercise in idolatry, betraying a failure to grasp the significance of the incarnation, a failure to have learned Christ. Dietrich Bonhoeffer thus remarks:

> Christian belief deduces that the reality of God is not in itself merely an idea from the fact that this reality of God has manifested and revealed itself in the midst of the real world. In Jesus Christ the reality of God entered into the reality of this world. The place where the answer is given, both to the question concerning the reality of God and to the question concerning the reality of the world, is designated solely and alone by the name Jesus Christ. . . . In Him all things consist (Col. 1:17). Henceforward one can speak neither of God nor of the world without speaking of Jesus Christ. All concepts of reality which do not take account of Him are abstractions.[33]

And again:

> There are not two realities, but only one reality, and that is the reality of God, which has become manifest in Christ in the reality of the world. Sharing in Christ we stand at once in both the reality of God and the reality of the world. . . . The world has no reality of its own, independently of the revelation of God in Christ. One is denying the revelation of God in Jesus Christ if one tries to be "Christian" without seeing and recognizing the world in Christ.[34]

If the incarnation designates Jesus Christ as the content and meaning of reality, surely the incarnation designates Jesus Christ as the content and meaning of salvation. We observed that Gregory of Nazianzus attested to the profound gospel significance of the incarnation by stating that any humanity God the Son has not assumed is humanity God the Son cannot save; for only that assumed humanity can be brought into a true, full, perfect, and personal relationship with God in the person of Christ. To say

---

[32] Blaise Pascal, *Pensées*, no. 417, trans. A. J. Krailsheimer (New York: Penguin, 1995), 141.
[33] Dietrich Bonhoeffer, *Ethics*, ed. Eberhard Bethge, trans. Neville Horton Smith (1955; repr., New York: Macmillan Publishing, 1979), 194.
[34] Ibid., 197.

otherwise is to suggest that there are aspects of our humanity that do not need saving, or that fallen humans can receive the saving benefits of God independently of or remotely from Jesus Christ. Gregory's point reverberates through the thought of the two greatest shapers of the Protestant Reformation, and thus of historic evangelicalism. Luther marvels, "He [Jesus Christ] condescends to assume my flesh and blood, my body and soul."[35] And the point Calvin stressed before all others when discussing salvation is that we receive the saving benefits of God only as those benefits are mediated to us as humans in and through the humanity of Jesus Christ. Calvin proclaims:

> First, we must understand that as long as Christ remains outside of us, and we are separated from him, all that he has suffered and done for the salvation of the human race remains useless and of no value for us. Therefore, to share with us what he has received from the Father, he had to become ours and to dwell within us. . . . We also, in turn, are said to be "engrafted into him" [Rom. 11:17], and to "put on Christ" [Gal. 3:27]; for, as I have said, all that he possesses is nothing to us until we grow into one body with him.[36]

When the church dares to grasp the gospel significance of the incarnation according to the apostolic witness of Scripture and her Scripture-derived creeds, she refuses to separate Christ's person from his work, as if his incarnate humanity were little more than a prerequisite for his atoning activity. Likewise, the church refuses to separate Christ's saving benefits from Christ himself, as if salvation were the reception of an objectified commodity given on account of Christ yet apart from him—that is, as if Christ were the agent or condition of our salvation but not that salvation himself. Finally, the church refuses to separate the objective accomplishments of Christ's saving activity for his people from the subjective effects of Christ's being with and in his people, as if our relation to Christ were extrinsic and abstract—that which is merely metaphorical, moral, volitional, legal, or ideational—as opposed to an inner experience of the life-giving, life-transforming presence of God. The glorious reality of which the gospel speaks is not the reception of an impersonal benefit called salvation, but the reception of Christ, and thus salvation *in him*.

---

[35] "Sermon on the Gospel of St. John 6:47," in *LW*, 22:102.
[36] *Inst.*, 3.1.1.

FACING AND FILLING THE VOID: ABOUT THIS BOOK

Let us now call to mind the observation of Dorothy Sayers near the beginning of this chapter, namely, that to tell most modern Christians about the staggering reality of the incarnation is to invite a response of bewilderment. This situation is troubling and saddening, but not altogether perplexing, for telling people about the incarnation is telling them that Jesus Christ is not only the content and meaning of salvation, but also the content and meaning of reality, given that in him the reality of God entered into the reality of our human existence. However, most modern Christians do not sufficiently grasp that Jesus Christ holds all things together and is preeminent in all things, such that the meaning of God, and no less the meaning of human existence, must be revealed in him. Though perhaps not all that perplexing, this situation is certainly grave, and its gravity requires that it be faced squarely. It is a grave state of affairs that many modern Christians are unable to think and speak about the incarnation with any considerable sense of competency, let alone any particular sense of wonder and delight. After all, the very center of the Christian confession is the conviction that the Word became flesh, our flesh, in Jesus Christ; thus, this current state of affairs cannot help but have the most detrimental effects on every dimension of the Christian life, individually and corporately. Graver still, this state of affairs dishonors the incarnate God himself, who is supremely worthy of all our faith, hope, love, and worship.

This book is aimed at addressing and, in some modest measure, redressing this state of affairs by providing a sustained exploration of the inexhaustible wonders and vast implications of the incarnation. We shall proceed on the premise that the supreme mystery—and, indeed, scandal—at the center of Christian confession, and no less at the center of all reality, is the incarnation of God in and as the man Jesus Christ. As we immerse ourselves in the doctrine of the incarnation, our prayer is that the One to whom this doctrine sings, the incarnate Savior, will graciously impart to us a richer knowledge of himself and, in turn, of the triune God, ourselves, salvation, the church, and more. With a view to moving forward in this exploration, let us identify and briefly discuss a few core characteristics of this undertaking.

First, this book is a work in theology. As such, it prioritizes the question of *who* over the question of *what*. In other words, priority is given to the question, "Who is the incarnate Christ?" over the question, "What is the relevance of the incarnate Christ?" Ours is a pragmatic culture; it prizes and praises utility, efficiency, and expediency. Consequently, the latter question is routinely prioritized in contemporary Christian discourse, sometimes to such a degree and extent as to nearly eclipse the former question altogether. Let us speak plainly: this betrays an idolatrous tendency to place more value and interest in the blessings of Christ than in Christ himself, a tendency to see Christ not as a matchlessly beautiful end in himself, but as a means to other greater and grander personal, social, or cultural ends.[37] Because everything in the Christian confession depends upon knowing who Jesus Christ is, to begin by asking the wrong question is to make our first step a misstep, ensuring our failure to grasp the heart and significance of the gospel.[38] Is this to suggest that theology is not practical or pastoral? No! On the contrary, we should sooner ask if anything could be so impractical or nonpastoral as a lack of knowing God. Theology is both practical and pastoral for the express reason that it is *theological*, that its aim is to give true and accurate expression to the identity and acts of its subject: the triune God of the gospel, whose divine self-exposition of God and man is embodied in the incarnate Christ.[39]

Second, this book is a work in confessional theology, as distinguished from speculative or overtly apologetic theology, at least insofar as apologetics is often understood. As it is used here, the adjective *confessional* does not indicate an exclusive allegiance to the confessional documents of any one denomination. Rather, the adjective identifies an ecclesial and doxological posture that insists that Christian theology cannot be an exercise in convictional detachment, an exercise in which we step outside the presence of revelation, the practice of faith and worship, or participation in the church to adopt a different—a more abstract or supposedly neutral—stance toward the Christian confession. Used in this sense, confessional theology rejects as a piece of Enlightenment mythology the notion that the operations of reason are a sphere from which God's presence may be effectively banished.[40]

As such, this book prioritizes the question of *who* over the question

---

[37] James B. Torrance, *Worship, Community, and the Triune God of Grace* (Downers Grove, IL: IVP Academic, 1996), 28–29.
[38] Andrew Purves, "Who Is the Incarnate Saviour of the World?" in *An Introduction to Torrance Theology: Discovering the Incarnate Saviour*, ed. Gerrit Scott Dawson (London: T&T Clark, 2007), 23.
[39] Purves, *Reconstructing Pastoral Theology*, 7, 12.
[40] John Webster, *Holiness* (Grand Rapids: Eerdmans, 2003), 14–15.

of *how*. In other words, priority is given to the question, "Who is the in-carnate Christ?" over the question, "How could an incarnate Christ be possible?" As Bonhoeffer poignantly attests, the latter question is a godless question inasmuch as it seeks to establish the possibility and knowledge of God apart from God—that is, it tacitly denies not only that God alone is able to reveal and authenticate God, but also that Jesus Christ is God in-carnate. To demand an answer to the question of how an incarnate Christ could be possible is to tacitly deny that Christ's witness to himself is either self-authenticating or sufficient. Such a denial requires a search above and beyond Christ for reasons independent of or remote from Christ that are deemed capable of rendering Christ's witness to himself legitimate and viable.[41] At bottom, those who will not confess Jesus Christ as the incarnate Lord according to his own witness must establish the conditions for this possibility according to other self-identified, self-appointed, and, at least in effect, self-verifying standards of authentication. The legitimacy and vi-ability of Jesus Christ's being the incarnate Lord must then be evaluated and concluded by those standards, with his claim to lordship being rejected or conferred accordingly.

Confessional theology maintains that conferred lordship is a contradic-tion in terms. If Jesus Christ is Lord, and thus Lord of his own self-disclo-sure, then the conditions of his lordship can only and ever be set by him, not his followers or his critics. The incarnation is the God-given reality from which theology begins, not a plausible possibility toward which theology moves. Is the charge of "foolishness" sometimes waged against confessional theology by those who prefer "the free play of intellectual judgment"? In-deed. This charge "is a permanent accompaniment for any authentically Christian theology."[42] Does confessional theology have a low estimation of reason? No. Confessional theology simply insists that our reason is not a transcendent and autonomous entity before which God is summoned and by which God is judged. On the contrary, our reason is summoned into the presence of God, where it must be purged of idolatry and self-lordship by being crucified and raised to new life in Jesus Christ if it is to be made a fit handmaiden to faith in praise of God and service to his church.[43]

---

[41] Dietrich Bonhoeffer, *Christ the Center*, trans. Edwin H. Robertson (New York: Harper & Row, 1978), 30–37.
[42] Webster, "Incarnation," 204, 207–8.
[43] Webster, *Holiness*, 8, 17; Kelly M. Kapic, *A Little Book for New Theologians: Why and How to Study Theology* (Downers Grove, IL: IVP Academic, 2012), 49–63.

Confessional theology insists that the incarnation of God is and shall always remain a mystery. In no sense does this imply that nothing may be known about the incarnation. Rather, it means that the incarnation's depth and breadth are such as to prohibit its ever being plumbed or spanned. The incarnation can never be exhaustively explained, much less explained away. Far from being a concession to irrationality, acknowledging the irreducibly mysterious nature of the incarnation is a mark of intellectual maturity, displaying sanctified reason's proper suspicion of all ostensibly sophisticated forms of infidelity that presume to "solve" the One who became what he created without ceasing to be God. In other words, confessional theology refuses to degrade biblical mysteries by reducing them to problems. Problems are subject to solution by the application of an appropriate technique, whereas biblical mysteries transcend every conceivable solution or technique. Problems elicit frustration and invite resolution, whereas biblical mysteries elicit contemplation and invite adoration. Problems obscure other related matters until solved, whereas biblical mysteries illumine related matters without ever surrendering their own inherent inscrutability.[44] Such is the mystery of the incarnation, splendidly set to song by H. R. Bramley:

> A Babe on the breast of a Maiden he lies,
> Yet sits with the Father on high in the skies;
> Before him their faces the Seraphim hide,
> While Joseph stands waiting, unscared, by his side. . . .
> O wonder of wonders, which none can unfold,
> The Ancient of Days is an hour or two old;
> The Maker of all things is made of the earth,
> Man is worshiped by Angels, and God comes to birth.[45]

Third, this book is a work in evangelical theology in two important senses. On the one hand, the adjective *evangelical* aptly locates this book's authors within the evangelical tradition—that tributary within the broader stream of Christian expression rooted in classical Christian orthodoxy and shaped by the sixteenth-century Protestant Reformation and its heirs. Our work on the incarnation is thus grounded in Scripture, committed to

---

[44] Vernon C. Grounds, "The Postulate of Paradox," *Bulletin of the Evangelical Theological Society* 7, no. 1 (Winter 1964): 4–5 (hereafter *BETS*).
[45] H. R. Bramley, "The Great God of Heaven Is Come Down to Earth," no. 29 in *The English Hymnal* (London: Oxford University Press, 1933), 51.

Christian orthodoxy as articulated in the Nicene Creed and the Definition of Chalcedon, and informed by a wide range of theologians within the broader Christian tradition, both past and present. On the other hand, the adjective *evangelical* also describes a theological conviction of this book's authors that was quite simply bedrock to the theology of sixteenth-century Reformers such as Luther and Calvin, but is often absent from the thought of many who now consider themselves heirs of those Reformers. The conviction is that theology is faithful to Jesus Christ and beneficial to his church only when the living Truth himself prescribes the method by which God is known and confessed. The God-given vocation of theology is to be a servant of the Truth, never his self-appointed master. Thus, theology adopts a posture of suspicion and incredulity toward its Lord and his claim to be the divine self-exposition of God and man whenever it prescribes a method of its own choosing and assumes for that method an independent and authoritarian role in its vocation.[46] For this reason, Webster notes that perhaps the primary mark of authenticity for any theologizing on the incarnation is whether it resists the temptation of self-lordship, "or prefers, instead, to establish an independent colony of the mind from which to make raids on the church's confession."[47] As such, we maintain that theology is aptly called "evangelical" when it relates to Jesus Christ in a way that is specifically ordered by the "theo-logic" of the gospel, when it refuses to undermine and obscure the identity and significance of Jesus Christ by lifting him from the habitat of scriptural witness or laying for him a foundation alien to his own self-authenticating lordship.

CHAPTER PROSPECTUS

The remaining chapters of this book fill in the skeletal structure provided in the present chapter by exploring the relation of the incarnation to other major facets of the Christian faith. Chapter 2 is about the incarnation in relation to the Trinity. Here we discuss how the incarnate Jesus Christ manifests the inner being and heart of God by disclosing the intimate and eternal relationship enjoyed by God the Father, God the Son, and God the Spirit. Further, we discuss how believers are granted saving experiential knowledge of the triune God of the gospel as they are joined to the incarnate Jesus

---

[46] Torrance, *The School of Faith*, l.
[47] Webster, "Incarnation," 204.

Christ so as to partake in the life and love Christ shares with the Father in the communion of the Spirit.

Chapter 3 looks at the incarnation in relation to the attributes of God. Here we discuss how beholding the face of God in the face of Jesus Christ radically challenges all our self-styled expectations and assumptions regarding the nature and character of God. The attributes of God are indelibly Trinitarian and definitively displayed in the incarnate Christ, and so must be understood in dynamic, relational, and communicative terms. Christ assumed our flesh not to provide an object lesson on divine attributes, but to participate as God in our humanity, redeeming and remaking us, so that the life of God might be imaged in the life of Christ's body and bride, the church.

Chapter 4 moves our exploration of the incarnation more decidedly and explicitly into the realm of salvation by discussing the kind of humanity that God the Son assumed in becoming flesh. Because most modern Christians think our Lord assumed a human nature different and dissociated from our own, they tend to view the incarnation as merely an incidental prerequisite for our redemption. Here we propose that our redemption began with the incarnation, when God the Son penetrated the depths of our darkness to seize our corrupted and estranged humanity and make it his own, re-creating and reorienting our humanity by taking it into the very life of God.

Chapter 5 moves us more deeply still into the realm of salvation by discussing how the incarnation is inherently and dynamically related to the entire scope of our salvation, given that the incarnate Christ is himself the very substance and sum of that salvation. Here we propose an understanding of salvation with the incarnation at its center. The great soteriological significance of Christ's vicarious humanity is addressed with respect to his birth, life, death, resurrection, and ascension in the hope of deepening and broadening common notions of what it means to be reconciled to God in Christ by every aspect of our incarnate Savior's embodied existence.

Chapter 6 discusses the incarnation in relation to the application of Christ's reconciling activity, a topic commonly called applied soteriology. The logic of the incarnation indicates that salvation consists in nothing less or other than our being joined to the incarnate Christ, who has joined himself to us. Our incarnate Mediator comes to us clothed in his saving benefits, and he cannot be sundered from them. Thus, it is only by receiving Christ himself that we come to enjoy all he has done for us and our salvation. Here we address this glorious reality, giving particular attention to three major aspects of applied soteriology: justification, sanctification, and adoption.

Chapter 7 considers the incarnation in relation to the church. Seeing the church in light of Christ's humanity helps us grasp that the church is, in fact, the very body and bride of Christ. The incarnation also clarifies the nature and purpose of the preached word of God and the visible words of baptism and the Lord's Supper, constituting as they do the God-ordained means by which we commune with the living Word himself. This chapter aims to retrieve some of the richness found in historical evangelical ecclesiology so as to fortify the holiness and vitality of the contemporary evangelical church.

Finally, chapter 8 addresses the incarnation in relation to marriage and sex. Christians too often think and speak about these precious gifts of God in ways that abstract them from the *imago Dei* ("image of God") and the reality of Christ's intimate, saving union with his bride. Here we propose that our understanding of marriage and sex must not be detached from the union of God and man in Jesus Christ, because God intended marriage and sex to be life-affirming, life-enriching, life-giving manifestations of the gospel. Further, we propose that understanding marriage and sex in light of the incarnation punctuates the destructive and absurd nature of marital infidelity and sexual unholiness, which are, in effect, contradictions of the gospel.

2

Knowing the Father through the Son

THE INCARNATION AND
KNOWLEDGE OF GOD

The incarnation of the eternal Word of God is indeed the greatest and most profound mystery there is, for it leads to the following absolutely unique confession of the Christian church: God, without ever ceasing to be God, actually became what he created in order to reconcile us to himself. God's love is so great, his mercy and grace so persistent, and his desire to have us as his own so unrestrained that he performed an act of unparalleled condescension. According to Cyril, the fifth-century archbishop of Alexandria, the incarnation shatters the bounds of credulity:

> Indeed the mystery of Christ runs the risk of being disbelieved precisely because it is so incredibly wonderful. For God was in humanity. He who was above all creation was in our human condition; the invisible one was made visible in the flesh; he who is from the heavens and from on high was in the likeness of earthly things; the immaterial one could be touched; he who is free in his own nature came in the form of a slave; he who blesses all creation became accursed; he who is all righteousness was numbered among the transgressors; life itself came in the appearance of death. All this followed because the

body which tasted death belonged to no other but to him who is the Son by nature.[1]

The "incredibly wonderful" mystery the church confesses when we say Jesus Christ is both fully God and fully man is that God has joined himself to us forever. As the eternal Son of God, the incarnate Jesus is fully God without reserve and fully man without reserve, and he is fully God and man in his one person. In the words of the Chalcedonian Definition, the Lord Jesus Christ is "of the same reality as God . . . as far as his deity is concerned and of the same reality as we are ourselves . . . as far as his humanness is concerned."[2] The incarnate Son of God is, in other words, exactly as God is and exactly as we are. By becoming human, the eternal Son of the eternal Father took our humanity into union with himself in order to bridge the divide between God and man; thus, God and man are united in the incarnate One. This is why the starting point for all theological reflection is the incarnation.

We will explore the implications of this staggering reality for our understanding of God's character and attributes, sin, salvation, the church, and marriage and sex in the chapters that follow. But before we do so, let us pause in this chapter to reconsider the mystery of Christ's person from a perspective that is often overlooked.

THE INCARNATE SON AND KNOWLEDGE OF GOD

It is commonplace in evangelical theology to tie the incarnation directly to Christ's reconciling and atoning death and resurrection—that is, to assert, rightly, that the Son of God took on our flesh in order to bear our sin on the cross and raise us to new life. But what is often overlooked is the corresponding reality that in joining himself to humanity, the Son came to reconcile and atone for—to crucify and resurrect—our broken and corrupted *knowledge* of God. The divide that Christ came to bridge between humanity and God includes the deep chasm in our hearts and minds between what we think we know about God and who God really is.[3] Just as

---

[1] Cyril of Alexandria, *On the Unity of Christ*, trans. John Anthony McGuckin (New York: St. Vladimir's Seminary Press, 1995), 61.
[2] "The Definition of Chalcedon (451)," in *CC*, 36.
[3] John Webster notes: "Sin involves forfeit of knowledge of God and the replacement of that knowledge by illusion. We are fallen creatures, we do not know, and we do not know what we do not know." "Principles of Systematic Theology," in *International Journal of Systematic Theology* 11, no. 1 (January 2009): 61–62 (hereafter *IJST*).

crucial is the divide he came to bridge between how *we want* to know God and how *he actually wants* to be known. "Human reason," writes John Calvin, "neither approaches, nor strives toward, nor even takes a straight aim at, this truth: to understand who the true God is or what sort of God he wishes to be toward us."[4]

The advent of Christ constitutes an epistemological upheaval for fallen humanity, exposing and disrupting our twisted and rebellious human reasoning about God, and bringing into our humanity knowledge of *who* God really is and *how* he wishes to be known—all the makings of a truly merry Christ-mas! Jesus compels us to repentantly rethink, and then rejoice in, the reconciliation he has enacted between our fallen knowledge of God and his own perfect knowledge of God. Essential to the grand mystery of the incarnation is that the One who has come among us knows God *as God knows himself.* And he knows God in this most remarkable way *in our humanity*— Jesus Christ is fully God and *fully human.* This is gloriously good news for sinners, who have in Christ the reality of God's self-knowledge opened up into our human existence. The Son of God has joined himself to us for nothing less than to heal our corrupted minds and hearts, reconciling our false knowledge of God with his own true knowledge, making atonement ("at-one-ment") between our knowing and his. The incarnation constitutes Christian epistemology.

The unveiling of God in our human flesh, his stunning self-disclosure in our creaturely existence, was simultaneously scandalous and saving. In other words, the *kind* of knowledge Jesus of Nazareth claimed to have of God was both a stumbling block and the offer of eternal life at the same time.

What does it mean to say his knowledge proved scandalous, that it was a stumbling block? It means, for one thing, that Christ uncovered a beautiful and intimate complexity in God. The advent of God the Son revealed that the one God of Israel, who created the heavens and the earth, and who brought all creatures into existence, the one Sovereign over all the universe, is a complex unity. God is God the Father, God the Son, and God the Spirit, and is all the while one God. This revelation of God's eternal triune existence is punctuated by Jesus's outrageous personal claims. He scandalized those who claimed to truly know God by insisting time and again that true

---

[4] *Inst.*, 2.2.18.

knowledge of God requires true knowledge of the Son. Knowing God as he really is means knowing him as Father, but the Father is known only by and through the Son: "No one knows the Son except the Father," Jesus asserted, "and no one knows the Father except the Son and anyone to whom the Son chooses to reveal him" (Matt. 11:27). In other words, to know the Son *is* to know the Father: "If you had known me, you would have known my Father also. . . . Whoever has seen me has seen the Father" (John 14:7, 9). Claims like these proved so scandalous that they led Jesus straight to Golgotha, proving not only that we do not know God, but that we do not want to know him as he wishes to be known—as God the Father of his Son. And herein lies the scandal: there is no access to God the Father Almighty except through the one Lord Jesus Christ. Thus, Jesus's knowledge of God proved to be scandalous because it meant that this man from Nazareth—"Is not this Joseph's son?" (Luke 4:22)—knew God as only God could.

But Jesus's knowledge of God also proved to be the offer of eternal life. How was this so? To answer, we must pay attention to the *nature* of the Son's knowledge of the Father. It is common to children of modernity, reared in the epistemological abstractions of post-Enlightenment rationalism, to conceive of the term *knowledge* in merely cognitive or cranial ways. Knowing something or someone is often reduced to little more than knowing *about* that something or someone. Knowledge tends to have a data-driven orientation in our minds, and this orientation can have a deadening effect on our understanding of Jesus's knowledge of his Father. But knowledge has a very different orientation in Scripture, so when Jesus declares that he has come to make the Father known to us, he means much more than that he has come to transmit *information about* God the Father. Jesus did not come to dispense arcane, previously hidden factoids about God that we are to mentally appropriate. Rather, the Son of God came to share with us his knowledge of God his Father. He came, in other words, to incorporate us into his *experiential, relational knowledge* of the Father through the Spirit, to share the intimacy that characterizes their knowing of one another. The knowledge of which Jesus speaks is not speculative, theoretical, or philosophical knowledge, but the intimate fellowship he has eternally enjoyed in relation to the Father and Spirit. To *know* God is to *participate in* the very life and love that the Father has for the Son by the power and presence of the Spirit (John 14:20). The Son of God has joined himself to us so that we might partake of the life-giving intimacy he has always enjoyed with his Father: "And this is eternal life, that they know you the only true God, and Jesus Christ whom you have sent" (John 17:3).[5]

T. F. Torrance articulates the life-giving implications of this incarnational reality in a poignant way:

> By drawing near to us in Jesus Christ who took our human nature upon himself and lived out his divine life within it as a human life, God has opened up to us knowledge of his innermost Self as a fullness of personal being and brought us into intimate personal communion with himself as Father, Son and Holy Spirit.[6]

As the Son of God assumed our humanity into union with his divinity, he revealed not simply knowledge *about* who God is in his personal relations as Father, Son, and Spirit, but granted us participation in his intimate, relational knowing of the Father in the Holy Spirit. The incarnation assures us that to know God in Christ is nothing less than to *experience* the Son's life-giving knowledge of the Father—eternal life indeed.[7]

There is an axiomatic theological principle at work here that needs to be especially stressed among modern evangelicals, and it is this: Only God knows God, so only God can make himself known. To say it another way, anything or anyone that is not God cannot make God known. Or, from the lips of Jesus: "No one knows the Father except the Son." There is no true, saving knowledge of God except as he is experienced in the Son, as Father, through the Spirit. There is, quite simply, no other God than he, and no way to know him except as he really is. For modern evangelicals, this calls for a theological expansion of our biblical confession that "there is one God, and there is one mediator between God and men, the man Christ Jesus" (1 Tim. 2:5). Evangelicals faithfully stress that Christ is the sole Mediator of *salvation* between God and men, yet demonstrate a curious equivocation about whether Christ is the sole mediator of *knowledge* between God and men.

---

[5] In Scripture, life and death are primarily relational, rather than biological, realities. Life and death are descriptions about our existence in communion with, or alienation from, God.

[6] Thomas F. Torrance, *The Trinitarian Faith: The Evangelical Theology of the Ancient Catholic Church* (London: T&T Clark, 1991), 65–66.

[7] Andrew Purves reminds us that this reality applies to Christian doctrine as well: "There is no neutral knowledge of God, no sense in which Christian doctrine apart from faith in and relationship with God in Jesus Christ could exist as an independent item of information that did not stake an absolute claim upon us." *Reconstructing Pastoral Theology: A Christological Foundation* (Louisville, KY: Westminster John Knox Press, 2004), 16.

A testimony to this uncertain commitment to Christ's sole mediation is the prevalence among evangelicals of highly rationalistic forms of apologetics, or the related preoccupation with erecting epistemological frameworks for our theological confession unhinged from the revelation of Jesus Christ, which frameworks attempt to provide the conditions for the possibility of God apart from his triune revelation in Christ.[8] Regarding salvation, in other words, modern evangelicals tend to be robustly Augustinian-Reformational, and yet in relation to revelation, they often succumb to a dangerous rationalism, which Alister McGrath aptly refers to as "epistemic Pelagianism."[9] Apologetic methodologies and theological prolegomena that exhibit a rationalist tendency carry with them the implicit assumption that not only can knowledge of God be nonrelational, and thus nonsalvific, but also that our cognitive capacities have either escaped the devastating effects of the fall or have come out only limping, transcending the need for redemption and sanctification in Christ.[10] Such a view either leads to outright epistemic Pelagianism, in which it is assumed that God can be truly known apart from his self-revelation in Christ, or to epistemic semi-Pelagianism, in which it is assumed that true knowledge of God may begin with unsanctified human reason, needing only the "assisting" revelation of Christ to render it complete.[11] In either case, this remains a curious theological position for the evangelical heirs of Martin Luther and Calvin, the latter of whom wrote:

> For Christ proves that he is *the life*, because God . . . cannot be enjoyed in any other way than in Christ. Wherefore all theology, when separated from Christ, is not only vain and confused, but is also mad, deceitful, and spurious; for though the philosophers sometimes utter excellent sayings, yet they have nothing but what is short-lived, and even mixed up with wicked and erroneous sentiments.[12]

---

[8] As John Webster so forcefully states, "Because [Jesus Christ] is Lord, he can only be thought of as Lord; if he is not thought of as Lord, and with the rational deference which is due him as Lord, then he is not thought of at all." "Incarnation," in *BCMT*, 206.

[9] Alister E. McGrath, "The Doctrine of the Trinity: An Evangelical Reflection," in *God the Holy Trinity: Reflections on Christian Faith and Practice*, ed. Timothy George (Grand Rapids: Baker Academic, 2006), 19.

[10] Conversely, Dietrich Bonhoeffer asserts, "There are only two ways possible of encountering Jesus: man must die or he must put Jesus to death." *Christ the Center*, trans. Edwin H. Robertson (New York: Harper & Row, 1978), 35.

[11] Curious also on this note is the persistent evangelical flirtation with natural theology, which is thought to provide valid, if incomplete, knowledge of God. We say curious because, according to Scripture, even a theology that begins with the created order must of necessity be thoroughly christocentric (John 1:1–3; Col. 1:16–17; Heb. 1:1–3). To reject a purely natural theology is by no means to reject a theology of nature, in which, under the impress of God's self-revelation in Christ, theology comes to expression via the created order.

[12] John Calvin on John 14:6, *Calvin's Commentaries*, Calvin Translation Society (Edinburgh: 1844–56; repr. in 22 vols., Grand Rapids: Baker, 2003), 18/1:85–86 (hereafter *Comm.*).

A truly *Christ*ian epistemology, therefore, involves the assertion, even insistence, that apart from Christ, true knowledge of God (wisdom) is no more accessible to us than is his love, holiness, redemption, or life (1 Cor. 1:30). Any presumption of the knowledge of God apart from his self-revelation and self-giving in Christ is necessarily idolatrous. Because Jesus is himself fully God and fully man, he is the *self*-manifestation of God in our humanity. He is not a pointer *to* God or a revealer of information *about* God; he is the Way, Truth, and Life of God in our existence.[13] He is the Way because he is the union of God and man in his person; he is the Truth because he alone knows the Father; and he is the Life because he alone brings us to share in his life with the Father through the Spirit. Genuine knowledge of God can never be anything less or other than a sharing in God the Son's knowledge of God the Father through God the Spirit. The French Protestant preacher Adolphe Monod (1802–1856) expresses this reality splendidly:

> The relation of the Father, the Son and the Holy Spirit to man corresponds to a relationship in God between the Father, the Son and the Holy Spirit; and the love which is poured out to save us is the expression of that love which has dwelt eternally in the bosom of God. Ah! The doctrine then becomes for us so touching and profound! There we find the basis of the Gospel, and those who reject it as a speculative and purely theological doctrine have therefore never understood the least thing about it; it is the strength of our hearts, it is the joy of our souls, it the life of our life, it is the very foundation of revealed truth.[14]

This means, further, that Christian epistemology is not only coincident with Christian soteriology, but that a truly *Christ*ian epistemology and soteriology is inescapably triune. God became incarnate in order to reveal to us, and in us, the incredibly good news that he deigns to be our Father by joining us to himself in his Son the Savior by the power of the Spirit. To *know* God is to experience him as the saving Trinity. The eternal life he gives to us is the eternal life and love he intrinsically and eternally is as Father,

---

[13] Thomas Smail: "Many can say, Go to God, but only Jesus can say Come to me, for to come to him is to come to God." *The Forgotten Father* (Grand Rapids: Eerdmans, 1981), 56. Unlike the prophets who preceded him, the Prophet Jesus does not point away from himself but to himself.

[14] Adolphe Monod, *Adophe Monod's Farewell to His Friends and to His Church*, trans. Owen Thomas (London: Banner of Truth Trust, 1962), 114, quoted in Fred Sanders's excellent book *The Deep Things of God: How the Trinity Changes Everything* (Wheaton, IL: Crossway, 2010), 166.

Son, and Spirit. There is no other God except the triune God, and so any other supposed knowledge of God is by definition religious fantasy:

> The bedrock of our faith is nothing less than God himself, and every aspect of the gospel—creation, revelation, salvation—is only Christian insofar as it is the creation, revelation and salvation of *this* God, the triune God. . . . And so, because the Christian God is triune, the Trinity is the governing center of all Christian belief, the truth that shapes and beautifies all others. The Trinity is the cockpit of all Christian thinking.[15]

To confess God as Trinity is no mere conceptual apparatus by which we attempt to "explain" God; God simply is fundamentally and gloriously triune. The self-manifestation of God in the incarnation allows us to experience God as such, and teaches us to think, speak, and—as Charles Wesley teaches us—even sing of God in specifically this way:

> Veiled in flesh the Godhead see,
> Hail th' incarnate Deity!
> Pleased as man with us to dwell,
> Jesus, our Emmanuel.[16]

The Incarnate Son Reveals God as Father

The coming of the eternal Word and Son of God into our humanity precipitated a revolution in our understanding of who God is and who he is for us. After all, if God has a Son, then God must be a Father. And the fact that the Son does indeed have a Father is the best of all possible news for humanity. The Son's relationship with his Father is everything to him; he has eternally existed in the intimacy of his Father's loving embrace, enjoying the most perfect and intimate of all unions from before time began. The relationship that the Son and Father share (in the Spirit, see below) transcends the bounds of time and the limits of our imagination: "I and the Father are one," Jesus declares (John 10:30); and, as if to forestall any underinterpretation, he says later:

---

[15] Michael Reeves, *Delighting in the Trinity: An Introduction to the Christian Faith* (Downers Grove, IL: IVP Academic, 2012), 15–16.

[16] Charles Wesley, "Hark, the Herald Angels Sing," no. 24 in *The English Hymnal* (London: Oxford University Press, 1933), 43.

Do you not believe that I am in the Father and the Father is in me? The words that I say to you I do not speak on my own authority, but the Father who dwells in me does his works. Believe me that I am in the Father and the Father is in me. (John 14:10–11)

The Father has always been in the Son, and the Son has always been in the Father, and so the Son has known the Father's love from "before the foundation of the world" (John 17:24). In fact, the Father's eternal love for the Son is so immense and so extravagant that it overflowed into the creation of the world, and it is now overflowing again into the re-creation of the world through him. The Father not only created all things by and for his Son, he will also reconcile all things in heaven and earth in his Son (Col. 1:16; Eph. 1:9–10). It is this love, this life-giving, universe-creating love between the Father and the Son, that the Son came to make known among us—he came to preach the gospel of his Father's love to us. But, more amazing still, he came to make this gospel known *in* us:

If anyone loves me, he will keep my word, and my Father will love him, *and we will come to him and make our home with him.* (John 14:23)

O righteous Father, even though the world does not know you, I know you, and these [those given to the Son by the Father] know that you have sent me. I made known to them your name, and I will continue to make it known, *that the love with which you have loved me may be in them, and I in them.* (John 17:25–26)

If any point bears repeating, it is this: Jesus came to do more than disseminate information about the Father; he came to join himself to us that we might be brought *into* the eternal love that he and the Father simply are. Jesus shares with us his Father's love by sharing himself. It is no wonder, then, that whoever has the Son has eternal life (1 John 5:12). Likewise, it is no wonder that Jesus was so insistent that we can truly know God as the Father he really is only if we know him through the Son—apart from whom the Father is not God! That is why those who rejected Jesus, while still claiming to know God, always struck Jesus as literally absurd.[17] Such a claim was, for him, self-evidently self-refuting, for there is no other God

---

[17] Literally, *absurdity* means "the state or condition in which human beings exist in an irrational and meaningless universe and in which human life has no ultimate meaning." *Merriam-Webster's Collegiate Dictionary*, 10th ed. (Springfield, MA: Merriam-Webster, Inc., 2002), 5.

than his very own Father, so there is no other God than who the Son is *with* the Father: "I and the Father are one." The claim to know God apart from the Son amounted to the absurdity of claiming to know God while at the same time rejecting who God essentially is. There is no knowledge of God—and, thus, no knowledge of God's love—apart from the Son's experiential knowledge of his Father's love. It is exactly this kind of knowing that the Son came to bring to us and in us.

Jesus reserved his harshest condemnations for those who questioned his sonship with the Father. We might begin to understand why this was so when we realize that Jesus's self-testimony was at the same time his testimony to his Father. He said this in many ways: he was sent by his Father; he came to do the will of his Father; he came to glorify his Father; and he came to make his Father's love known. Nothing was more certain to Jesus than that to reject him, to repudiate his sonship with the Father, was to reject God, to repudiate God as the Father he is. This explains his stern rebuke of the Pharisees, who dared to question Jesus's sonship. "Where is your Father?" they asked disingenuously. "You know neither me nor my Father," Jesus answered. "If you knew me, you would know my Father also" (John 8:19).[18] The extended interchange that ensued is remarkable and arresting. After all, nothing was more certain to the Pharisees than that they really did know God, studied as they were in the Law and the Prophets, and being descendants of Abraham himself. They were equally certain that knowing God did not require knowing his Son: "We have one Father—even God," they insisted (John 8:41). This claim struck at what is absolutely unique to Jesus, and what is most precious to him; after all, if their claim were true, it would have meant that Jesus himself did not really know his Father! And so it was *this* claim, to know God as Father without embracing his eternally beloved Son, that provoked perhaps the harshest and most shocking words Jesus ever spoke:

> If God were your Father, you would love me, for I came from God and I am here. I came not of my own accord, but he sent me. Why do you not understand what I say? It is because you cannot bear to hear my word. You are of your father the devil, and your will is to do your father's

---

[18] Calvin has wise words for those of us who would disassociate ourselves from the Pharisees: "Let us know that the same thing is spoken to us all; for whoever aspires to know God, and does not begin with Christ, must wander—as it were—in a labyrinth." Calvin on John 8:19, *Comm.* 17/2:329.

desires. . . . Whoever is of God hears the words of God. The reason why you do not hear them is that you are not of God. (John 8:42–47)

These words rumble like thunder. They proceeded from the heavens with terrific gravity, meant to shake his hearers awake from their godless slumber: "You are of your father the devil. . . . You are not of God." There is no God, Jesus insists, other than the God who is Father and Son: to know, hear, and love the Son is the same as to know, hear, and love God. Jesus is, in other words, the *self*-revelation of God. This means that God the Father does not wish to be known in any other way than in God the Son, and, furthermore, that God is not, and cannot be, God apart from his Son. Thus, to reject the Son is to belong, by definition, to one who is other than God. "Belief in the 'one Lord Jesus Christ,'" John Webster writes, "is not a supplement to belief in one God but rather a precise statement of the content of such a belief, in which it is an ingredient."[19]

The Son's testimony to the Father is an echo of the Father's testimony to the Son. The Son came to make his Father's love known among us, and the Father sent his Son so that we would know and experience that love. In fact, God chose to speak from heaven on exactly three occasions after the incarnation of his Son—that is, in the whole of the New Testament—and on these occasions, he directed us to his Son and to the love he has for him: "This is my beloved Son, with whom I am well pleased; listen to him" (Matt. 17:5; cf. Mark 1:11; 9:7; Luke 3:22; 9:35; 2 Pet. 1:17). The Father and the Son share precisely the same desire—to open up to us the love they eternally share with one another. And so the Father directs us to his Son, his eternally beloved, and the Son directs us to himself, the bearer and bestower of that love.

It is here that the *incarnation* of the Son is so monumentally significant. God does not just tell us *about* his love for his Son, nor does Jesus merely tell us *about* the love his Father has for him. Such knowledge would perhaps be interesting, even novel—but it would not require the enfleshing of God's Son, and it would not be *saving, eternal-life-giving* knowledge. The stunning reality of the incarnation is that the love that God the Father has

---

[19] Webster, "Incarnation," 216. We wish to add here that the Old Testament saints did indeed truly know God; not apart from Christ, however, but insofar as Christ was always the substance of that knowledge, proleptically. As Jesus told the Pharisees in the context at hand: "Your father Abraham rejoiced that he would see my day. He saw it and was glad" (John 8:56).

for God the Son *has come into our humanity through the enfleshing of the Father's Son.* The love of God for his Son has actually entered into our humanity, allowing our humanity entrance into that love.

With such an astonishing realization in mind, consider again Jesus's words: "I am the way, and the truth, and the life. No one comes to the Father except through me" (John 14:6). When Jesus said that he is the "way" to the Father, and that it is only "through me" that one comes to the Father, it surely makes all the difference in the world that it is specifically the *incarnate* Son of God who said so! The incarnate Son is *himself* our Way to the Father, precisely because he is the union of God and our humanity in his one person. By becoming human, the Son joined our humanity to the Father—only God incarnate could do that! This is what it means to say that when the incarnate Son reveals God as Father, it is supremely good news (gospel).

To be a recipient of the love of God in Christ is to really experience this love *in Christ himself*, in the Son who unites God and man. Christ does not provide *a way* to God the Father; he himself is that Way, for he is God in our flesh. This amazingly good news ought to keep us from reductionistic sentimentalizing of God's love. The love that God has for us sinners is not a dispositional adjustment effected in God because of something Jesus has done. Neither is eternal life a commodity that Jesus dispenses as a reward for belief in him. God's merciful and grace-filled offer of life and love in Christ is far more beautiful, intimate, and *real* than that. In Christ, God gives us a share in the very life and love that the Son and the Father have always been. As Donald Fairbairn notes:

> Jesus is not saying eternal life is something that he will give us. He is not saying that because of what he has done, or what he will do or what we do, then we will get *x*, *y* or *z* while living forever in heaven. Eternal life is knowing Christ and his Father, God. At the heart of the central idea of Christianity lies the reality that Christians will know the Father and the Son.[20]

To know the Father through the Son is also no mere dispositional change or cognitive re-adjustment on the part of sinners. To *know* the Father through the Son is to be *joined* to the Father through the incarnate

---

[20] Donald Fairbairn, *Life in the Trinity: An Introduction to Theology with the Help of the Church Fathers* (Downers Grove, IL: IVP, 2009), 29.

Son. The early church fathers were known for expressing the gospel in this way, but many evangelical Christians may be surprised to find that Luther concurred vigorously:

> For the Son comes down to us from the Father and attaches Himself to us; and we, in turn, attach ourselves to Him and come to the Father through Him. This is the reason for His incarnation and His birth from the Virgin Mary, that He might mingle with us, be seen and heard by us, yes, be crucified and put to death for us, and draw and hold us to Him. He was sent to draw up to the Father those who would believe in Him, just as He is in the Father. He forged these links between Himself and us and the Father, thus enclosing us in this circle, so that now we are in Him, and He in us, just as He is in the Father and the Father is in Him. Through such a union and communion our sin and death are abolished, and now we have sheer life and blessedness in their stead.[21]

THE INCARNATE SON REVEALS GOD AS THE SPIRIT OF THE FATHER AND THE SON

The incarnation, as Luther wrote, performed the miracle of "enclosing us in this circle" of the Son and the Father so that we would have "sheer life and blessedness." Could there be any better news than this? Well, in truth, yes! It turns out that the circle of which Luther spoke is actually bigger, if you will, than the circle of the Father and the Son. We might call this circle three-dimensional or, better, three-personal. While it is most certainly true that the Father is God and the Son is God, it is also true that neither of them is God without the Holy Spirit, who is himself God. God is always one God, and he is always three persons. In other words, God is always the eternal love, life, and communion of Father, Son, and Spirit. If this is true, then we might expect that the relational knowledge of God the Father that we have through God the Son necessarily involves God the Spirit. As we have shown, the knowledge of God that we have in Christ is none other than a sharing in God's self-knowing—Jesus Christ is God. Let us now expand the circle of that astonishingly good news into the following: our knowledge of God in Christ is none other than a sharing in God's self-knowing through the Spirit—the Spirit is God. As Victor Shepherd aptly states:

---

[21] "Sermon on the Gospel of St. John 14:28," in *LW*, 24:139.

In Scripture, to know God is to participate in the reality of God and so to be rendered forever different. Our knowledge of God is precisely the *difference* our engagement with this "Other" has made to us when we meet this "Other" as *Person*. Only if the Spirit is God (i.e., homoousially identical with the Father and Son) is the activity of the Spirit that act of God whereby the God who knows himself includes us in his self-knowing.[22]

God cannot be known as God apart from his triune existence because God *is not God* apart from his triune existence: God cannot be other than who he is as he includes us in his self-revelation. It is this tripersonal divine gospel reality that the incarnate Son presses upon us when he speaks of our knowledge of God. As Jesus repeatedly insisted, the knowledge we have of the Father through the Son is mediated to us through the presence of the Holy Spirit: we know God as Father only *in* the Son and always *through* the Spirit. This should bring to mind a point made earlier in this chapter: only God knows God, and so only God can make himself known. Because God is intrinsically triune, he makes himself known in no other way than as Father in the Son through the Spirit, and so any other supposed knowledge of God can be nothing other than religious fantasy. An assertion like this may strike many Christians as excessive, perhaps a bit theologically high-handed or pedantic, implying that a full-orbed understanding of Trinitarian doctrine is necessary before one can really know God. We admit that the assertion is indeed striking and excessive, though not because of its theological sophistication, but because of the excessive beauty of God's self-disclosure. What *ought* to be striking to us, as it was to Jesus's disciples, is what the Son actually reveals about how we come to know the Father:

> If you love me, you will keep my commandments. And I will ask the Father, and he will give you another Helper, to be with you forever, even the Spirit of truth, whom the world cannot receive, because it neither sees him nor knows him. You know him, for he dwells with you and will be in you. I will not leave you as orphans; I will come to you. . . . In that day you will know that I am in my Father, and you in me, and I in you. (John 14:15–20)

---

[22] Victor Shepherd, "Thomas F. Torrance and the *Homoousion* of the Holy Spirit," in *Canadian Evangelical Review* 32, no. 22 (Fall 2006–Spring 2007), 9.

Jesus spoke these words not to confuse but to comfort his disciples, then and now, troubled by his earthly departure. In this sublime passage, Jesus disclosed the tripersonal reality of knowing God. To know God is to know the Father in the Son through the Spirit, as the Spirit brings us into the Son who is in the Father: a triune circle of knowing. This is the basis for the assertion that God makes himself known precisely and only as he really is— Father, Son, and Spirit. The eternal Son of God became incarnate to bring into our humanity his knowing of the Father, and he does so by his sending of, and indwelling through, the Spirit: "I will not leave you as orphans; I will come to you." The role of the Spirit in the economy of salvation (knowing God) is to intimately acquaint us with Jesus Christ, and in so doing, to bind us so closely to him that we share in his riches with the Father:

> I still have many things to say to you, but you cannot bear them now. When the Spirit of truth comes, he will guide you into all the truth, for he will not speak on his own authority, but whatever he hears he will speak, and he will declare to you the things that are to come. He will glorify me, for he will take what is mine and declare it to you. All that the Father has is mine; therefore I said that he will take what is mine and declare it to you. (John 16:12–15)

The disciples, Jesus said, could not bear these things. Can we bear them now? Can we bear in humble boldness the truth that God the Spirit brings us to enjoy all that God the incarnate Son has with God the Father? Can we really know God like this? We not only can, but must, for there is no other way to know him except in the lavish and indescribable triune love that he is.

Paul learned to bear these things. On the road to Damascus, Saul the Pharisee encountered the incarnate Son of God and left as Paul the apostle of Jesus Christ. He left that encounter, in other words, knowing God. Only God can make God known, he learned, because only God knows God:

> For who knows a person's thoughts except the spirit of that person, which is in him? So also no one comprehends the thoughts of God except the Spirit of God. Now we have received not the spirit of the world, but the Spirit who is from God, that we might understand the things freely given us by God. . . . The natural person does not accept the things of the Spirit of God, for they are folly to him, and he is not able to un-

derstand them because they are spiritually discerned. . . . "For who has understood the mind of the Lord so as to instruct him?" But we have the mind of Christ. (1 Cor. 2:11–16)

Knowledge of God, as Paul knew only too well, has a distinctly and exclusively Trinitarian shape. We have access to God's knowing of himself only through the mind of God the Son, and this only through God the Spirit. The man Jesus Christ is indeed the one Mediator between God and men. He is both the Mediator of our salvation *and* the Mediator of our knowledge of God in one act of mediation through the Spirit: "For through [Christ] we both have access in one Spirit to the Father" (Eph. 2:18). Thus, while the knowledge of God that we have in Christ through the Spirit is never less than the redemption of our cognitive awareness of God, it is always more than this. "Knowledge of God in his revelation is no mere cognitive affair," says Webster; "it is to know *God* and therefore to love and fear the God who appoints us to fellowship with himself, and not merely to entertain God as a mental object, however exalted."[23] The revelation of God in Christ through the Spirit is reconciling, redemptive, saving knowledge because to know God in this way is to experience the fellowship that the Father, Son, and Spirit share; after all, the triune persons do more than entertain one another as mental objects! The Son of God has come to share with us his knowing of God the Father through God the Spirit. It is the saving grace of Christ to bring us into God's love through the fellowship of the Spirit. Bearing this in mind and heart, we may come to see that Paul's concluding words to the Corinthians are more than poetic sentiment: "The grace of the Lord Jesus Christ and the love of God and the fellowship of the Holy Spirit be with you all" (2 Cor. 13:14). Paul is simply and profoundly expressing what is true of every Christian, then and now—we have come to know *God*.

To reiterate what we have said previously: the role of God the Spirit in the economy of salvation is to intimately acquaint us with God the Son and, in so doing, to bind us so closely to him that we share in his knowing of God the Father. In this respect, consider the words of the Nicene-Constantinopolitan Creed (381): "We believe in the Holy Spirit, the Lord, the giver of life, who proceeds from the Father and the Son." This historic

---

[23] John Webster, *Holy Scripture: A Dogmatic Sketch* (Cambridge: Cambridge University Press, 2003), 16.

confession, enjoined upon the one, holy, catholic, and apostolic church, urges us to think of the Spirit in properly Trinitarian ways. The Spirit is "the Lord"—he is God—because the Spirit has eternally been the One who proceeds from the Father and the Son; he is not Lord in some other way. The Spirit is also "the giver of life," and he is so (note the qualifier) *as he proceeds from the Father and the Son*—not otherwise. The Spirit is the giver of life, not abstractly considered, but rather precisely as he is joined to and proceeds from the Father and Son. Just as the eternal love that the Father has for the Son overflows into creation for our salvation, so the eternal procession and fellowship of the Spirit, with the Father and Son, overflow into creation to join us to that love. The Son sends the Spirit from the Father in order that, in that procession, we may experience the love of the Father in the Son. And it is for this reason that, despite the disciples' initial grief and anxiety, Jesus insisted that his earthly departure was in fact very good news. For he was returning to the Father in order to send the Spirit from him, and this would mean that Jesus would be present to them, and us, in an unimaginable way: "In that day you will know that I am in my Father, and you in me, and I in you."

The Spirit, thus, is never to be conceived of apart from the Father and the Son, any more than the Son is to be thought of apart from the Father, or the Father from the Son. The procession of the Spirit from the Father and the Son—"I will ask the Father, and he will give you another Helper"—constitutes the fulfillment of God's revelation as *triune*. The Spirit is not sent as a replacement or substitute for the Father and the Son, he is sent as the One who brings us into union with Christ so that we experience his loving communion with the Father.[24] The Spirit, in other words, performs a specifically Trinitarian and christological redemptive role. "The Holy Spirit," Calvin writes, "is the bond by which Christ effectually unites us to himself."[25] The Spirit binds us to Christ so that we may experience all that the Father has given the Son.

This gospel reality is important to stress given the pneumatological ambiguity prevalent in much contemporary evangelical theology, which often conceives of the Spirit as a surrogate for an absent Christ. When

---

[24] J. I. Packer writes, "[T]he distinctive, constant, basic ministry of the Holy Spirit in the New Covenant is . . . to mediate Christ's presence to believers." *Keep in Step with the Spirit* (Grand Rapids: Fleming H. Revell, 1984), 49.
[25] *Inst.*, 3.1.1.

our pneumatology becomes nonchristological in this way, and thus non-Trinitarian, the "Spirit" may be invoked to bolster any number of false theologies or, better, ideologies. Loosed from his role as the One who comes to acquaint us with God by joining us to the Son, the Spirit can be manipulated to serve our speculative religious agendas, movements, and "spiritual giftings." Worse still, we may begin to lose sight of the spectacular work of the Spirit, who is sent to join us to the incarnate Son of God that we may share in his knowing of the Father.

Indeed, the indwelling Spirit is the Spirit of Jesus Christ, who indwells the children of God, incorporating us into the loving fellowship of God *through the Son*: "And because you are sons, God has sent the Spirit of his Son into our hearts, crying, 'Abba! Father!'" (Gal. 4:6; cf. Rom. 8:9–10, 15). So intimately does the Spirit bind us to the incarnate Son that we even share in the cry of the incarnate Son to his Father, who uttered these same words in his deepest hour of need—"Abba, Father" (Mark 14:36). The danger of abstracting the Spirit from his Trinitarian role of making the Father known through the Son is that we risk losing what is so glorious and life-giving about the procession of the Spirit: the Spirit is "the giver of life" to us *because* he joins us to the incarnate Son of God, who has brought us life from the Father.

Here again we are reminded of the extraordinary significance of the incarnation. The incarnate Son is our only way to know God as the Father he is, because Christ alone has assumed our humanity into union with himself. It is not the Spirit but the Word who became flesh, and in so doing sanctified and justified our fallen knowledge of God. The Spirit brings the Word into us and us into him. This is why, following the apostolic testimony, we confess that in the incarnate Savior, and through the Spirit, we come to experience God as he truly is: "In [Christ Jesus] you also are being built together into a dwelling place for God by the Spirit" (Eph. 2:22). And elsewhere:

> By this we know that we abide in [God] and he in us, because he has given us of his Spirit. And we have seen and testify that the Father has sent his Son to be the Savior of the world. Whoever confesses that Jesus is the Son of God, God abides in him, and he in God. (1 John 4:13–15)

PERICHŌRĒSIS, HOMOOUSION . . .
AND THE GOSPEL OF JESUS CHRIST?

Given what we have just written, we are in a position to return to, and expand upon, the point made in chapter 1 regarding the Trinitarian and christological expressions of the early church—in other words, how Nicene and Chalcedonian orthodoxy bears directly upon our saving knowledge of the triune God. The incarnation of the Son of God—the revelation of God himself in the flesh and blood of Jesus of Nazareth—compelled humanity to answer the most important question that has ever been or ever will be asked: "Who do you say that I am?" It seems fair to say that the entire New Testament is an extended answer to and reflection upon this one question. There is good reason for this. After all, the incarnation of God in his eternal Son opened up to humanity the glorious and mysterious complexity of God's triune existence. So the question from Jesus's lips, "Who do you say that I am?" is monumentally and fundamentally significant. If Jesus is indeed the eternal Son of God in flesh and blood, then this means everything for how we conceive of and come to know God. Consequently, it means everything for how we understand what it means to be the recipients of God's saving love. The mystery of Christ's person is both the mystery of God's being and the mystery of our salvation.

From the very beginning, the church, under the kindling of God's burning love, came to confess and adore the mystery of Christ's person. She delighted in and praised Jesus Christ as God himself, exulting in the good news that through him and all that he had done, the church was the recipient of the love of the heavenly Father, and this through the power and presence of the Spirit. Also from the very beginning, the church was forced to safeguard this precious, saving mystery of Christ's person against the constant threat of those who would have obscured or denied it. The church knew very well that her one hope of salvation was that Jesus Christ is God himself in flesh and blood, and that to know the Son is to be reconciled to God the Father through God the Spirit. To obscure or deny who Jesus is would mean nothing less than to obscure or deny who God is, resulting in the obscuring or denying of the gospel—that *God* has reconciled us to himself in Christ through the Spirit (1 John).

The early church came to employ two especially rich words in her efforts to both confess and protect the wonder of God's triune being as disclosed through the revelation of the mystery of the incarnate Son of God. One of these words was *perichōrēsis* and the other *homoousion*. Although words such as these tend to be relegated to the domain of ivory-tower theologians or church historians, or regarded as philosophical jargon that unnecessarily complicates the simplicity of the gospel,[26] we wish to show, on the contrary, that these are the kinds of words that serve to *articulate exactly why the gospel is such good news*. These words expressed the beauty and depth of the good news of Jesus Christ, and, if they are seen for what they are, can express the same good news for the contemporary church.

Let us begin with *perichōrēsis*.[27] Defined succinctly by Miroslav Volf, *perichōrēsis* expresses "the mutual internal abiding and interpenetration of the divine persons."[28] The term was coined by John of Damascus in the eighth century, although as Robert Letham notes, the conceptual reality was present and "was already widely accepted" by early church figures such as Athanasius and the Cappadocians.[29] The term speaks to the mutual interpenetration and indwelling that exists within the three-person unity of God the Father, Son, and Spirit. *Perichōrēsis* describes, in other words, the intense intimacy that binds Father, Son, and Spirit together as one God. It has been used to attempt to speak of the mystery of the holy and beautiful interpersonal communion that is intrinsic to God's being, a mystery that is repeatedly opened up to us in the Scriptures: "Do you not believe that I am in the Father and the Father is in me?" (John 14:10); "I and the Father are one" (John 10:30); "For the Spirit searches everything, even the depths of God" (1 Cor. 2:10). Consider the way Torrance describes the perichoretic relations in God's inner being:

> [*Perichōrēsis*] expressed the truth that the Father, the Son and the Holy Spirit are distinctive persons each with his own communicable properties, but that they dwell *in* one another, not only *with* one another in such an intimate way . . . that their individual characteristics instead

---

[26] There is a common misconception that the early church borrowed from Greek philosophy in an attempt to elucidate the gospel. Far from it. The church's use of *homoousion*, for example, would have horrified the philosophers. J. B. Torrance writes, "What could be more un-Hellenic than the statement of the Creed that God 'was made man'!" "The Vicarious Humanity of Christ," in *The Incarnation: Ecumenical Studies in the Nicene-Constantinopolitan Creed A.D. 381*, ed. T. F. Torrance (Eugene, OR: Wipf & Stock, 1998), 132.

[27] *Perichōrēsis* derives from the Greek prefix *peri*, which indicates enclosing or surrounding, and the words *chōra* ("space or room") or *chōrein* ("to extend or contain").

[28] Miroslav Volf, *After Our Likeness: The Church as the Image of the Trinity* (Grand Rapids: Eerdmans, 1998), 208.

[29] Robert Letham, *The Holy Trinity: In Scripture, History, Theology, and Worship* (Phillipsburg, NJ: P&R, 2004), 178.

of dividing them from one another unite them indivisibly together, the Father in the Son and the Spirit, the Son in the Father and the Spirit, and the Spirit in the Father and the Son. The Father is not Father apart from the Son and the Spirit, the Son is not the Son apart from the Father and the Spirit, and the Spirit is not the Spirit apart from the Father and the Son, for each is who he is in his wholeness as true God of true God in the wholeness of the other two who are each true God of true God, and yet in the mystery of their perichoretic interrelations they are not three Gods but only one God, the Blessed and Holy Trinity.[30]

Although the term *perichōrēsis* was meant to bring doctrinal clarity to the church's confession that God is one and that the persons of the Father, Son, and Spirit are coequally God—a unity in Trinity and a Trinity in unity—the reality it expresses also brings to light the innermost and profoundly intimate relations that the divine persons enjoy together. Our one God has eternally been, and will eternally be, a mutually indwelling and interpenetrating communion of persons who exist in self-giving and life-giving love: indwelling and interpenetrating personal love is *who God is*. The Father has always loved the Son, the Son has always loved the Father, and that love has always existed in the loving fellowship of the Spirit. Thus, when the church confesses that God is love, we ought to mean much more than that God *loves* or *is loving*. We ought to mean principally that God is himself the love from which he loves. Just as there was never a time when God was not Father to his Son, so there was never a time when God was not love. Love is not a disposition in God that comes to expression only in the creation and redemption of the world; rather, God simply *is and always has been* the love by which he loves the world. "The Gospel does not rest simply on the fact that God loves us," writes Torrance, "but on the fact that he loves us with the very same love which he is in the eternal communion of Love which God is in his Triune Being."[31]

This already sounds like fantastic news, but let us pause for a moment and consider our second word: *homoousion*. This term originally was used to express the incarnate Christ's absolute unity with God the Father. We first encounter it in the Nicene Creed (325) in the following phrase: "We

---

[30] T. F. Torrance, *The Christian Doctrine of God: One Being, Three Persons* (Edinburgh: T&T Clark, 1996; repr., 2006), 172.
[31] Ibid., 253.

believe . . . in one Lord Jesus Christ, the Son of God, begotten of the Father as only begotten, that is, from the essence of the Father . . . God from God, Light from Light, true God from true God, begotten not created . . . *of the same essence [homoousion] as the Father . . .*" (emphasis added).[32] This word protects and joyfully asserts the church's confession that Jesus Christ is none other than God himself, of one being or essence with the Father: Jesus is the selfsame God, and he is so as Son to the Father.

As staggering as this reality is, there is yet more. We encounter the word *homoousion* again in the equally majestic Chalcedonian Definition (451):

> Following, then, the holy fathers, we . . . confess the one and only Son, our Lord Jesus Christ. This selfsame one is perfect . . . both in deity . . . and also in humanness; this selfsame one is also actually . . . God and actually man, with a rational soul . . . and a body. He is of the same reality [*homoousion*] as God as far as his deity is concerned and of the same reality [*homoousion*] as we are ourselves as far as his human-ness is concerned.[33]

The words "same reality" are a translation of the Greek word *homoousion*. What is important to note here is that, while *homoousion* was originally applied in the Nicene Creed to Christ's unity with the Father, Chalcedon also applied the term to Christ's unity with us. Jesus is "of one substance" with the Father, and he is also "of one substance" with us; truly God and truly man. The holy mystery of the person of the incarnate Son means that he never ceases to be God when he takes on our flesh, but neither is he anything less than authentically human by reason of his divinity—he really is God and he really is human at one and the same time in his one person.[34] To put it as we have previously: God, without ever ceasing to be God, has become what he created in order to join us to himself.

With this brief explanation before us, we are now in a position to say why the words *perichōrēsis* and *homoousion*, far from being theologically elitist terms, are in fact critically important to a full-orbed appreciation of the gospel.[35] We made the point earlier that the Son of God became

---

[32] "The Creed of Nicaea (325)," in *CC*, 30.

[33] "The Definition of Chalcedon (451)," in *CC*, 35.

[34] This reality has been expressed by the equally rich ecclesiological phrase "hypostatic union," which expresses the gospel truth that in the one person of Jesus Christ there exists a union of a fully human and fully divine nature or "substance."

[35] Alasdair Heron writes: "The key to the gospel is not the word *homoousios*, but the Word made flesh, not the word chosen by the fathers of Nicaea, but the Word in whom our life has been chosen, redeemed and sanctified

incarnate to dwell among us not merely to tell us *about* the life and love he has always shared with his Father—which he might just as easily have done from afar or through another prophet—but rather to allow us to participate *in* that very life and love by joining himself to us. By becoming incarnate, the Son of God extended his relationship with his Father into our human existence, through the Spirit. In other words, the perichoretic relation of Father, Son, and Spirit—their mutual indwelling and interpenetration, the life and love they share together—has taken residence in our human flesh in the person of Jesus Christ. Thus, the love and life that God *is and always has been* as Father, Son, and Spirit comes to us as the Spirit joins us to the Son that we might know his Father. "In that day," says the Son, referring to the sending of the Spirit, "you will know that I am in my Father, and you in me, and I in you" (John 14:20).

When we couple this astounding fact with the reality that Jesus Christ, the eternal Son of God in our flesh, is *homoousion* with the Father and *homoousion* with us—he is unreservedly God and unreservedly human in his one person—we come face to face with the unutterably glorious depth of the gospel: God has given us *himself*. It would be difficult to improve on Torrance's words:

> In the outgoing movement of his eternal Love God himself has come among us and become one of us and one with us in the Person of his beloved Son in order to reconcile us to himself and to share with us the Fellowship of Love which he has within his own Triune Life. . . . The Love that God the Father, God the Son and God the Holy Spirit eternally are, has taken incarnate form in the Lord Jesus Christ for us and our salvation. The self-giving and self-sacrificial Love manifested in him flows from the self-giving and self-sacrificial Love of God and are that self-giving and self-sacrificial Love in redemptive action on our behalf in the world.[36]

The triune life and love of Father, Son, and Spirit have "taken incarnate form." This is the spectacular import of *perichōrēsis* and *homoousion*. Together, they help us to articulate what Jesus means when he says that he

to the glory of the Father. So long as *homoousios* is used to say *that*, it will have its place as the hall-mark of authentic Christian theology." "Homoousios with the Father," in Torrance, *The Incarnation*, 76. The same, of course, should be said of *perichōrēsis*.

[36] Torrance, *The Christian Doctrine of God*, 162.

comes to give us eternal life. The eternal life he comes to give is nothing other than the life and love he eternally shares with the Father and the Spirit; he has brought that life into our humanity that we might share in it. It is *eternal life* because it is a sharing in the life of all life, the life that generates and sustains all things. This life is available to us only in the incarnate Son of God: "And we know that the Son of God has come and has given us understanding, so that we may know him who is true; and we are in him who is true, in his Son Jesus Christ. He is the true God and eternal life" (1 John 5:20). Jesus Christ is himself the very life that he gives, for there is no other life that is eternal—the life of Christ is the life of God.

In the enfleshing of the Son of God, God has come to be with us and within our humanity, that we might enjoy the innumerable blessings of his love. After all, this is why we were created—to be the recipients of his lavish love. "What is the chief end of man?" the Westminster Shorter Catechism begins. Answer: "To glorify God and enjoy him forever." Indeed. And the incarnation accomplishes this in the most extravagant way. The Son came to make his Father *known* through the Spirit, and nothing would stand in his way—not humiliation, not nakedness, not suffering, not death, not hell itself. In fact, not even the most incredible of all obstacles could stand in his way: becoming what he created. And so it is that the mystery of the person of Christ is indeed the mystery of our salvation.

3

Beholding God in the Face of Jesus Christ

The Old Testament narrates the disruptive blessing of God drawing near to the Israelites. Through tabernacle and temple, law and liturgy, God dwelt *in their midst*, the contours of his visage slowly yet steadily emerging. Then, at last, out of the womb of Israel, God himself came forth *in our flesh*, revealing his face clearly and concretely in the face of Jesus Christ. But despite God's progressive self-disclosure to the Israelites, Jesus "came to his own, and his own people did not receive him" (John 1:11). "Is not this the carpenter's son?" hissed those in his hometown of Nazareth (Matt. 13:53–58). "He has a demon, and is insane; why listen to him?" sneered others (John 10:20). "He has uttered blasphemy," cried Israel's high priest. "He deserves death," seethed the scribes and elders (Matt. 26:57–68). "Let him be crucified!" howled the crowd to Pontius Pilate (Matt. 27:15–23).

Of course, rejection was not the totality of Israel's response to Jesus. Many received him. Yet even those closest to Jesus often stumbled and stammered over him, unsettled and perplexed by his presence. "Can anything good come out of Nazareth?" demurred Nathanael (John 1:46). "Lord, show us the Father, and it is enough for us," pleaded Philip (John 14:8).

"Far be it from you, Lord! This shall never happen to you," scolded Peter, offended by Jesus's talk of crucifixion (Matt. 16:21–23). "I do not know this man of whom you speak," swore the same apostle, his third denial of Jesus on the night of his arrest (Mark 14:66–72). "Unless I see in his hands the mark of the nails . . . I will never believe," announced Thomas, incredulous in the wake of Jesus's brutal and humiliating death (John 20:24–25).

The scandal Jesus presented to the ancient Israelites—foe and follower alike—had much to do with the challenges he posed to their common messianic expectations and assumptions. Yet we are no different from them in that scandal is inevitable when God confronts man face to face in the face of Jesus. All people this side of Eden harbor a deep desire to be gods, and thus to be the gods of God. Christians are not immune to this desire, as seen in our unholy habit of telling God who he can and cannot be, and what he can and cannot do, often apart from much serious consideration of the incarnation. The fullness and finality of God's self-disclosure in and as the man Jesus Christ radically exposes and attacks *all* self-styled expectations and assumptions about God.[1] Thus, T. F. Torrance writes:

> Israel teaches us . . . that divine revelation cuts against the grain of our naturalistic existence and calls into question the naturalistic patterns of human thought. . . . We must let the sword of divine truth that was thrust into Israel pierce our own heart also so that its secret contradiction of God may be laid bare. We must go to school with Israel and share with it the painful transformation of its mind and soul which prepared it for the final mediation of God's self-revelation in Jesus Christ, if we ourselves are to break free from our assimilation to the patterns of this world and be transformed through the renewing of our mind in Christ, for only then will we be in a position to recognize, discern and appreciate what God wills to make known to us.[2]

Chapter 2 explored the incarnation in relation to our knowledge of the triune God. There we made the point that contemporary evangelical theology often overlooks a basic and momentous implication of the incarnation: God the Son joined himself to humanity to overturn and set to rights—to crucify and resurrect—our broken and corrupted knowledge of God. The

---

[1] Kelly M. Kapic, "Christian Existence and the Incarnation: Humiliation of the Name," unpublished plenary address, Evangelical Theological Society, November 2011, San Francisco, CA, 2–3.
[2] Thomas F. Torrance, *The Mediation of Christ*, rev. ed. (Colorado Springs, CO: Helmers & Howard, 1992), 12.

second person of the Trinity has come to us in our flesh to bridge the divide between humanity and God that includes the chasm in our hearts and minds between what we presume to know about God and who God really is. Here we will continue exploring the incarnation in relation to our knowledge of the triune God, but will approach this topic from a different angle, namely, by way of the attributes of God. Because the fullness and finality of God's self-disclosure is given in and as Jesus Christ, his incarnate humanity is where the attributes of God are definitively displayed and properly understood. This thesis will be developed in two phases of roughly equal length. The first half of this chapter will explore how we ought to think about God's attributes in general, mapping the way forward and marking off stretches of hazardous terrain in the process. The second half of this chapter will narrow our focus to several divine attributes in particular, where we will pay special attention to how the redeemed ought to confess and image these attributes in light of the glorious reality that God is with, to, for, and in us in Jesus Christ.

How Ought We to Think about the Attributes of God?

Attributes are the properties or qualities of someone, something, or some place. When we speak of *God's* attributes, then, we are seeking to provide shorthand commentary on features of his nature and character. In other words, we are attempting to give voice to what God is like, to point out that which identifies and distinguishes him as uniquely himself, to describe him. If we are to think faithfully and skillfully in this regard, and avoid some significant pitfalls in the process, there are a few crucial issues we must consider.

God's Attributes Are Not Our Attributions

Right at the outset of this exploration, let us highlight a potential misunderstanding about the word *attributes* itself. Whenever it refers to the nature and character of God, the word *attributes* must never be thought to imply the act of *attribution* on our part, as though we were investing God with the attributes of which we speak. To miss this point would be to invert, and thus pervert, this entire undertaking. Our interest in God's attributes must never be a matter of what we presume to foist on God, but of who God reveals himself to be.[3] All too common is the notion that the human mind has an unmediated and intuitive—an *a priori*—knowledge of what God is like; that we innately perceive and accurately understand, for example, God's love, holiness, power, freedom, and glory. Yet whenever discussions of God's attributes are beholden to incipient naturalism, to rationalistic tendencies that suggest epistemic Pelagianism, God is invariably domesticated and distorted, reduced, in effect, to little more than a representation of some self-styled ideal. God becomes an instantiation of what we deem appropriate to a "supreme being," as opposed to the triune God of the gospel.[4] To think of God's attributes in this way is simply a thinly veiled attempt to be the god of God—an exercise in idolatry and self-lordship, whereby we forge a fictitious deity in our own image. Genuine knowledge of God is not the product of our self-projection. Moreover, knowledge of God's attributes cannot be a human achievement for the simple reason that knowledge of God is always conditioned by God himself, and thus never conditioned by our own analysis. Because only God knows God, he is revealed, not discovered; he is known only by his self-disclosure, never by way of our deduction or inference. We do not tell God who he is and what he is like; he tells us. As we proceed in our exploration of God's attributes, therefore, let us hear and heed this wise counsel from Hilary, the fourth-century bishop of Poitiers:

> Since . . . we are to discourse of the things of God, let us assume that God has full knowledge of Himself, and bow with humble reverence to His words. For He Whom we can only know through His own utterances is the fitting witness concerning Himself.[5]

God's Attributes Are Not "Parts" of His Being

God's attributes must not be considered "parts" of God because he is ontologically basic.[6] To say the same thing in more common and overtly theological language is to affirm the unity, or simplicity, of God. When we

---

[3] Colin E. Gunton, *Act and Being: Towards a Theology of the Divine Attributes* (Grand Rapids: Eerdmans, 2003), 8–9.

[4] Christopher R. J. Holmes, "The Theological Function of the Doctrine of the Divine Attributes and the Divine Glory, with Special Reference to Karl Barth and His Reading of the Protestant Orthodox," *Scottish Journal of Theology* 61, no. 2 (May 2008): 206–7 (hereafter *SJT*).

[5] Hilary of Poitiers, *On the Trinity*, 1.18, in *NPNF*, 9:45.

[6] Stephen R. Holmes, "Something Much Too Plain to Say: Towards a Defense of the Doctrine of Divine Simplicity," *Neue Zeitschrift für Systematische Theologie und Religionsphilosophie* 43 (2001): 139.

confess that God is *simple*, we mean that he is not a composition, compound, combination, or collection of disparate and separable properties, with the aggregate sum of these properties constituting his identity. God is not made up, as it were, of his attributes. When we affirm divine simplicity, we also mean that God's attributes are not *accidental*, or nonessential, to who he is. These properties cannot be added to or removed from God, given that they are not extrinsically and abstractly related to him. Stated positively, when we confess that God is simple, we mean that his attributes are intrinsic and inherent to his indivisible being.[7]

Granted, most Christians are not exactly breathless with interest over whether God is composite or simple. In this instance, however, interest is no indicator of importance. To deny divine simplicity would mean that God's attributes are only extrinsically and abstractly related to him. This would suggest: (1) that love, holiness, power, freedom, glory, and the like are but names we ascribe to God's actions—actions that can have no intrinsic and inherent relation to God's being, and that therefore are unable to be vehicles of God's self-disclosure and self-bestowal; and (2) that there are numerous impersonal and self-existent abstractions external to God that we call love, holiness, power, freedom, glory, and the like, and that these *things* determine, measure, and judge God's being and acts. On the other hand, to affirm divine simplicity is to confess that God's attributes cannot be meaningfully distinct from who God is in himself, that his attributes are differentiated properties of his indivisible being. God does not *have* a host of impersonal assets we call attributes. Rather, God's attributes are intrinsic and inherent to his being, to who God is in himself. Thus, to affirm divine simplicity is to confess that God *is* what his attributes are—not in the sense that God may be clumsily reduced to his attributes, but in the sense that God would not be himself apart from his attributes.[8]

The simplicity of God informs our present discussion in at least four momentous ways. First, because God's attributes are intrinsic and inherent to his being, God's actions are outward manifestations of his inner life, revealing who God is in himself. In other words, God does who he is. Second, because God's attributes are intrinsic and inherent to his being, these

---

[7] John Webster, *Holiness* (Grand Rapids: Eerdmans, 2003), 37.
[8] Stephen R. Holmes, "The Attributes of God," in *The Oxford Handbook of Systematic Theology*, ed. John Webster, Kathryn Tanner, and Iain Torrance (New York: Oxford University Press, 2007), 63.

attributes cannot be descriptive of God only some of the time. God is not sometimes loving, sometimes holy, and sometimes glorious, for example, because for God to *be* is for God to be the love, holiness, and glory that he is in himself. God is who he is all of the time. Third, because God's attributes are intrinsic and inherent to his being, these attributes are wholly integrated and consistent with one another. As such, God's attributes cannot be separated from or opposed to one another, as if some attributes were more important, more appropriate, or more characteristic of God than others. For example, God's love cannot be separated from or opposed to his holiness or power. On the contrary, God's love, holiness, and power must be seen as interrelated and mutually qualifying, given that God's love is never less, different, or other than the holy and mighty love that God is in himself. Fourth, because God's attributes are intrinsic and inherent to his being, each attribute must describe the entirety of his being, not merely a "part" of his being. God is all he is all the time. Joyfully, then, we confess that God is entirely loving, entirely holy, entirely powerful, entirely free, entirely glorious, and so forth.

God's Attributes Are Indelibly Trinitarian

It is bedrock to Christian orthodoxy that God the Father, God the Son, and God the Spirit are of one and the same divine reality, three coequal and coeternal persons whose mutual interpenetration and indwelling is intrinsic and inherent to God's being. The three-person unity of God has placed an indelibly Trinitarian impress on the church's confession, echoed by Gregory of Nazianzus, who declares, "When I say God, I mean Father, Son, and Holy Ghost."[9] Because God is essentially triune, he cannot be rightly thought or spoken of except as triune, as Gregory so aptly illustrates:

> No sooner do I conceive of the One than I am illumined by the Splendour of the Three; no sooner do I distinguish Them than I am carried back to the One. When I think of any One of the Three I think of Him as the Whole. . . . I cannot grasp the greatness of That One so as to attribute a greater greatness to the Rest. When I contemplate the Three together, I see but one torch, and cannot divide or measure out the Undivided Light.[10]

---

[9] Gregory of Nazianzus, *Orations*, no. 38.8, in *NPNF*, 7:347.
[10] Ibid., no. 40.41, 7:375.

Together, the Father, Son, and Spirit are one God without remainder, co-inhering in perfect interpersonal communion. Thus, the God who is Trinity is not constituted of disparate and separable persons who can be added to or removed from one another, but of persons who are forever differentiated yet never divisible. God is not a composition, compound, combination, or collection of persons, with the aggregate sum of these persons constituting his identity. God is not made up, as it were, of three persons; nor are these persons accidental, or nonessential, to who God is. The persons of God, like the attributes of God, are not extrinsically and abstractly related. Rather, the persons of God, like the attributes of God, are intrinsic and inherent to his indivisible being.

The fact that this description of God's triunity bears a striking resemblance to our description of his simplicity is no mere coincidence. The resemblance is intentional and crucial, so as to accentuate this point: God's simplicity is rightly understood only when informed and normed by his triunity. God's simplicity affirms his unity, but in no sense does this affirmation imply a unitarian notion of God. Rightly understood, in fact, God's simplicity is utterly opposed to divine solitariness, in that God's simplicity is necessarily a triune reality. Not only must God's triunity inform and norm our understanding of his simplicity, then, but God's triunity also demands that *all* divine attributes be understood through the lens of his Trinitarian *perichoresis*—that mutual interpenetration and indwelling of the Father, Son, and Spirit in perfect interpersonal communion.[11]

For the express reason that God's attributes are intrinsic and inherent to the Father, Son, and Spirit alike, we must beware not to think of these attributes as if they were properties of a unitary, solitary, undifferentiated "god." This is an all too real and present danger. Robert Letham notes that a common and chronic problem regarding Trinitarian doctrine in the Western church is the tendency to blur or even eclipse the personal distinctions among the Father, Son, and Spirit. Contemporary evangelicals are certainly not immune to this tendency. On the contrary, some of our most esteemed and influential theological textbooks contain long and detailed discussions on God's attributes that *begin and end* before God's triunity is even addressed.[12]

---

[11] Gunton, *Act and Being*, 122–23.

[12] Robert Letham, *The Holy Trinity: In Scripture, History, Theology, and Worship* (Phillipsburg, NJ: P&R, 2004), 2–4. For examples of this tendency in contemporary evangelical theology, see Charles Hodge, *Systematic Theology* (Grand Rapids: Eerdmans, 1977), 1:366–441, on the attributes of God; 1:442–82, on the Trinity; Louis

Discussing God's attributes in this largely extra-Trinitarian manner dichotomizes God's attributes from Jesus Christ, as if he were not the fullness and finality of God's self-disclosure, and as if his incarnate humanity were not where God's attributes are definitively displayed and properly understood. Whether intended or not, moreover, largely extra-Trinitarian discussions of God's attributes encourage practical unitarianism, prompting God's attributes to be understood in primarily static, nonrelational, and noncommunicative terms.

The God who is Trinity reveals himself to be none other than a communion of Father, Son, and Spirit. This means God is outgoing and effusive by very nature, his orientation being naturally with, to, and for the other. As such, God's attributes must be understood in dynamic, relational, and communicative terms. To facilitate our understanding of God's attributes in these terms, let us note the distinction commonly made between the *economic* and *immanent* Trinity. The economic Trinity refers to the triune God's relations *ad extra*, or outside himself—to his relations with us, his creatures. The immanent Trinity, on the other hand, refers to the triune God's relations *ad intra*, or inside himself—to the inner relations of Father, Son, and Spirit.

This distinction does not suggest that there are two Gods or two Trinities. Rather, it helps us frame and articulate the conviction that two distinct yet indivisible affirmations must be made about God's triunity from two distinct yet indivisible angles of vision: (1) that God reveals himself to us as triune in time; and (2) that God's triunity is intrinsic and inherent to his eternal inner life. Thus, the distinction between the economic and immanent Trinity helps us grasp that the order of God's being grounds the order of our knowing, insomuch that what God does in time is a function and manifestation of who God is eternally and antecedently in himself. God's being is known from God's acts, given that God reveals who he is under the economy of what he does. Again, God does who he is. Consequently, our discussion of God's attributes must be indelibly Trinitarian from the outset; and this Trinitarianism must bring together God's being and our knowing—ontology and epistemology—in the gloriously stunning confes-

---

Berkhof, *Systematic Theology* (Grand Rapids: Eerdmans, 1996), 52–81, on the attributes of God; 82–99 on the Trinity; Wayne Grudem, *Systematic Theology: An Introduction to Biblical Doctrine* (Grand Rapids: Zondervan, 2000), 156–225, on the attributes of God; 226–61, on the Trinity.

sion that who God reveals himself to be with, to, and for us in his acts of creation and redemption is who God has ever been with, to, and for himself in his eternal inner-triune life.[13]

God's Attributes Are Definitively Displayed in the Incarnate Christ

The question of who God is finds its definitive answer in who Jesus Christ is with, to, and for us in the power of the Spirit. Let us revisit two interactions between Jesus and his apostles that we cited at the start of this chapter.

The first took place amidst the so-called Upper Room Discourse, when Jesus addressed pointed questions from his apostles as to how the Father is seen, known, and apprehended. To Philip's plea for him to reveal the Father, Jesus replied: "Have I been with you so long, and you still do not know me, Philip? Whoever has seen me has seen the Father. How can you say, 'Show us the Father?' Do you not believe that I am in the Father and the Father is in me?" (John 14:8–10). Do not allow familiarity with this passage to obscure the scandal of Jesus's point: to see, know, and apprehend him is precisely what it means to see, know, and apprehend the Father. "I am the way, and the truth, and the life," declared Jesus. "No one comes to the Father except through me. If you had known me, you would have known my Father also. From now on you do know him and have seen him" (John 14:6–7).

The second interaction occurred when the desolate Thomas encountered the resurrected Jesus, transforming Thomas's emphatic "I will never believe" into the ringing confession "My Lord and my God!" Jesus did not propose merely to show Thomas something *about* God, nor did Jesus point Thomas away from himself to a God behind his back or over his head. Jesus pointed to himself *as* God. Again, do not let familiarity blunt the force of Thomas's confession: to believe in Jesus is precisely what it means to believe in God (John 20:24–29; cf. John 12:44–45).

Because the Son is in the Father and the Father is in the Son, Jesus Christ is the effectual presence of God. "I and the Father are one," is Jesus's witness (John 10:30); therefore, "no one knows the Father except the Son and anyone to whom the Son chooses to reveal him" (Matt. 11:27; cf. Luke 10:22). The incarnate God, who is forever "at the Father's side, he has made him known" (John 1:18). Thus, Scripture testifies that "there is one God,

---

[13] Gunton, *Act and Being*, 94–98.

and there is one mediator between God and men, the man Christ Jesus" (1 Tim. 2:5). This one man, *as man*, is the "image of God" (2 Cor. 4:4; Col. 1:15), "the exact imprint of his nature" (Heb. 1:3), the One in whom "the whole fullness of deity dwells bodily" (Col. 2:9). Or as stated by Irenaeus, the second-century bishop of Lyons, "the Father is the invisible of the Son, but the Son is the visible of the Father."[14] In other words, the face of God is definitively displayed in the face of Christ, rendering knowledge of the Father *through* the Son and knowledge of the Son *from* the Father one and the same. Knowledge of Christ is thus the same as, and *simultaneously* the same as, knowledge of God, given that knowing Christ is neither the first step toward, nor an additional step beyond, knowing God.

We are bold to confess, then, that the God who meets us in and as Jesus Christ is the only God there is, that in Christ we are granted to know the very being of God, because in Christ we encounter the outward expression of who God is in himself.[15] To confess otherwise would be to imply that Christ does not truly and fully participate in the divine nature, that to behold Christ is ultimately not to behold God. This would not be a confession of the gospel, but of agnosticism. God cannot be known apart from himself, apart from his own *self*-disclosure. At the same time, we can know God only as humans, and thus only as God discloses himself to us in accord with our human modes of knowing. As John Calvin famously remarked, God lisps to us like nurses do with infants.[16] God condescends to accommodate, or adapt, himself to our humanity, and the incarnation of God in and as the man Jesus Christ is the absolute apex of God's self-adaptation.

Such divine condescension is staggering, to say the least. Yet the incarnation neither contradicts nor obscures who God is, as if God were known more fully and clearly prior to or apart from the appearing of Immanuel. God the Son come in the flesh is not an instance of divine *retreat*, the *regressive* revelation of God! On the contrary, in this stunning act of divine *invasion*, of *progressive* revelation, God accommodates himself to us in the humanity of Jesus Christ to reveal himself all the more radiantly. The incarnation does not attest to God's self-abdication, but to his omnipotent self-possession, to his boundless plenitude. The condescension of God in

---

[14] Irenaeus, *Against Heresies*, 4.6.6, in *Ante-Nicene Fathers*, ed. Alexander Roberts and James Donaldson (Peabody, MA: Hendrickson Publishers, 2004), 1:469 (hereafter *ANF*).
[15] Gunton, *Act and Being*, 93, 111.
[16] *Inst.*, 1.13.1.

and as Jesus Christ does not contradict or obscure God's divine majesty, but is his freely chosen mode of exalting his divine majesty. Thus, the incarnation demonstrates that God's self-emptying and self-fulfillment are not antithetical, but identical.[17] The incarnation illumines rather than beclouds who God is, in that God's self-disclosure in and through the humanity of Christ corresponds to our human modes of knowing. Furthermore, the union of God and man in the person of our incarnate Mediator teaches us that what it means for Jesus Christ to be a divine person is at once what it means for him to be a human person, given that the acts of this man, *as man*, are at once the acts of God.[18] The fullest and clearest manifestation of God's nature and character is distinctly Christ-given and Christ-shaped, which is to say that God's attributes are definitively displayed in the incarnate Christ.

Understanding God's attributes in a distinctly and robustly christological manner calls into serious question the legitimacy of the *viae*, or "ways"—a method of discussing divine attributes that originated in the ancient Greek philosophical tradition, and that was regrettably adopted and popularized by later Christian writers such as Pseudo-Dionysius, John of Damascus, Thomas Aquinas, and Francis Turretin. The *via causalitatis*, or "way of causality," ascribes attributes to God from what can be observed in the cause-and-effect occurrences of creation. The *via eminentiae*, or "way of eminence," ascribes attributes to God by projecting every perceivable excellence in creation to its highest degree, based on the assumption that God, the supreme and perfect being, must possess these qualities in infinite proportion. And the *via negativa*, or "way of negation," attempts to understand God's attributes by setting him in opposition to everything in creation, conceiving of God chiefly in terms of who and what he is not.

Common to these "ways" is the presumption that we innately and intuitively know what must be affirmed and denied of God, for these "ways" are exercises in natural theology, misguided attempts to pronounce on the nature and character of God apart from his own self-disclosure, without respect to Jesus Christ.[19] There is but "one mediator between God and men," and that Mediator is not creation (1 Tim. 2:5). Creation cannot mediate God's *self*-disclosure for the simple reason that creation is categorically,

---

[17] John Webster, "Incarnation," in *BCMT*, 218.
[18] Thomas F. Torrance, *The School of Faith: The Catechisms of the Reformed Church* (New York: Harper and Brothers Publishers, 1959), xxii; idem, *Theology in Reconstruction* (Eugene, OR: Wipf & Stock, 1996), 113–14.
[19] Holmes, "The Attributes of God," 56–58.

qualitatively *not* God. Were this not the case, and creation itself could produce true and accurate knowledge of God, the mediation of Jesus Christ as revealer of God would be superfluous.

Thus, these "ways" expose the fact that Christians are not immune to indulging sinful humanity's unholy habit of projecting onto God preconceived presumptions about who he can and cannot be, and what he can and cannot do. At bottom, these "ways" serve to highlight the scandal of the incarnation. There is no host of self-styled, naturalistic ways to God. Jesus Christ, conceived in Mary's womb by the Spirit, is himself *the* Way to God, the one man, *as man*, in whom God is seen, known, and apprehended.

God's Attributes Are Imaged in Our Redeemed Humanity

Jesus Christ is at once the true, full, perfect image of both God and man, and so the true, full, perfect image of God *as* true, full, perfect man. This has momentous implications for our present discussion. Because Jesus Christ is the very image of God in and as the very image of man, the *imago Dei* finds in him a clear and concrete expression that is at once authentically divine and authentically human. Consequently, he clearly and concretely displays not only what original humanity made in God's image *was to be*, but also what redeemed humanity remade in God's image *is to be*. Thus, Irenaeus of Lyons writes:

> For in times long past, it was *said* that man was created after the image of God, but it was not [actually] *shown*; for the Word was as yet invisible, after whose image man was created. . . . When, however, the Word of God became flesh, He confirmed both these: for He both showed forth the image truly, since He became Himself what was His image; and He re-established the similitude after a sure manner, by assimilating man to the invisible Father through means of the visible Word.[20]

Yet being the very image of God in and as the very image of man does not render Jesus Christ merely the supreme object lesson on God's attributes, the grand exemplar whom we are to emulate from afar by our own industry and resolve. We must never think of the incarnation as if Christ's humanity were displayed for our mere observation and imitation, all the while providing a bulwark to insulate and isolate God from us. This would

---

[20] Irenaeus, *Against Heresies*, 5.16.2, in *ANF*, 1:544 (emphasis original).

be anything but the good news of the gospel. In such a case, the incarnation would signal that life-giving, life-transforming communion with God is not possible, thrusting us back on ourselves. Thankfully, the incarnation signals an altogether different reality, namely, that God has come to share who he is with us! The Father, Son, and Spirit ever exist with, to, for, and *in* one another by the mutual indwelling of God's inner-Trinitarian *perichōrēsis*; and in Jesus Christ, God exists with, to, for, and *in* the redeemed by the indwelling Spirit, the personal agent of Christ's presence and power (John 14:16–20; Rom. 8:9–11; Gal. 4:6). In the person of our incarnate Mediator, God participates unreservedly in the same human nature that we ourselves possess, that the Head and Bridegroom might humanly mediate the very life of God to those who together constitute his body and bride (Rom. 6:1–11; Gal. 2:20; Eph. 1:22–23; 5:23–32; Col. 2:6–15; 3:1–4). As Jesus Christ continually imparts himself to the redeemed, then, they are progressively conformed to him, progressively remade in the image of Christ, who is at once both the very image of authentic humanity and the very image of God. As such, God's attributes, imaged forth clearly and concretely in the humanity of Jesus Christ, are to be imaged forth in our redeemed humanity, the corporate dimension of which is the church, the communion of saints created and sustained in Christ by the Spirit. Definitively displayed in the incarnate Christ, God's attributes are to be displayed—truly and increasingly, if not yet fully or perfectly—in those united to Christ by Spirit-wrought faith.

We repeat: *the incarnation signals that God has come to share with us who he is!* Though this point is routinely undervalued and overlooked by contemporary evangelicals, the leading architects of the evangelical tradition grasped it with clarity and conviction. Martin Luther declares:

> Because He lives in me, whatever grace, righteousness, life, peace, and salvation there is in me is all Christ's; nevertheless, it is mine as well, by the cementing and attachment that are through faith, by which we become as one body in the Spirit. . . . But faith must be taught correctly, namely, that by it you are so cemented to Christ that He and you are as one person, which cannot be separated but remains attached to Him forever and declares: "I am as Christ." And Christ, in turn, says: "I am as that sinner who is attached to Me, and I to him. For by faith we are joined together into one flesh and bone." Thus Eph. 5:30 says: "We are members of the body of Christ, of His flesh and of His bones," in

such a way that this faith couples Christ and me more intimately than a husband is coupled to his wife.[21]

Calvin heartily agrees, stating:

God's natural Son fashioned for himself a body from our body, flesh from our flesh, bones from our bones, that he might be one with us. . . . Ungrudgingly he took our nature upon himself to impart to us what was his, and to become both Son of God and Son of man in common with us.[22]

God's attributes are often seen as belonging to one of two broad categories, being either *communicable* or *incommunicable* attributes. In one sense, this distinction is appropriate and helpful, in that it relates what the Definition of Chalcedon confesses of Christ's person to his redeemed people. That is to say, the hypostatic union of the divine and human natures in the person of Christ upholds the integrity of both natures, undermining or overturning neither, and this informs the nature of the union between the redeemed and Christ. God the Son assumed what is ours to impart what is his, to humanly mediate the very life of God to us. The redeemed are rendered authentically human as a result, *not* denatured or deified, as if our humanity were mixed or intermingled with Christ's deity. One with us, Christ also remains utterly and uniquely himself.

As helpful as the distinction between communicable and incommunicable attributes may be, two important qualifications are in order. First, lest we suppose this distinction means that God is unable to accomplish his intentions, we must understand that God's attributes are not so much communicable and incommunicable as *communicated* and *uncommunicated*. Second, we must understand that none of God's attributes are strictly uncommunicated. For instance, while God does not grant the redeemed omnipotence, or almightiness, his omnipotence enables him to communicate resurrection power to us in Jesus Christ (Rom. 8:11; Eph. 1:19–20; Phil. 3:9–10). Likewise, while God does not grant the redeemed aseity, or self-existent life from oneself, his aseity enables him to communicate new and eternal life to us in Jesus Christ (John 6:35–59; 10:22–30; 17:1–3). All this to say, it does not follow from the sheer and singular majesty of God that

---

[21] *Lectures on Galatians* (1535), in *LW*, 26:167–68.
[22] *Inst.*, 2.12.2.

he is the insular Other in isolation from us, or worse still, the insular Other in opposition to us. On the contrary, in Jesus Christ, God is the Other with, to, for, and *in* us, the God whose uncommunicated attributes are the basis and impetus for his effectual self-communication.[23]

How Ought We to Confess and Image the Attributes of God?

Because the fullness and finality of God's self-disclosure is given in and as Jesus Christ, his incarnate humanity is where the attributes of God are definitively displayed and properly understood. Having discussed how we ought to think about God's attributes in general, let us now narrow the focus of our exploration to several divine attributes in particular. We will not attempt the impossible task of discussing all of God's attributes. Nor will we provide a systematic taxonomy of God's attributes. Talk of God's attributes is not primarily about classification and categorization, but about confession—the confession of who God is and how he relates to us.[24] We will thus give special attention to how the redeemed ought to confess and image the attributes of God in light of the glorious reality that God is with, to, for, and in us in Jesus Christ.

The Love of God

Scripture announces not that God is capable of love, nor that he tends to be loving, but that love is of the very nature of God—that God *is* love (1 John 4:8, 16). J. I. Packer rightly observes that this "is one of the most tremendous utterances in the Bible—and also one of the most misunderstood."[25] Talk of God's love is increasingly sanitized, domesticated, and distorted. Shorn of theological content and purged of all that moves against the prevailing narrative of contemporary culture, this grand reality is often reduced to little more than amicable impotence, well-intentioned indulgence, or feckless sentimentality.[26]

But wherever the church is faithful and sane, we find her confessing that God loves us freely and truly because, prior to and apart from us, his love

---

[23] Gunton, *Act and Being*, 124; Holmes, "The Attributes of God," 59.

[24] Webster, *Holiness*, 37.

[25] J. I. Packer, *Knowing God*, 20th anniversary ed. (Downers Grove, IL: IVP, 1993), 117.

[26] D. A. Carson, *The Difficult Doctrine of the Love of God* (Wheaton, IL: Crossway, 2000), 9–16.

is characterized by the mutual love of the Father and the Son in the communion of the Spirit. In the eternal inner life of God, the loving Father and the beloved Son fulfill their love for one another in the unity of the Spirit, the living love who perfects that bond of fellowship.[27] In fact, when Jesus said that he and the Father are *one* with each other and in each other, he was speaking of the love that he and the Father have shared from "before the foundation of the world" (John 17:20–24).[28] Thus, we must beware of contradicting the good news of the gospel by suggesting that God created the world *so that* he might know interpersonal love, or that the Father sent the Son to redeem sinners *so that* God might once again love them. God's acts in creation and redemption are prompted by, and are profound demonstrations of, the love that God is.

The mutual love of the Father and the Son is the blueprint for creation, in that creation is an overflow of the effulgent love of God, a celebration of the Father's love for the Son, that the Son might be the firstborn of many siblings (Rom. 8:29; Eph. 1:3–6). From before the creation of time itself, the Father delighted in showering love on his Son, and the Father desired to create so he could delight in showering that very same love on the children he would gather to himself in his Son. This is put beautifully by Jonathan Edwards: "God created the world for his Son, that he might prepare a spouse or bride for him to bestow his love upon; so that the mutual joys between this bride and bridegroom are the end of the creation."[29]

Moreover, God's love for his fallen creation motivated his sending of the Son (John 3:16). Whereas it cost God nothing to make all things in their primal splendor, to make us new creations in Christ cost God everything—he exhibits a self-giving, self-sacrificial love "in that while we were still sinners, Christ died for us" (Rom. 5:8; cf. Eph. 2:1–7). And just as the Father delights to include us in his love for the Son, the Son delights to include us in his love for the Father. Jesus came in our flesh to make us *one* with him and with each other, just as he is *one* with the Father; to include us *in* himself, just as he is *in* the Father; to share with us the same love he has ever shared with the Father (John 17:20–26). The church confesses that

---

[27] Thomas A. Smail, *Like Father, Like Son: The Trinity Imaged in Our Humanity* (Grand Rapids: Eerdmans, 2005), 154–55.

[28] Donald Fairbairn, *Life in the Trinity: An Introduction to Theology with the Help of the Church Fathers* (Downers Grove, IL: IVP, 2009), 33.

[29] Jonathan Edwards, *Miscellanies* (No. 271), in *The Works of Jonathan Edwards*, ed. Thomas A. Schafer (New Haven, CT: Yale University Press, 1994), 13:374.

God is love, then, because love is the nature of the Son's relationship with the Father in the communion of the Spirit, and the redeemed are made to participate in this very love.[30]

The love of the Father for the Son, and of the Son for the Father, was poignantly revealed in Christ throughout the entire course of his earthly ministry. Indeed, the love revealed to us in Christ is precisely the love that God is. Had Christ revealed anything less or other than that love, we would be forced to confess that Christ did not truly reveal the God who is love, and that we, in turn, remain unacquainted with that God, a God who would necessarily be different from Christ. Stunningly, then, the incarnation demands that we speak univocally about divine love and human love in the case of Christ, given that he, *as man*, is the "exact imprint of [the Father's] nature" (Heb. 1:3), and thus the embodied love of God in action. Perhaps more stunning still, inasmuch as that divine love has become human love in Christ, the incarnation demands that the love of God revealed in Christ is precisely the pattern for the human love to be imaged in and by the church. The apostle John makes this quite clear, writing: "In this the love of God was made manifest among us, that God sent his only Son into the world, so that we might live through him. . . . Beloved, if God so loved us, we also ought to love one another" (1 John 4:9–11).[31]

If the church is to be the church in any authentic sense, she must reflect the love of God manifested for her and communicated to her in Christ. The church is constituted by the love of God in Christ and is called to bear witness to that love. Of course, we cannot fulfill this calling in any capacity unless we abide in Christ, as he shares himself—his very life and love—with us by the indwelling ministry of the Spirit (John 15:1–17). Jesus declared that as a result of his coming to reside in the redeemed by the Spirit, we are made to know that he is *in* the Father, just as we are *in* the Son and the Son is *in* us (John 14:16–20). Just as the Spirit has ever been the living bond of love between the Father and the Son, the Spirit will ever be the living bond of love between the Son and his members. The personal agent of Christ's presence and power, the Spirit pours into our hearts the knowledge and

---

[30] Michael Reeves, *Delighting in the Trinity: An Introduction to the Christian Faith* (Downers Grove, IL: IVP Academic, 2012), 43–44; Mark Achtemeier and Andrew Purves, *Union in Christ: A Declaration for the Church* (Louisville, KY: Witherspoon Press, 1999), 42–43.

[31] Gunton, *Act and Being*, 70, 147.

efficacy of the Father's love for us in his beloved Son (Rom. 5:5; Titus 3:4–6; 1 John 4:13–21).

Because our triune God is outgoing and effusive by nature, the Christian life is not lived in and for oneself, but in and for others. Together, Christ's members live *in* him by Spirit-wrought faith and *for* others—our neighbors, both near and far—by Spirit-wrought love, imaging forth faith active in love. How do we love others as God in Christ loves us? Displays of this love are as numerous and multifaceted as the situations in which the church finds herself in this world. Yet in every situation, we are called to love others by meeting them in their need; more costly still, by meeting them in their suffering; and most costly of all, by meeting them in their shame, for was not Christ "numbered with the transgressors" (Isa. 53:12; Luke 22:37)? Let us heed these words regarding our high calling:

> Christ's love is a love that went all the way into the hell of our separation from God in order to restore us to union and communion with God. To share in that love by our union with Christ is to share in the fellowship of his suffering. To share in his love of the Father is also to share in his mission from the Father, which is the outpouring of his love for the sake of the world. It is to share in his obedience, for there is no sharing in Christ's love of God without a sharing also in his obedience to the will of God. . . . Thus a sharing in Christ's love of the Father means a sharing in what that love led him to do, and to take up our cross daily and follow him. Surely there is no greater desentimentalizing of love than this![32]

The Holiness of God

The nature of God's triune life is that of holy love, for just as God is love, God is holy (Ex. 15:11; Isa. 6:3; Rev. 4:8; 15:4). To confess God's holiness is to confess his tripersonal transcendence, his distinct differentiation from all else, his sheer otherness. For God to be holy is for God to constitute the sole and absolute standard of himself, eclipsing and eluding the measure of all but himself. God's holiness denotes his perfection and purity, his utter lack of defect or deficiency. Stated negatively, this means God is free *from* all that is unclean and profane, from all that corrupts and compromises. Stated positively, this means God is free *for* the completeness and wholeness

---

[32] Achtemeier and Purves, *Union in Christ*, 44.

of the perfect and pure love of the Father and the Son in the communion of the Spirit. Some are accustomed to conceiving of God's holiness as that which denotes the antithesis of relationship, that which debars God from all that is unholy into the separateness of absolute isolation. Were this true, there would be no gospel, as God neither could nor would come near us; and should the church seek to image this false notion of God's holiness, the integrity of her inner life and mission to the world would be forfeit. Thankfully, God's holiness is a *relational* reality, marking not only the character of his transcendent inner-Trinitarian life, but also the character of his condescension to us, informing the manner and goal of God's relation to his fallen creation.[33]

As the Holy One of Israel *in their midst* (Isa. 12:6; 43:3, 15; Jer. 50:29; Ezek. 39:7; Hab. 1:12), God demonstrated his holiness by calling Israel to himself, by bestowing law and liturgy to expose sin and purify sinners, and by struggling with Israel amid her flights from God into the self-contradiction of unholiness, that Israel might be his own possession—a holy people, as the Lord their God is holy (Lev. 19:2). In establishing, maintaining, and perfecting fellowship with his people, God redeems and purifies them, negating their unholiness by judging and eradicating sin.[34] This judging, eradicating action is what Scripture calls God's wrath. Far from petulance, ill temper, or blind rage, God's wrath is inseparably related to his holy love; for God's wrath is but the willed shape of that holy love when it is defied, violated, and mobilized by sin. In other words, wrath, unlike love or holiness, is not an attribute of God, but rather a particular expression of the attributes of love and holiness. God is love and God is holy, but God is not wrath, inasmuch as wrath, unlike love and holiness, is not intrinsic and inherent to who God is; thus, there is no divine wrath where there is no human sin. Yet the bracing reality of God's wrath cannot be diluted without also diluting the beautiful reality of God's holy love, seen in his refusal to deny or compromise himself even as he refuses to abandon his fallen creation or leave his sinful people in ruin.[35]

God's holiness takes definitive form and expression in Jesus Christ, the Holy One of God *in our flesh* (Mark 1:24; Luke 1:35; John 6:69). In Christ,

---

[33] Webster, *Holiness*, 43–47.
[34] Ibid.
[35] Carson, *The Difficult Doctrine of the Love of God*, 66–73; Packer, *Knowing God*, 148–57; Donald G. Bloesch, *Essentials of Evangelical Theology* (Peabody, MA: Prince Press, 1998), 1:32–34.

the transcendent God, "who dwells in unapproachable light" (1 Tim. 6:16), condescends to approach man *as man*. Jesus neither dissipates nor dulls the blazing light of God's holiness. Rather, he focuses and intensifies that holiness, his incarnate presence exposing and even agitating the sin-darkened world's unholiness—its unbelief, self-lordship, and thinly veiled contempt for God (John 1:1–14; 3:19–20; 8:12–19; 12:44–46). For us and for our salvation, the Holy One of God mysteriously assumes us into his incarnate existence and vicariously represents us in living faithfully, lovingly, and obediently before the Father. Culminating his fulfillment of all righteousness on our behalf, he voluntarily offered himself a perfect and pure sacrifice to the Father—the holiness of God rendered to God by God *as man*. Bearing the full force of our guilt and shame in his very body and soul, Jesus Christ effectively bore away the full force of our alienation, condemnation, and death. This jarring display of divine wrath, which was anything but the contradiction of God's character or the frustration of his purposes, served as the triumph of his holy love, for here he upheld all that his holiness required in lovingly fashioning a people for himself—a people holy as God is holy, precisely because in Jesus Christ, God gives what he demands. Jason Goroncy writes:

> Creation's disorder, chaos, pollution and guilt have been taken up in this Man who gathered all the cesspool of the confusion of human hell into the depths of his own being as he fulfilled the Father's will in becoming a curse for us. . . . And in his crucified humanity, he suffered all unholy corruption and guilt until it was annihilated. He made purification for our sins and in bringing us into the holy presence of God he sanctified us, and perfected us in himself. . . . God does not merely dispense judgment. He bears it, praises it, hallows it and absorbs it on the tree; and his resurrection announces that he exhausts it. . . . He who shared the wrath of the Father (Rev. 6:16–17) as well as his love for humanity (Jn. 3:16; 13:1), entered humanity to stand as humanity's vicar, answering the prayer "Hallowed be thy name" at the cross.[36]

The Father has placed the redeemed *in* Jesus Christ, who is our righteousness, redemption, and sanctification (1 Cor. 1:30). The Father sent the Son so that our fallen selves could be assumed into his incarnate humanity

---

[36] Jason Goroncy, "The Elusiveness, Loss and Cruciality of Recovered Holiness: Some Biblical and Theological Observations," *IJST* 10, no. 2 (April 2008): 203–4.

and made holy, so that we could share in the holiness that God is. In one sense, our holiness is a finished reality, as we were purged *from* the unclean and profane in our crucifixion with Christ, and set apart *for* God in our resurrection with Christ, so that we are even now sharing in the completeness and wholeness of his perfect and pure life with the Father in the communion of the Spirit (Rom. 6:1–11; Col. 2:11–13). In another sense, our holiness is an ongoing work of God, as the Father, through the Spirit, continues to forge Christ ever more deeply into our hearts, progressively conforming us to the One who is at once the express image of both God and man, the very embodiment of God's holiness *as man*.

But in no sense should holiness be confused with the sham substitute of moralism. Moralism is self-styled, self-satisfied self-righteousness, a smug and sanctimonious attempt to be holy on one's own terms, a sometimes subtle form of self-lordship that inevitably renders Jesus Christ superfluous. The incarnation confronts sinful humanity with the scandal that holiness is not something to achieve but someone to receive: the tripersonal, thrice-holy God (Isa. 6:3; Rev. 4:8), who shares what is his in the self-bestowal of God the Son. Because God alone is holy in himself, there is no holiness to be found or had apart from this sole Mediator between God and men.

Christ offered himself as a perfect and pure sacrifice for the church, "that he might sanctify her, having cleansed her by the washing of water with the word, so that he might present the church to himself in splendor . . . that she might be holy and without blemish" (Eph. 5:26–27). The Spirit of holiness has given new life—first to Christ in his resurrection from the dead, and then to Christ's members (Rom. 8:9–11). As such, our concern must not be with the *acquisition* of our own holiness, but with the progressive *manifestation* of our identity in Christ, with imaging the One to whose holy image we are being conformed. The church is not the communion of saints because of her self-possessed, self-professed sanctity, but because she belongs to Christ and participates in his hallowing of God's name in his mission to the world.[37] The church's holiness is thus imaged in all her acts of worship, in all her acts of confessing God's holy name—that is, in hearing and heeding the promise and command of the gospel, in repenting of sin, in proclaiming Christ in Scripture and sacrament, and in turning toward the world in word and deed to gather strangers and sinners, exiles and aliens into the peace of Christ's

---

[37] Ibid., 205–6.

victory over disorder, chaos, and death.[38] The church is never more authentically human or holy than in her worship, for there she becomes ever more like the One she worships, fulfilling God's purpose in creation and redemption by reflecting the splendor of him who is the epitome of God's holiness.

The Omnipotent Freedom of God

"Whatever the LORD pleases, he does, in heaven and on earth, in the seas and all deeps," proclaims the psalmist (Ps. 135:6; cf. Ps. 115:3; Isa. 46:10; Dan. 4:35; Eph. 1:11). *Omnipotence* is a compound of two Latin words: *omni*, which means "all," and *potens*, which means "power." To confess that God is omnipotent is thus to confess that he is sovereign, all-powerful, or almighty.

Is this to suggest that God is capable of anything and everything? No! Power exercised in the name of power alone is sheer and unqualified power, arbitrary and capricious power, the power of terrorists and despots. Such may befit Satan, but certainly not God. Consequently, confessing God's omnipotence does not preclude the confession that there are some things God simply cannot do. For instance, God is unable to lie or be unfaithful, because God does who he is, and is unable to do who he is not (2 Tim. 2:13; Titus 1:2; Heb. 6:18). In other words, God's purposes and his power to accomplish them are informed, qualified, and determined by his character, which neither his purposes nor power contradict. Thus, God's omnipotence is not about the exertion of indiscriminate force, but about his unfettered ability to actualize his altogether magnificent intentions.

For God to be omnipotent is for God to be free. Indeed, God is not free in the way that benighted humans sometimes understand freedom—that is, free to be and do whatever serves one's fickle and fitful sense of self-realization. This is no freedom at all, but only the random and tyrannical bondage of self-centered existence. Rather, God is free to be his triune self, free to be with, to, for, and in the other in holy love—first the divine Other in the relation of the Father and the Son in the communion of the Spirit, and then the human other in God's acts of creation and redemption. To be sure, then, God's omnipotent freedom can never be properly understood apart from his holy love, for when God creates in omnipotent freedom, he

---

[38] Webster, *Holiness*, 64–76.

creates in and for holy love. Likewise, when God judges his fallen creation in omnipotent freedom, he judges because his creatures are living and acting in defiant contradiction of that holy love. And when God redeems a people in omnipotent freedom, he establishes, maintains, and perfects his communion with them because the God who is holy love cannot relinquish them to ruin.[39]

Just as Jesus Christ is one in nature with the Father and the Spirit, so too he is one with the Father and the Spirit in the omnipotent freedom of holy love. Truly, fully, perfectly, and simultaneously both God and man, Christ is free to be his incarnate self. He is free to be the only Mediator between God and men, free to be with, to, for, and in both God and men in holy love. In the omnipotent freedom of God's holy love *as man*, Christ is the "only Sovereign, the King of kings and Lord of lords" (1 Tim. 6:15; cf. Rev. 1:8; 19:15–16). Dwelling in the world created through and for him (John 1:1–3; Col. 1:15–16; Heb. 1:1–2), Christ showed himself almighty over the elements of nature, turning water into wine and calming turbulent storms (John 2:1–11; Matt. 8:23–27). Further, he showed himself almighty over demonic affliction (Mark 5:1–20; Luke 4:31–37), over sickness and disease (Mark 7:31–37; Luke 4:38–41; 5:12–26), even over death (Matt. 9:18–26; John 10:17–18; 11:1–44).

Yet these mighty acts were but anticipations of the first Good Friday and Easter Sunday, when we find the ultimate expression of God's omnipotent freedom. Without giving himself *over* in the surrender of his lordship, Christ freely gave himself *up* to humiliation and death, transforming that suffering into his almighty triumph over every malevolent power, toward the eschatological summation of all things in himself (Eph. 1:7–10; Col. 1:19–20; Revelation 5). Power is often understood in terms of self-preservation, the ability to protect oneself from any and all perceived threats. What commonly follows is an unqualified identification of vulnerability and suffering with weakness, even impotence. The incarnation forcibly overturns all such notions, seeing that the characteristic expression of God's omnipotence is the effectual suffering of Christ. God does not exercise his omnipotence remotely, from above or afar, as if insulated and isolated from the suffering of his fallen creation. Rather, God exercises his omnipotence by freely entering our suffering, not merely in our midst but *in our flesh*. Christ's almighty

---

[39] Smail, *Like Father, Like Son*, 155.

brokenness is the sin-defeating, death-destroying, creation-renewing victory of God's holy love.

Although God does not grant us omnipotence, his omnipotence is the
basis and impetus for his effectual self-communication. Those who are in
Christ by the Spirit share in the same power that raised Christ from death
to newness of life (Rom. 8:11; Eph. 1:19–20). Those who are in Christ by
the Spirit are thus free to be authentically human, free to realize God's purpose in creation and redemption to authentically relate to God and others:
"If the Son sets you free, you will be free indeed" (John 8:36; cf. Gal. 5:1);
"Where the Spirit of the Lord is, there is freedom" (2 Cor. 3:17). Freedom
is often understood as the untrammeled exertion of self-will in the service
of self-defined self-actualization. Far from freedom, this is the very epitome
of sin, the primal sin of our first parents and the prevailing sin of every aspiring god and goddess thereafter. Freedom is neither a human entitlement
nor a human achievement. More to the point, apart from Christ, authentic
freedom is not even a human possibility. In other words, freedom is a divine
attribute that finds human expression first in the incarnate Christ, and then
in his members through the liberating self-communication of Christ by
the Spirit. However imperfectly, freedom is imaged in redeemed humanity
just as freedom is perfectly imaged in the incarnate Christ, namely, in the
ability to be with, to, and for the other—both the divine and the human
other—in holy love.[40]

What is more, just as the characteristic expression of God's omnipotence is the effectual suffering of Christ, redeemed humanity's freedom to
image God's holy love is made powerful in cross-bearing. Our Lord promises that nothing, not even the gates of hell, shall prevail against his church.
Yet he promptly adds that the shape of our life in Christ is necessarily
cruciform, stating, "If anyone would come after me, let him deny himself
and take up his cross and follow me" (Matt. 16:24). Accentuating the bond
between the effectual suffering of Christ and our cross-bearing, the apostle
Paul announces that the surpassing worth of being "found in [Christ]"
entails knowing by experience "the power of his resurrection," so as to
"share his sufferings, becoming like him in his death" (Phil. 3:8–10).[41] Let us

---

[40] Gunton, *Act and Being*, 105.

[41] John Calvin noted that it is but a "little thing" to have a merely conceptual grasp that Christ is crucified and
raised from the dead, because Christ is "rightly known" only "when we feel how powerful his death and resurrection are, and how efficacious they are in us." Calvin on Phil. 3:10, *Calvin's New Testament Commentaries*,

be altogether clear: we could not bear Christ's cross. The cross that Christ bore was his and his alone, in that he alone put away sin and reconciled us to God. But even as he bore a cross we could not take, Christ bestows a cross we cannot refuse, for to refuse the cross Christ bestows would be to repudiate our discipleship, even to repudiate Christ himself.

If Christ's suffering from manger to cross were but an unsavory episode he left behind in his resurrection, the church's cross-bearing would be retrograde and pointless. In that case, Paul might do well to say that knowing the power of Christ's resurrection means *never* sharing in his suffering. But Christ was raised wounded, his exaltation exhibiting the indelible impress of his humiliation, not a decisive break from it. Christ did not leave the cross behind in his resurrection. Rather, his resurrection made his cross effective, and his almighty brokenness constitutes the leading edge of his victory in and over the world. Our Head and Bridegroom identifies so closely and thoroughly with us, his body and bride, that he continues to suffer in our suffering, calling the world's hatred for the church hatred for him (John 15:18–19) and the world's persecution of the church persecution of him (Acts 9:5). In other words, Christ shares in the suffering that the church receives from a hostile world as the church shares in Christ's mission of holy love to the world, and Christ uses the church's suffering to effect his redemptive purposes for the world. Imaging the omnipotent freedom of God's holy love must never be confused with triumphalism, given that the power of Christ's resurrection is tasted by sharing—not spurning—his suffering, and thus not by political, fiscal, cultural, or any other sort of ascendency. At the same time, while we need never deny nor even diminish the difficulty of our calling, cross-bearing must never be confused with cross-counting. The omnipotent freedom of God's holy love is not imaged in unremitting morbidity, gloom, self-absorption, or self-pity, but in peace, courage, and good cheer *amidst* the tumult of the world, for it is precisely this tumultuous world that the crucified One has overcome (John 16:33).

The Immutability of God

To affirm God's immutability is to confess that he does not change, that from everlasting to everlasting he is God (Ps. 90:2; cf. Ps. 102:25–27; Isa.

---

12 vols., ed. David W. Torrance and Thomas F. Torrance (Grand Rapids: Eerdmans, 1959–1972)., 11:275 (hereafter *CNTC*).

48:12). But what does this mean? Is this to imply that God is unmoved and immobile, nonrelational and unresponsive? Perhaps mountains or mathematical principles could be described as immutable in this sense, but not the God who acts in creation and redemption to reveal himself as a communion of Father, Son, and Spirit. God always has been, now is, and forever will be no one or nothing other than his triune self. God is who he is all the time. Thus, we confess that God is immutable in the sense that he is perfectly consistent and constant in his nature and character.[42] "I AM WHO I AM," God said to Moses at the burning bush (Ex. 3:14). And because God's nature and character are perfectly consistent and constant, so too are his promises and purposes (Ps. 33:11). That is to say, what God does in creation and redemption is perfectly consistent and constant with who God is, as he is ever and always his immutable self: "For I the LORD do not change; therefore you, O children of Jacob, are not consumed" (Mal. 3:6).

Divine immutability described in static, nonrelational, unresponsive terms is alien to the God we encounter in the Old Testament, and the incarnation culminates God's frontal attack on all such notions. In this astonishing act of omnipotent self-possession, God the Son freely assumed our humanity without forfeiting or curtailing his divinity, becoming what he previously was not without ceasing to be who he always had been. In this thrilling exhibition of boundless plenitude, God the Son demonstrates that while God is who he is all the time, God refuses to be who he is apart from us.[43] As such, Jesus Christ identifies himself as the very God who seized upon Moses at the burning bush, announcing, "Truly, truly, I say to you, before Abraham was, I am" (John 8:58). So perfectly does Jesus claim to reveal the nature and character of God the Father that he cries: "Whoever believes in me, believes not in me but in him who sent me. And whoever sees me sees him who sent me" (John 12:44–45). Yet again, testifying that his acts show him to be the very God of Moses and Abraham *as man,* Jesus declares: "The Father who dwells in me does his works. Believe me that I am in the Father and the Father is in me, or else believe on account of the works

---

[42] John H. Leith, *Basic Christian Doctrine* (Louisville, KY: Westminster John Knox Press, 1993), 54.

[43] Ephesians 1:23 says the church is "his [Christ's] body, the fullness of him who fills all in all." Calvin believed that while God the Son lacks nothing in himself, God's overflowing goodness compels him to be filled and in some sense perfected, or completed, by joining the redeemed to himself. Calvin proclaims: "This is the highest honour of the church, that, unless he is united to us, the Son of God reckons himself in some measure imperfect. What an encouragement it is for us to hear, that, not until he has us as one with himself, is he complete in all his parts, or does he wish to be regarded as whole!" Calvin on Eph. 1:23, *CNTC,* 11:138.

themselves" (John 14:10–11). One with the Father in the communion of the Spirit, the man Jesus embodies the nature and character of God with perfect consistency and constancy, carrying out the promises and purposes of God in identical manner. The church may joyfully confess, then, that God's immutability is definitively displayed in the incarnate Christ, that "Jesus Christ is the same yesterday and today and forever" (Heb. 13:8). Tasting the perfect consistency and constancy of God's holy love in the Son, the children of God are free to image steadfast stability and endurance amidst the vicissitudes of life this side of Eden, utterly assured that with "the Father of lights . . . there is no variation or shadow due to change" (James 1:17).

Rejecting any notion of divine immutability that speaks of God's being changeless in static, nonrelational, unresponsive terms, let us also reject the notion of divine *impassibility* common to the classical Greek philosophical tradition. This notion of divine impassibility, or divine *apatheia*, maintains that God cannot be affected by anything outside himself, and thus that God is without passions, or *pathos*. Not only incapable of suffering, God is without emotion, painful or pleasurable. Because God cannot be affected by anything outside himself, there can be no assurance that who God reveals himself to be in his acts of creation and redemption is who God is in himself. Those acts may be described as acts of disinterested benevolence, expressions of willed altruism devoid of both suffering and emotion.[44] We should be quick to assert that God is not manic, prone to mercurial mood swings. Neither is he pathetic, subject to the whims of his creatures in a way that renders him malleable and manageable, freely manipulated and therefore unfree to be himself. Nonetheless, this Hellenistic notion of divine impassibility is profoundly unbiblical, for it reduces the rich emotional life of God, found at virtually every turn throughout the Old Testament, to nothing more than anthropopathism—that literary device that ascribes emotions to an emotionless God in order to accommodate the sensitivities of emotive readers.[45] Moreover, this notion blunts any full-throated confession that God is triune or that Jesus Christ is God incarnate. On the one

---

[44] Richard Bauckham, "'Only the Suffering God Can Help': Divine Passibility in Modern Theology," *Themelios* 9, no. 3 (April 1984): 7–8. Divine *pathos* is attracting growing interest among evangelicals. Two books of particular note in recent years are: Dennis Ngien, *The Suffering of God according to Martin Luther's Theologia Crucis* (Vancouver, BC: Regent College Publishing, 2005); Richard J. Mouw and Douglas A. Sweeney, *The Suffering and Victorious Christ: Toward a More Compassionate Christology* (Grand Rapids: Baker Academic, 2013).

[45] Bauckham, "Only the Suffering God Can Help,'" 9–10; Carson, *The Difficult Doctrine of the Love of God*, 48–49, 58–59.

hand, it implies an Arian dichotomization of the Father from the Son in that the passions of the Son are not those of the Father; this means that to see the Son is *not* to see the Father. On the other hand, it implies a Nestorian dichotomization of Christ's humanity from his divinity in that the passions of Christ are not those of God *as man*; this means that Christ's passions must either be interpreted as unreal—feigned stagecraft—or isolated to his humanity, so as to be insulated from his divinity.[46]

Distinctions between the persons of the Trinity and the natures of the incarnate Christ must be accentuated, not merely acknowledged. But distinctions must never be confused with divisions. Christ assumed our humanity without forfeiting or curtailing his divinity in order to humanly manifest God's nature and character with perfect consistency and constancy, and this necessarily entails the manifestation of God's emotional life. In fact, if Christ does not definitively display the emotional life of God, the church has precious little good news to herald. In such a case, our confession would be that Christ's passions are not God's passions, because God is incapable of allowing himself to be affected by us, and thus incapable of any impassioned involvement with us.[47] At bottom, our confession would not be that God *is* love, but that God is loveless and unable to be otherwise. Remarkably, however, Christ's love for us is precisely that of the Father's love for him: "As the Father has loved me, so have I loved you" (John 15:9). Consequently, our Lord implores, "This is my commandment, that you love one another as I have loved you" (v. 12; cf. 1 John 4:7–11). The progression is clear: the Father's love for the Son is the very love the Son shares with us; and that love, God's inner-Trinitarian love turned outward, is the love that the redeemed are called to image. Tellingly, then, Paul says that we could undertake heroic feats of self-denial, giving away all we possess or even surrendering our bodies to the flames of persecution, but without love, such feats would be hollow (1 Cor. 13:1–3). Why? Because Christian love is denatured when it is expressed in even extraordinary acts of disinterested benevolence, given that God's love can never be reduced to willed altruism independent or devoid of emotion.[48]

Here God's love serves as the rule, not an exception. Because Jesus

---

[46] Gunton, *Act and Being*, 125.
[47] Bauckham, "'Only the Suffering God Can Help,'" 10.
[48] Carson, *The Difficult Doctrine of the Love of God*, 28, 48; Gerald W. Peterman, *Joy and Tears: The Emotional Life of the Christian* (Chicago: Moody Publishers, 2013), 103–15.

Christ is the visible image of the invisible God, in whom the fullness of deity dwells bodily, he humanly manifests with perfect consistency and constancy—that is, immutably—what we find throughout the Old Testament: the rich emotional life of God. To be sure, Christ humanly manifests God's joy and peace, and he shares this very joy and peace with the redeemed (John 14:27; 15:11; 16:33; 17:13). Yet, as Christ embodies and expresses God's holy love this side of Eden, he is deeply moved by other emotions as well. He displays compassion in suffering with those who suffer (Matt. 9:35–36; 20:29–34; Mark 1:40–41; 8:1–2; Luke 7:11–14), grief over a world blinded by sin and bound to death (Luke 19:41–44; John 11; 13:21), anger at hardness of heart (Mark 3:5; 10:13–16; 11:15–18), and distress amidst what he selflessly embraced to make many sons and daughters of God (Matt. 26:36–38; Mark 14:32–34).

Seeking to image the holy love of her Head and Bridegroom, the church must resist a failure of faith and nerve by discerning God's holy love from the costless counterfeit of benign cordiality, or that most prized attribute of our present socio-political milieu, what we might call *omni-affirmation*. So, too, must we beware of doing violence to the legitimacy and complexity of human emotions, because the affective domain is a constituent aspect of the divine image in which humans are created. Redemption should not blunt the intensity of our emotional life, prompting us to aspire to something like the Stoic ideal of apathy. Neither should redemption reduce the scope of our emotional life, prompting us to repudiate all expressions of emotions sometimes seen as inherently bad or negative, such as grief, anger, and distress. Redemption means the crucifixion, the resurrection, and the ongoing sanctification of our entire persons, resulting in the whole of our emotional life being progressively purged and healed of all that corrupts, perverts, and distorts, so that our emotions might be expressions of authentic humanity made and remade in God's image. Our ongoing sanctification in Jesus Christ is ongoing conformity to him who is the image of God in and as the image of man—the One who clearly and concretely displays what humanity made and remade in God's image is to be. Consequently, the church's inward and outward activity should be marked by impassioned involvement, as the redeemed image, with progressive authenticity, the richness and complexity of God's holy love, the same holy love humanly manifested to perfection in Christ.

The Glory of God

God's glory denotes his inestimable weight, worth, and splendor, the effulgent radiance of the One who is holy love in all his wisdom, goodness, and beauty. When Moses pleaded to behold God's glory, that glory was at once revealed and concealed. God graciously condescended to make his presence accessible to Moses in the fiery cloud called the Shekinah, proclaiming his name—that is, his nature and character—while insisting "you shall see my back, but my face shall not be seen" (Ex. 33:17–23; 34:5–7). The Shekinah was the characteristic manifestation of God's glory in the Old Testament (Ex. 13:17–22; 16:7, 10; 24:15–18), and it was especially associated first with the tabernacle (Ex. 40:34–38; Lev. 9:23–24; Num. 9:15–23) and then with the temple (1 Kings 8:10–11; Ezek. 8:4; 9:3; 10:4; 11:22–23), those divinely appointed places where God deigned to meet his people, putting himself on show *in their midst.*

Though the lineaments of God's face progressively emerged through Israel's tabernacle and temple, the apostle John notes that God himself remained unseen by all. But in the fullness of time, "the Word became flesh and dwelt among us, and we have seen his glory, glory as of the only Son from the Father, full of grace and truth" (John 1:14, 18). The Greek word translated "dwelt" in this text is σκηνόω, which can also be translated as "tabernacled," alluding to the tabernacle in the Old Testament. The point is that Jesus Christ is the very embodiment of the Shekinah, the visible manifestation of God's glory, put on show *in our flesh.* The face of God, concealed from Moses and all others until the incarnation, is revealed clearly and concretely in the face of Christ, the effulgent radiance of God's glory *as man* (2 Cor. 4:6; Heb. 1:3). Sacred place has thus given way to sacred person in that the aim of Israel's temple is fulfilled and transformed by the incarnation of God. Christ declares that his very body is the temple, where divinity and humanity meet, where God has deigned to make himself accessible to us (John 2:18–22).

The manifestation of God's glory, like all divine attributes, is an eternal inner-Trinitarian reality turned outward. Our Lord made this clear in his High Priestly Prayer by stating, "And now, Father, glorify me in your own presence with the glory that I had with you before the world existed" (John 17:5). In this same prayer, offered on the eve of his betrayal and arrest, Christ exclaimed that he had glorified the Father on earth, having manifested his name—that is, having exalted and amplified the Father's nature and character. Here Christ was referring to his embodiment of God's glory throughout his first advent, from manger to cross. Yet the shadow of the cross loomed over the entirety of Christ's first advent, even as the whole course of that advent moved inexorably toward the cross and was characterized by the cross. For Christ identified his crucifixion as that unique hour when the Father would glorify the Son, and the Son, in turn, would glorify the Father—that unique hour when God's nature and character would be most brilliantly and definitively put on show (John 17:1–6; cf. 12:27–28; 13:31–32). Cornelius Plantinga highlights this paradox in gripping fashion: "'The hour has come for the Son of Man to be *glorified*,' says Jesus. How can this be? Being glorified on a cross? Is that like being enthroned on an electric chair? Is it like being honored by a firing squad?"[49] And if the force of this paradox were not unyielding enough, Jesus sent the redeemed into the world in the same manner that the Father sent him, granting us a share in the same glory that he has with the Father (John 17:18, 22). As the church shares in Christ's mission from the Father, Christ is with her always, continuing to conform her to himself, that she might shine with the radiance of his glory, and he might be known, worshiped, and obeyed to the ends of the earth (Matt. 28:18–20).

Recalling what we said at the start of our discussion of God's attributes, the fullness and finality of God's self-disclosure in Jesus Christ radically challenges *all* self-styled expectations and assumptions about who God is, what he is like, and what his mission entails. God's glory is but a case in point. Looking upon the crucified Christ, the world sees only weakness, shame, and folly, the occasion for death to boast over the perceived barrenness of a bankrupt God. But the church confesses with Christ himself that the cross was the very hour of his glory, the occasion of the mightiest, wisest, and most characteristic display of who God is and what he is like, the occasion that gives an indelibly cruciform shape to the church's sharing in Christ's mission from the Father. The world tends to confuse glory with egoism, self-regard, and self-aggrandizement. Thus, glory tends to be understood in terms of an ascent to greatness, often through competition, and often at the expense—sometimes the immense detriment—of

---

[49] Cornelius Plantinga, "Deep Wisdom," in *God the Holy Trinity: Reflections on Christian Faith and Practice*, ed. Timothy George (Grand Rapids: Baker Academic, 2006), 151.

others. But God manifests his glory by descent to greatness, descent at his own expense for the immense benefit of others. This definitive display of God's glory is the definitive triumph of his holy love, wherein the incarnate God freely spends himself that others might flourish. The redeemed image Christ's glory as we share in his descent of self-giving love, as we freely spend ourselves that others might flourish, and as we joyfully discover, perhaps to our repeated surprise, that self-emptying and self-fulfillment are not antithetical, but identical (Matt. 16:24–25; Mark 8:34–35). Here God is supremely on show, for as the redeemed are conformed to him who is the express image of both God and man, the express image of God *as man*, we are "transformed into the same image from one degree of glory to another" (2 Cor. 3:18).[50]

---

[50] Ibid., 151–55.

4

Becoming Human, Becoming Sin

THE LIGHT SHINING IN OUR DARKNESS

The language of the Christian confession contains few words as precious as *atonement*, for this word speaks to the reconciliation, or "at-one-ment," between God and the redeemed secured in Jesus Christ. More to the point, *atonement* speaks to our Lord's making amends and assuaging enmity between God and the redeemed, to his healing of estrangement and alienation, and to his restoration of a ruptured relationship. Regrettably, however, modern Christians often imbibe and perpetuate two momentous misconceptions about this grand reality called atonement. First, we commonly attribute atonement to the *work* of Christ but not to the *person* of Christ; thus, we dichotomize Christ's work from his person. Second, we commonly equate atonement with the *death* of Christ, as if his death constitutes the totality of the atonement he secured for us; thus, we dichotomize Christ's atoning *death* from his atoning *birth*, not to mention his atoning *life, resurrection,* and *ascension.* Both of these dichotomies have become so engrained in our habits of thought that associating Christ's atonement with his person, to say nothing of his birth, will surely strike some readers as odd.

Lest any readers harbor doubts about just how pervasive these dichotomies are among modern Christians, let us take a moment to consider our habits of speech. We often talk, for instance, about trusting the finished work of Christ rather than the living person of Christ for our salvation. We talk about our sins being nailed to the cross rather than our sins being borne away in the body and soul of Christ. We even talk about taking our prayers to the cross rather than taking them to our resurrected and ascended Lord. The situation demands that we be altogether clear: these dichotomies diminish the scope of our salvation and the grandeur of the gospel. What is more, these dichotomies not only reflect but also reinforce our tendency to miss that the incarnation is central to our reconciliation with God, that the reality of Christ's atonement is grounded in the reality of his incarnation.

Modern Christians often view the incarnation as an incidental prerequisite for salvation, a mere prelude to the real drama of redemption. In other words, the incarnation is often recognized as a reconciling, atoning reality only insofar as it makes possible Christ's eventual crucifixion. After all, the thought goes, our Lord could hardly have died for us unless he first had been born. Many modern Christians, it seems, have forgotten or never fully grasped that our redemption *began* with the incarnation.[1]

As our exploration of the incarnation now moves more decidedly and explicitly into the realm of salvation, this chapter and the next are together intended to demonstrate that a proper estimation of the incarnation deepens and broadens common notions of what it means to be reconciled to God in Jesus Christ. Ultimately, we must grasp that not only is Christ's death atoning, but the whole of his ministry is atoning, from incarnation to ascension. In view of that end, the aim of this chapter is to discuss the kind of humanity that God the Son assumed in becoming flesh.

What Kind of Humanity Did God the Son Assume?

Christian orthodoxy, as articulated by the Definition of Chalcedon, maintains that God the Son took upon himself a human body and soul, participating unreservedly in "the same reality as we are ourselves [*homoousion hēmin*] as far as his human-ness is concerned; thus like us in all respects, sin only excepted."[2] At the same time, the apostle Paul declares that the

---

[1] Oliver D. Crisp, "By His Birth We Are Healed: Our Redemption, It Turns Out, Began Long Before Calvary," *Christianity Today* 56, no. 3 (March 2012): 31.

[2] "The Definition of Chalcedon (451)," in CC, 36.

Father sent "his own Son in the likeness of sinful flesh and . . . condemned sin in the flesh," making "him to be sin who knew no sin, so that in him we might become the righteousness of God" (Rom. 8:3; 2 Cor. 5:21). What is the likeness of *sinful flesh*? When and how was sin condemned *in Christ's flesh*? In what sense was Christ *made to be sin*, and when did this frightful event occur? These inquiries are all comprehended in a more basic question: What kind of humanity did God the Son assume in order to secure our salvation? Let us consider some prominent answers and their implications.

The Official Answer of Modern Roman Catholicism

The fifteenth century brought decisive developments in the Roman Catholic Church's growing desire to assert and extol the sinlessness of the Virgin Mary. The Council of Basel officially affirmed the legitimacy of this belief in 1439, and ten years later, the Sorbonne required all doctoral candidates in theology to swear an oath to defend it. Other universities soon followed. The Council of Trent (1545–63) explicitly declared that its decree on original sin did not include "the blessed and immaculate Virgin Mary," and from the sixteenth century forward, the doctrine of the immaculate conception was defended by the Franciscans, the Carmelites, many Dominicans, and especially the Jesuits.[3] Finally, in December 1854, Pope Pius IX issued the papal bull titled *Ineffabilis Deus*, or "Ineffable God." This document defines and declares what was thereafter the Roman Catholic Church's official dogma on the immaculate conception: Mary was conceived free, or exempt, from original sin. Pius IX writes:

> The most Blessed Virgin Mary was, from the first moment of her conception, by a singular grace and privilege of almighty God and by virtue of the merits of Jesus Christ, Savior of the human race, preserved immune from all stain of original sin.[4]

Christology drives Roman Mariology. In this instance, then, an ultimate concern with the human nature of Jesus Christ gave rise to an immediate concern with the human nature of the Virgin Mary, for the human nature that

---

[3] "Immaculate Conception of the BVM," in *The Oxford Dictionary of the Christian Church*, 3rd ed., ed. F. L. Cross and E. A. Livingstone (New York: Oxford University Press, 1997), 821–22; "The Canons and Decrees of the Council of Trent (1563)," in *CC*, 408.

[4] *Catechism of the Catholic Church*, 2nd ed. (Città del Vaticano: Libreria Editrice Vaticana, 1997), 124.

Mary possessed was, of course, the human nature that Christ assumed. The immaculate conception of Mary is thus the Roman Church's attempt to explain the sinlessness of Christ by insulating and isolating his humanity from our humanity—that is, humanity in need of redemption. The organic structure and stream of human heredity is thought to have been divinely interrupted between Mary's parents and Mary herself, with the result that Mary's humanity was humanity in its original, primal state. Mary possessed a prefall Adamic human nature, and God the Son united that prefall Adamic human nature to himself in Mary's womb. Consequently, the immaculate conception safeguards Christ's humanity from ours by segregation, as ours is not the humanity he assumed.

The Common Answer of Modern Protestant Evangelicals

The Roman Catholic dogma of the immaculate conception is not officially espoused by any of the Protestant traditions, and Protestant evangelicals have rightly been quick to point out that this teaching finds no explicit scriptural warrant. Yet Scripture does explicitly teach the virgin birth of Christ (Matt. 1:18–25; Luke 1:26–38). All Protestant evangelicals believe that Christ's virgin birth has a terrific bearing on the kind of humanity he assumed, though Protestants have no official position on this matter, as do Roman Catholics. The answer of most modern Protestant evangelicals may be aptly represented by referencing two of the most highly esteemed and widely used theology textbooks in present-day evangelical churches, colleges, and seminaries. On the significance of the virgin birth to Christ's humanity, Louis Berkhof writes:

> If Christ had been generated by man, He would have been a human person . . . and as such would have shared the common guilt of mankind. But now that His subject, His ego, His person, is not out of [i.e. from] Adam, He . . . is free from the guilt of sin. And being free from the guilt of sin, His human nature could also be kept free, both before and after His birth, from the pollution of sin.[5]

Wayne Grudem states the significance of the virgin birth to Christ's humanity similarly:

---

[5] Louis Berkhof, *Systematic Theology* (Grand Rapids: Eerdmans, 1996), 336.

The virgin birth also makes possible Christ's true humanity without inherited sin. . . . . All human beings have inherited legal guilt and a corrupt moral nature from their first father, Adam (this is sometimes called "inherited sin" or "original sin"). But the fact that Jesus did not have a human father means that the line of descent from Adam is partially interrupted. Jesus did not descend from Adam in exactly the same way in which every other human being has descended from Adam. And this helps us to understand why the legal guilt and moral corruption that belongs to all other human beings did not belong to Christ. . . . Such a conclusion should not be taken to mean that the transmission of sin comes only through the father, for Scripture nowhere makes such an assertion. It is enough for us merely to say that *in this case* the unbroken line of descent from Adam was interrupted, and Jesus was conceived by the power of the Holy Spirit. . . . Reflection on that fact allows us to understand that through the absence of a human father, Jesus was not fully descended from Adam, and that this break in the line of descent was the method God used to bring it about that Jesus was fully human yet did not share inherited sin from Adam.[6]

Here most modern Protestant evangelicals differ from modern Roman Catholics not in the end to which they aspire, but only in the means by which they attain that end. On the one hand, modern Roman Catholics attempt to explain the sinlessness of Christ by maintaining that the organic structure and stream of human heredity was divinely interrupted between Mary's parents and Mary herself, with the immaculate conception of Mary resulting in Christ's assumption of a prefall Adamic human nature. On the other hand, modern Protestant evangelicals such as Berkhof and Grudem attempt to explain the sinlessness of Christ by maintaining that the organic structure and stream of human heredity was divinely interrupted between Mary and Christ himself, with the virgin birth of our Lord resulting in his assumption of a prefall Adamic human nature. When understood in this way, the virgin birth of Christ serves the same end as the immaculate conception of Mary: both safeguard Christ's humanity from ours, precisely because both segregate Christ's humanity from humanity in need of redemption.

---

[6] Wayne Grudem, *Systematic Theology: An Introduction to Biblical Doctrine* (Grand Rapids: Zondervan, 2000), 530–31 (emphasis original).

The Common Answer of Modern Protestant Liberals

Suspicion and skepticism of established sources of knowledge marked the eighteenth-century Enlightenment, its architects and advocates calling people to emerge from the self-imposed tutelage of others by daring to follow the dictates of their own unaided reason. Modern Protestant liberals answered the call of the Enlightenment insofar as their self-understanding, not God's self-disclosure, constituted the starting point and controlling principle of their revisionist approach to the Christian faith. Friedrich Schleiermacher (1768–1834), often called the "father of modern theology," found the church's confession of Jesus Christ, as articulated by the Definition of Chalcedon, to be illogical. Christ, he said, cannot be God the Son in and as man. He must be a man like all others, distinguished only "by the constant potency of His God-consciousness, which was a veritable existence of God in Him."[7] Christ's God-consciousness should not be confused with divine self-knowledge, for that it is not. Yet the ideal God-consciousness that Christ possessed and exhibited suffices for what Christians have called his "divinity." Moreover, Christ's ability to model his fully realized God-consciousness *for* others, and summon forth the latent God-consciousness *of* others, constitutes his redemptive activity.[8] Schleiermacher's Christ signals the prospect of human ascent without the paradox of divine descent, man's coming of age without God's coming in flesh.

Protestant liberalism, shaped by the likes of David Strauss, Albrecht Ritschl, Wilhelm Herrmann, Walter Rauschenbusch, and Ernst Troeltsch, greatly influenced academic theology in Europe and North America throughout the nineteenth and early twentieth centuries. Yet none delineated and popularized this movement with the proficiency of Adolf von Harnack. He insisted that "the Gospel, as Jesus proclaimed it, has to do with the Father only and not with the Son."[9] Jesus draws our attention to the "great questions" of life regarding the Fatherhood of God and the brotherhood of mankind—not to himself, and certainly not to "christology."[10]

---

[7] Friedrich Schleiermacher, *The Christian Faith*, eds. H. R. Mackintosh and J. S. Stewart (New York: Harper Torchbooks, 1963), 385.

[8] Donald G. Bloesch, *Essentials of Evangelical Theology* (Peabody, MA: Prince Press, 1998), 1:120–21; Stanley J. Grenz and Roger E. Olson, *20th-Century Theology: God and the World in a Transitional Age* (Downers Grove, IL: IVP Academic, 1992), 49.

[9] Adolf von Harnack, *What Is Christianity?*, trans. Thomas Bailey Saunders (1902; repr., Philadelphia: Fortress, 1986), 144.

[10] Ibid., 143.

And because "the whole of the gospel" concerns "God and the soul, the soul and its God," the gospel must be kept "free from the intrusion of any alien element."[11] Tragically, the "alien element" Harnack had in mind was the incarnation, the church's confession that Jesus Christ is God the Son in and as man. Harnack deemed the incarnation to be a distortion of the gospel introduced by the apostle Paul and augmented by the Hellenization of the early post-apostolic church, a distortion assaulting not merely the simplicity but the very point and purpose of Jesus's own teaching, which "summarily confronts every man with his God."[12]

Protestant liberalism desires to maximally *adopt* the cultural and intellectual movements of the modern milieu, and maximally *adapt* the church's confession to the perceived preferences of modern men and women. Therefore, Protestant liberals tend to reduce the Christ of Christian orthodoxy to a master teacher, a sage spiritual guide, a great religious personality, or the prophet of socio-ethical ideals. If Christ was "divine," it was merely in the sense that he was unusually godly, having lived in volitional and moral harmony with God. And if Christ was different from other humans, it was in the sense that he possessed and exhibited fully realized human qualities. Because Protestant liberals tend to embrace the Enlightenment notion of humankind's natural goodness and inevitable progress, however, those qualities are considered obtainable merely by emulation and effort. The significance of Christ, then, lies in his moral instruction and example, in his religious genius, and in his profound experience of God—not in his person.[13] Christ's humanity may indeed be our humanity, but the presuppositions of Protestant liberals render the matter of little importance. Attempts to explain the sinlessness of Christ or the atoning effects of his sharing our human heredity are superfluous, given that our inherited corruption and estrangement from God are denied. Equally superfluous is any talk of Christ's *assumption* of human nature, for he is not believed to be God the Son come in flesh.

---

[11] Ibid., 142.

[12] Ibid., 184.

[13] Bloesch, *Essentials of Evangelical Theology*, 1:109, 120–21; Alister E. McGrath, *Christian Theology: An Introduction*, 2nd ed. (Oxford: Blackwell Publishers, 1997), 344–45.

A Gospel of Extrinsic and Abstract Relations

Modern Protestant liberalism is profoundly problematic, differing far more deeply and decidedly from both its Roman Catholic and Protestant evangelical counterparts than these latter two traditions differ from one another. Yet all three of these traditions share a troubling feature that is common to modern Christians: the tendency to view the incarnation in a way that dichotomizes either God from Christ or Christ from us. The result is a gospel fractured and fragmented by extrinsic and abstract relations.

Protestant liberals recoil at the incarnation of God. Thus, as Christ is not believed to be God the Son in and as man, the Father's relationship with Christ is merely generic, not unique. In other words, the tendency of Protestant liberals is to dichotomize *God from Christ* by denying that Christ is the eternally begotten Son of the Father, by denying that while Christ is indeed fully human, he is no less fully God. By denying the *homoousion* of the Father and the Son, the difference between Christ's sonship and ours becomes only a matter of degree, not of essence. His sonship is seen as a common sharing in the human spirit of brotherhood, not an eternal sharing in the being and life of God the Father Almighty. Here Christian orthodoxy is denatured, recast in unitarian, moralistic, and individualistic terms around the core conviction that each of us has the innate right and ability for an immediate and unmediated relationship with God. Christ's redemptive activity is thus interpreted in extrinsic and abstract categories because Christ himself is seen as merely an external influence upon us—an instructive and inspiring model of suffering love in our struggle for justice, an example of God-consciousness that should educate and motivate us to actualize the same in our own lives.[14]

On the other hand, modern Roman Catholics and modern Protestant evangelicals tend to dichotomize *Christ from us* by claiming that he assumed a prefall Adamic human nature—that is, a humanity different and dissociated from our own. To be sure, both traditions confess that Christ is God the Son, and that he is truly and fully human. But if Christ assumed human nature in a state that no longer exists—his humanness not touching ours—then his relation to us and redemptive activity for us must necessarily be interpreted in extrinsic and abstract categories. In other words, God

---

[14] James B. Torrance, *Worship, Community, and the Triune God of Grace* (Downers Grove, IL: IVP Academic, 1996), 25–26; Elmer M. Colyer, "The Incarnate Saviour: T. F. Torrance on the Atonement," in *An Introduction to Torrance Theology: Discovering the Incarnate Saviour*, ed. Gerrit Scott Dawson (London: T&T Clark, 2007), 41.

the Son's relation to us and redemptive activity for us cannot be seen as intrinsically and concretely rooted in the incarnate Christ's participation in the *actual* being and life of humanity if he did not assume the same human nature that we ourselves possess—that is, human nature in its *actual* state of existence, that is, in *actual* need of salvation. Here Christ's humanity is only representational in relation to us, and therefore only instrumental in relation to our redemption. The incarnation, in turn, is reduced to little more than the means by which God provided a sinless human surrogate, One able to live in perfect obedience to God's law and endure God's judgment against transgressors of that law. Christ died for us so that we need not die ourselves. He was the proxy who completed a legal transaction on our behalf, suffering in our stead, so as to fulfill the condition by which his saving benefits might be transferred to us.

Perhaps an incarnate Savior with his humanity insulated and isolated from our own could exert an external influence upon us to free us from the *penalty* of sin. But the *power* of sin, rooted in the depths of our fallen and corrupt human nature, would necessarily remain untouched. Roman Catholics and Protestant evangelicals who interpret Christ's redemptive activity in this way must look elsewhere for the internal renovation of our otherwise untouched human nature. The former usually appeal to the merits that Christ gained for us on the cross, which are thought to be deposited in the Roman Church and dispensed to the faithful as infusions of sanctifying grace. The latter often see our sanctification as the sole province of the Spirit, thereby separating the Spirit's work *in* us from Christ's work *for* us. The perichoretic relation between Christ and the Spirit is thus bifurcated, with the Spirit acting as a stand-in for a Savior who is now distant or absent from us—a stand-in, moreover, who in himself cannot sanctify our humanity given that he has not assumed it.

Further, an incarnate Savior with humanity insulated and isolated from our own may well be confessed as the one Mediator between God and men *as man* (1 Tim. 2:5). But in practice, he could easily be perceived as far more divine than human, and thus as remote from us. Roman Catholics and Protestant evangelicals routinely exhibit this perception. The former multiply human mediators between God and men, petitioning those to whom they more readily relate—the venerated saints—for empathy and advocacy in times of need. The latter frequently overlook the bidirectional nature of

Christ's mediation, acknowledging that God came near to us in Christ but failing to grasp that in Christ we now share in his vicarious human response to the Father. This failure to grasp that our human-Godward movement also takes place in Christ suggests that Christ fulfilled the conditions of our salvation only to throw us back upon ourselves, only to be far from us as we seek to draw near to God. This prompts preoccupation with *our* faith, *our* repentance, *our* decision, *our* response, *our* industry, and *our* resolve—a veneration of the saints of quite another sort, resulting in frenetic busyness and the crushing internalization of sin, guilt, fear, and shame.[15]

To dichotomize either God from Christ or Christ from us is to rip God's saving acts and benefits from their ontological mooring in the humanity of our Savior, stripping the incarnation of its tremendous soteriological, mediatorial significance. Consequently, proponents of both tendencies cannot help missing that the mystery of the incarnation is the very foundation of the gospel. It is no wonder, therefore, that modern Christians often proclaim a gospel fractured and fragmented by extrinsic and abstract relations. They tend to separate Christ's work from his person, as if his incarnate humanity were little more than the outward apparatus prerequisite for his atoning death. Moreover, modern Christians tend to separate Christ's saving benefits from Christ himself, as if salvation were an objectified commodity given on account of Christ yet apart from him, as if Christ were the agent of our salvation but not that salvation himself. Finally, modern Christians tend to separate Christ's saving activity *for* us from the internal renovation of Christ's being *in* us, as if our relation to Christ were only metaphorical, moral, volitional, legal, or ideational, not our life-giving, life-transforming participation in him who assumed the same humanity that we ourselves possess. Modern Christians tend to proclaim a gospel that is mechanistic and transactional in character. Yet the gospel proclaimed by the apostles, many early Christians, and the sixteenth-century Protestant Reformers was relational and participationist in character, for they heralded the glorious reality of receiving Christ and being saved in Christ, as opposed to obtaining an impersonal asset called salvation based on what Christ has done.[16]

---

[15] Torrance, *Worship, Community, and the Triune God of Grace*, 29; Colyer, "The Incarnate Saviour," 39–43.

[16] For two superb studies that deal with this dichotomizing impulse among modern Christians in general, and post-Reformation Protestants in particular, see Trevor Hart, "Humankind in Christ and Christ in Humankind: Salvation as Participation in Our Substitute in the Theology of John Calvin," *SJT* 42 (1989): 67–84; William B. Evans, "Twin Sons of Different Mothers: The Remarkable Theological Convergence of John W. Nevin and Thomas F. Torrance," *Haddington House Journal* 11 (2009): 155–73.

The Most Satisfying, Scandalous Answer

If Christ's humanity is true and full, rather than illusory or partial, and if Christ did not assume a human nature different and dissociated from our own, then what kind of human nature did he assume? What did Paul mean by declaring that the Father sent his Son in the likeness of sinful flesh and condemned sin in the flesh (Rom. 8:3)? According to the renowned New Testament scholar C. E. B. Cranfield, Paul clearly meant that God the Son assumed a fallen human nature, the selfsame fallen human nature that is ours, and that God's condemnation of sin took place in the flesh of Christ, in the human nature he holds unreservedly in common with us.[17] Thus, the condemnation of sin in Christ's flesh that surely *culminated* at the cross can neither be totalized by the cross nor isolated to the cross, as this condemnation *commenced* at his conception. Far from an incidental prerequisite or mere prelude to the real drama of redemption, therefore, the incarnation is the foundation of redemption. This is because the incarnation attests to the reality that God the Son seized us in the state in which he found us, a state of condemnation, corruption, and alienation—assuming the only kind of human nature that exists east of Eden, the only kind that actually needs redeeming.

Perhaps Christ's assumption of a hypothetical human nature would suffice if we were but hypothetical sinners in need of a hypothetical Savior. Yet sin is not a notion or concept, and it has no independent existence apart from sinners. Our Lord did not assume human nature to affect an ethereal entity called sin, but to decisively destroy sin in the lives of sinners. Thus, the incarnation is not a divine *interruption* in the organic structure and stream of human heredity, whereby God the Son wields an external influence on an abstract generality—all the while remaining safeguarded and segregated from us. Rather, the incarnation is a divine *invasion* of the organic structure and stream of human heredity, wherein God the Son attacks sin in its concrete reality by penetrating the depths of our actual fallen human existence, cleansing our corruption at its root and eradicating our estrangement from God in his very person.

---

[17] C. E. B. Cranfield, *The Epistle to the Romans*, ICC (Edinburgh: T&T Clark, 1998), 1:379–82. Fellow commentator Anders Nygren remarks: "In that expression [i.e., "the likeness of sinful flesh"] there is no trace of docetism. Christ's carnal nature was no unreality, but simple, tangible fact. He shared all our conditions. He was under the same powers of destruction. Out of 'the flesh' arose for Him the same temptations as for us." *Commentary on Romans*, trans. Carl C. Rasmussen (Philadelphia: Muhlenberg Press, 1949), 315.

Once again we are confronted by the unrelenting, irreducible mystery and scandal of the incarnation. How could Christ save us if he became a human just like us, entering the fallen condition from which we need saving? Many modern Roman Catholics and Protestant evangelicals might raise this objection, though the objection itself is as ancient as the christological controversies that precipitated the Council of Chalcedon (451). In fact, let us recall from chapter 1 that this was precisely the objection that compelled Apollinarius, the fourth-century bishop of Laodicea, to deny Christ's assumption of a true and full human mind, given that Apollinarius identified the human mind as the seat, or root, of our fallen condition. Let us also recall that famous response to Apollinarianism from the fourth-century archbishop of Constantinople, Gregory of Nazianzus: "For that which He [Christ] has not assumed He has not healed; but that which is united to His Godhead is also saved."[18] Gregory's maxim that the unassumed is the unhealed turns the objection at hand on its head, asking, in effect, *How could Christ save us if he did not become a human just like us, if he did not enter the fallen condition from which we need saving?* Is it not precisely our fallen humanity that needs to be assumed because it needs to be saved by an encounter with God in Christ? Is it not then the case that an incarnation that fails to heal what actually ails fallen humans is an incarnation that leaves us in a state of corruption and estrangement from God?

To deny that the enfleshment of Christ marks his entrance into the very condition from which fallen humans need saving is to fundamentally misunderstand the incarnation, declares Basil, the fourth-century archbishop of Caesarea:

> For if what was reigned over by death was not that which was assumed by the Lord, death would not have ceased working his own ends, nor would the sufferings of the God-bearing flesh have been made our gain; He would not have killed sin in the flesh; we who had died in Adam should not have been made alive in Christ; the fallen to pieces would not have been framed again; the shattered would not have been set up again; that which by the serpent's trick had been estranged from God would never have been made once more His own. . . . And if the God-bearing

---

[18] Gregory of Nazianzus, "To Cledonius the Priest against Apollinarius," *Letters on the Apollinarian Controversy*, no. 101, in *NPNF*, 7:440.

flesh was not ordained to be assumed of the lump of Adam, what need was there of the Holy Virgin?[19]

Note that unlike many modern Protestant evangelicals, Basil did not find Christ's virgin birth significant because it resulted in his assumption of a prefall Adamic human nature, thereby segregating his humanity from ours. On the contrary, the significance of Christ's being born of the Virgin Mary was that the human nature "assumed by the Lord" was human nature "assumed of the lump of Adam"—that is, human nature "reigned over by death . . . , fallen to pieces . . . , shattered . . . , [and] estranged from God."

Gregory and Basil are merely echoing an affirmation made by many of their predecessors in the early post-apostolic church. Irenaeus of Lyons (ca. 120–202) poignantly proclaims that Christ redeemed us from sin and death by being born of flesh subject to sin and death:

> For it behoved Him who was to destroy sin, and redeem man under the power of death, that He should Himself be made that very same thing which he was, that is, man; who had been drawn by sin into bondage, but was held by death, so that sin should be destroyed by man, and man should go forth from death.[20]

Tertullian (ca. 145–220), a church father from Carthage, North Africa, heartily agrees:

> Now, it would not contribute to the purpose of Christ's abolishing sin in the flesh, if He did not abolish it in that flesh in which was the nature of sin, nor (would it conduce) to His glory. For surely it would have been no strange thing if He had removed the stain of sin in some better flesh, and one which should possess a different, even a sinless, nature![21]

In the sixteenth-century Protestant Reformation, Martin Luther plainly and forcibly reiterated Christ's assumption of our fallen humanity. Like Tertullian and many other early Christians before him, Luther not only recognized but reveled in the strange and staggering reality that God the

---

[19] Basil of Caesarea, "To the Sozopolitons," *The Letters*, no. 261, in *NPNF*, 8:300.
[20] Irenaeus, *Against Heresies* 3.18.7, in *ANF*, 1:448.
[21] Tertullian, *On the Flesh of Christ*, in *ANF*, 3:535–36. For several similar quotes from the church fathers, see Thomas Weinandy, *In the Likeness of Sinful Flesh: An Essay on the Humanity of Christ* (Edinburgh: T&T Clark, 1993), 23–38; Thomas F. Torrance, *The Trinitarian Faith: The Evangelical Theology of the Ancient Catholic Church* (London: T&T Clark, 1991), 161–68.

Son saved us not *in some better flesh*, but in the *sinful human nature* that was united to God in the person of Christ. Luther muses:

> And if we really ponder the matter, we cannot but conclude that it would have been far more reasonable and honorable for God to adopt the nature of His noblest creatures, the angels, than that of sinful human nature, which had imbibed the poison of the old serpent, the devil, in Paradise. God's assumption of human nature and the union of God and man in the person of Christ is comparable to placing a filthy sow at table and chasing away holy and pious people.[22]

In fact, Luther did not seem to see his affirmation that Christ assumed our fallen human nature as new or novel, but as a result of his return to the sources of Scripture and the church fathers, over and against at least some medieval theologians. He declares:

> The scholastic doctors argue about whether Christ was born from sinful or clean flesh, or whether from the foundation of the world God preserved a pure bit of flesh from which Christ was to be born. I reply, therefore, that Christ was truly born from true and natural flesh and human blood which was corrupted by original sin in Adam, but in such a way that it could be healed.[23]

Let us not miss the fact that Luther's reply to medieval theologians who denied Christ's assumption of our fallen humanity was essentially the same as Gregory's reply to the Apollinarians: that which God the Son has not assumed he has not healed. Luther deemed such persons *sophists*—teachers of specious and unsound doctrine, doctrine that is ostensibly pious but pastorally cruel. This was because if Christ did not assume flesh *corrupted by original sin in Adam*, then the incarnation punctuates that our Lord remained segregated from us, that he did not bear away the sin of our bodies and souls in his body and soul. This signals that the incarnation failed to heal what ails us, given that God the Son's coming in flesh stopped short of his penetrating the depths of our actual fallen human existence. Luther insists:

---

[22] "Sermon on the Gospel of St. John 6:47," in *LW*, 22:104.
[23] Ibid., 7:12–13.

Christ was not only found among sinners; but of His own free will and by the will of the Father He wanted to be an associate of sinners, having assumed the flesh and blood of those who were sinners and thieves and who were immersed in all sorts of sin. . . . Of this the sophists deprive us when they segregate Christ from sins and from sinners and set Him forth to us as only an example to be imitated. In this way they make Christ not only useless to us but also a judge and a tyrant who is angry because of our sins and who damns sinners. But just as Christ is wrapped up in our flesh and blood, so we must wrap Him and know Him to be wrapped up in our sins, our curse, our death, and everything evil.[24]

Though characteristically more measured in expression than Luther, John Calvin also reveled in the scandal that our reconciliation with God entails God the Son's having assumed precisely the same humanity that we ourselves possess. On Colossians 1:22, Calvin comments:

The expression seems absurd; but the "body of his flesh" means that human body which the Son of God had in common with us. He [Paul] meant, therefore, to express that the Son of God had put on the same nature with us, that He took upon Him this lowly and earthly body, subject to many infirmities, that He might be our Mediator.[25]

Had Christ been born of flesh other than our own, he might be our *intermediary*—an indirectly related agent who facilitates extrinsic transactions between God and us, and transmits abstract benefits from God to us. But Christ was born of our flesh so as to be our *Mediator*. God the Son became the Son of man together with us—assuming what is ours to impart what is his, healing the human nature he took from us—that the self-giving of God might be accomplished in and through the incarnate humanity of the God-man, our Lord Jesus Christ. Thus, Calvin exclaims:

This is the wonderful exchange which, out of his measureless benevolence, he has made with us; that, becoming Son of man with us, he has made us sons of God with him; that, by his descent to earth, he has prepared an ascent to heaven for us; that, by taking on our mortality, he has conferred his immortality upon us; that, accepting our weakness,

---

[24] Ibid., 26:278.
[25] Calvin on Col. 1:23, in *CNTC*, 11:314–15.

he has strengthened us by his power; that, receiving our poverty unto himself, he has transferred his wealth to us; that, taking the weight of our iniquity upon himself (which oppressed us), he has clothed us with his righteousness.[26]

Likewise, writing in 1846 with the overt aim of calling American Reformed churches back from pseudo-Protestantism to their doctrinal roots, John Williamson Nevin unflinchingly declared, "The humanity which he [Christ] assumed was fallen, subject to infirmity, and liable to death."[27] And the Dutch Calvinist Abraham Kuyper could scarcely articulate his insistence on this point more stridently, stating:

> Throughout the ages the Church has confessed that Christ took upon Himself real human nature from the virgin Mary, not as it was before the fall, but such as it had become *by* and *after* the fall. . . . Upon the authority of the divine Word we cannot doubt then that the Son of God became man in our fallen nature. . . . Hence it cannot be too strongly emphasized that the Son of God, walking among men, bore the same nature in which we spend our lives; that His flesh had the same origin as our flesh; that the blood which ran through His veins is the same as our blood, and came to Him as well as to us from the same fountain in Adam.[28]

The host of Scripture-honoring advocates of Christ's assumption of a fallen human nature ranges from early champions of Christian orthodoxy, such as Irenaeus of Lyons and Gregory of Nazianzus, to Protestant stalwarts such as Martin Luther and Abraham Kuyper. This alone should give doubtful modern Christians, particularly modern evangelicals, more than ample reason to reconsider.[29]

---

[26] *Inst.*, 4.17.2.

[27] John Williamson Nevin, *The Mystical Presence: A Vindication of the Reformed or Calvinistic Doctrine of the Holy Eucharist* (Philadelphia: J. B. Lippencott, 1846), 223.

[28] Abraham Kuyper, *The Work of the Holy Spirit*, trans. Henri De Vries (1900; repr., Grand Rapids: Eerdmans, 1941), 84 (emphasis original).

[29] Some Christians who affirm that Christ assumed a fallen human nature observe, often in the form of lament, that theirs is not the traditional position. See D. M. Baillie, *God Was in Christ: An Essay on Incarnation and Atonement* (New York: Charles Scribner's Sons, 1948), 16; Cranfield, *The Epistle to the Romans*, ICC, 1:380; Weinandy, *In the Likeness of Sinful Flesh*, 17–18. For an evenhanded overview of the debate, see Kelly M. Kapic, "The Son's Assumption of a Human Nature: A Call for Clarity," *IJST* 3, no. 2 (July 2001): 154–66.

WHAT ARE WE SAYING AND NOT SAYING?

Some crucial clarifications and implications still need to be highlighted.[30]

1. When Paul informs us that God the Son came "in the likeness of sinful flesh" and "condemned sin in the flesh" (Rom. 8:3), he employs the Greek word *sarx*, or "flesh," twice. The first usage indicates the kind of humanity God the Son assumed, and the second usage identifies where the condemnation of sin occurred. Paul's word choice is telling, due to the fact that he characteristically distinguishes *sarx* from *sōma* throughout his epistles. Paul generally employs the word *sōma* to mean "body" when referring to the human constitution as created by God, and thus without an inherently negative connotation. But Paul generally employs *sarx* to mean "flesh" when referring to the human constitution as ruined and wrecked by sin, and thus with a decidedly negative connotation. In other words, Paul's usage of "body" tends to connote human creatureliness, whereas his usage of "flesh" tends to connote human fallenness. As such, Paul proclaims that the *body* can be transformed and raised to newness of life (1 Cor. 15:44), but the *flesh* cannot (1 Cor. 15:50), and that there is redemption for the *body* (Rom. 8:23), but this redemption demands the dissolution and destruction of the *flesh* (1 Cor. 5:5).[31]

We confess, then, that God the Son's coming in the likeness of sinful flesh means that he became man in our fallen nature, that he assumed a human constitution created by God yet ruined and wrecked by sin—not human nature as it was before or apart from the fall, but human nature as it exists by and after the fall. In his eternal, preincarnate existence, of course, God the Son knew no sin. But in order that we might become the righteousness of God *in him*, he who knew no sin was made to be sin *in us* (2 Cor. 5:21). This is basic to the "wonderful exchange" Calvin describes above. Yes, Christ was surely made to be sin at the cross. But our Lord's sin-bearing, sin-defeating death was no isolated anomaly in his redemptive activity, no aberrant oddity that came from nowhere and stands alone, as it were, so as to be pared and parceled off from the whole course of his sin-bearing, sin-defeating life. What is more, the cross could entail nothing beyond the virtual reality of mere extrinsic representation if it were not

---

[30] The following discussion of clarifications and implications reflects our grateful indebtedness to R. Michael Allen for his laudable analysis of Christ's assumption of fallen human nature. See Allen, *The Christ's Faith: A Dogmatic Account*, T&T Clark Studies in Systematic Theology (London: T&T Clark, 2009), 126–35.

[31] James D. G. Dunn, *The Theology of Paul the Apostle* (Grand Rapids: Eerdmans, 1998), 70–73.

grounded in the incarnation. The frightful reality of Christ's *actually* being made sin in us reaches its culmination and completion at the cross precisely because it commenced at Christ's conception in the womb of Mary—with that astonishing act of omnipotent self-possession wherein God the Son freely became what we are without ceasing to be his immutable self. He gloriously assumed our fallen humanity in order to act upon sin from the inside, to destroy sin from *within* the realm of sin, to condemn sin in the sinful flesh he took from us and joined to his own incarnate person.

2. Had God the Son assumed human nature as it was before or apart from the fall, Christ's incarnation would be merely the instrumental means by which he eventually effected our reconciliation with God by his *atoning death*. In no sense could an incarnation of this sort be seen as reconciling in itself; thus, in no sense could Christ be thought to inherently effect our reconciliation with God by his *atoning birth*. Consequently, those who maintain that God the Son assumed human nature as it was before or apart from the fall can hardly help but dichotomize, even if unintentionally, Christ's atonement from his incarnation, Christ's death from his birth, and Christ's work from his person. Here Christ might *achieve* our salvation. Yet Paul announces the supremely better news that Christ himself *is* our salvation, that the Father has made him to *be* our righteousness, our sanctification, and our redemption (1 Cor. 1:30).

We confess, then, that God the Son seized our fallen human nature in its actual state of estrangement and alienation from God so as to effect reconciliation, or "at-one-ment," between God and man within his very incarnate person. In other words, we confess that just as the atonement is inherently incarnational, the incarnation is inherently atoning. This is simply to affirm that God the Son assumed what needed healing and healed what he assumed. The hypostatic, or personal, union of the divine and human natures in Christ is a reconciling, atoning union in that God the Son has assumed our ruined and wrecked human constitution and made it his own. The second person of the Trinity has taken our humanity into himself, and thus into the very life of God, banishing the separation between God and man within the God-man himself.

Christian orthodoxy, as articulated by the Definition of Chalcedon, insists that the incarnation in no sense suggests the denaturing or deifying of

Christ's true and full humanity.[32] And for precisely this reason, the incarnation suggests nothing of the sort about us. Far from undermining or nullifying our humanity, the incarnation authenticates and validates our humanity by re-creating and reorienting it to God in Christ. What is more, to confess that the incarnation is a reconciling, atoning union is by no means to deny or diminish the soteriological significance of Christ's life, death, resurrection, and ascension—nor the reality that sinners are saved only by apprehending Christ in faith. Rather, this confession sets the whole of Christ's redemptive activity for us, and our Spirit-wrought response to him, firmly within the outworking of one grand, multifaceted atonement—an atonement that *begins* with a swaddled newborn at a stable in Bethlehem.[33]

3. To say that the incarnation is a divine invasion of the organic structure and stream of human heredity is to say that God the Son penetrated the depths of our fallen human existence and assumed a human nature like any other east of Eden: corrupted human nature decisively bent toward sin. At the same time, the Definition of Chalcedon states that Christ is "like us in all respects, sin only excepted."[34] More important, Scripture is absolutely clear: *our Lord never sinned in thought, word, or deed.* "He committed no sin, neither was deceit found in his mouth," writes Peter (1 Pet. 2:22). "He appeared in order to take away sins, and in him there is no sin," echoes John (1 John 3:5). Christ was the perfect sacrifice, who "offered himself without blemish to God," says the author of Hebrews (9:14). And our Lord himself asks, "Which one of you convicts me of sin?" (John 8:46). May none of us be so ignorant and arrogant, so foolish and blasphemous, as to do that! Together with all who embrace Christian orthodoxy across the globe and throughout the ages, we give joyful and full-throated affirmation to the sinlessness of Christ. Unlike some, however, we do not attempt to explain the sinlessness of Christ by insulating and isolating his humanity from ours, by claiming he assumed a prefall Adamic human nature separated and segregated from our own. God the Son assumed a human nature like any other east of Eden.

But more needs to be said. We confess, then, that Christ's humanity was immediately sanctified to God at the moment of his conception, at

---

[32] "The Definition of Chalcedon (451)," in CC, 35–36.
[33] Colyer, "The Incarnate Saviour," 36; Hart, "Humankind in Christ and Christ in Humankind," 83–84.
[34] "The Definition of Chalcedon (451)," in CC, 36.

the moment it was united with God the Son by the power of the life-giv-ing, communion-creating Spirit of holiness in the womb of Mary. In other words, we confess that God the Son *sinlessly* assumed our sinful flesh, such that *Christ never sinned in thought, word, or deed*.[35] This is precisely what Tertullian expresses when declaring, "For in putting on our flesh, He made it His own; in making it His own, He made it sinless."[36] Likewise, Hilary of Poitiers remarks, "For He took upon Him the flesh in which we have sinned that by wearing our flesh He might forgive sins; a flesh which He shares with us by wearing it, not by sinning in it."[37] Let us permit Luther to join the chorus as well; he states: "He wanted to be born from the mass of the flesh and from that corrupted blood. But in the moment of the Virgin's conception the Holy Spirit purged and sanctified the sinful mass and wiped out the poison of the devil and death, which is sin."[38] And John Webster adds a present voice to past saints with this incisive comment on Christ's sinless assumption of our sinful flesh:

> This re-making [of our humanity] takes place as he assumes *sinful* flesh, human existence in repudiation of and rebellion against its ordering by God to find fulfillment in fellowship with God. The Word assumes the full extent of human alienation, taking the place of humanity, existing under the divine condemnation. But his relation to the human alien-ation which he assumes is not such that he is swallowed up by it. He does not identify with humanity under the curse of sin in such a way that he is himself sinner. . . . He adopts the condemned human situation without reserve, but with a peculiar distance from our own performance of our humanness. By not following our path, by refusing complicity with the monstrousness of sin, he is and does what we are not and do not: he is human. In his very estrangement from us as the bearer rather than the perpetrator of sin, he takes our place and heals our corruption. That the Word became *flesh* means that he takes to himself the accursed

---

[35] Confessing that God the Son sinlessly assumed our fallen humanity highlights the distinction between *anhypos-tasis* and *enhypostasis* regarding the union of divine and human natures in Christ. The Definition of Chalcedon states that Christ's two natures are joined in one person and in one *hypostasis*, or personal subsistence. This *hypostatic*, or personal, union is *anhypostatic* in that the humanity of the man Jesus had no prior or independent existence apart from the Word, and *enhypostatic* in that his humanity only and ever exists within the Word. While the incarnate Word never existed sinfully, then, it is none other than our fallen humanity that he assumed. This distinction is beneficial in that it helps us articulate the mystery of the incarnation in a way that is faithful to scriptural witness. Even so, of course, a mystery this must always remain. See Allen, *The Christ's Faith*, 130–31.

[36] Tertullian, *On the Flesh of Christ*, in ANF, 3:536.

[37] Hilary of Poitiers, *On the Trinity*, 1:13, in NPNF, 9:44.

[38] "Lecture on Genesis 38:1–5," in *LW*, 7:13.

situation of humanity in sin. But he *takes* it to himself; he does not evacuate himself into our situation.[39]

4. Running through Webster's comment is an implicit point that must now be made explicit: the immediate sanctification of the sinful flesh that God the Son assumed in the womb of Mary must not be understood as Christ's immediate glorification. This would admit through the back door, as it were, what affirming Christ's assumption of a prefall Adamic human nature welcomes through the front—that is, an incarnation in which Christ did not enter our *actual* state of human existence east of Eden. Immediate glorification does not allow for the developmental maturation of humanity within the dynamic contours of Christ's life from manger to cross (Luke 2:52). Neither does immediate glorification allow for the humiliation of our Lord to the point of dereliction and death (Phil. 2:5–8). Glorification marks realized eschatological life, which means glorification cannot mark the life of a wayfarer.[40]

We confess, then, that just as the mortifying, vivifying power and presence of the Spirit immediately sanctified Christ at the moment of his conception, the Spirit continually and progressively sanctified Christ through the whole of his sojourn from Bethlehem to Golgotha.[41] Christ sinlessly assumed our sinful flesh in the womb of Mary, and then sinlessly bore our sinful flesh all the way to the cross, where that flesh met definitive dissolution and destruction. From incarnation to crucifixion, our sinful flesh was condemned in the flesh that Christ took from us and made his own, in order that our human constitution as created by God might be redeemed and transformed to newness of life. "In the days of his flesh," reads the epistle to the Hebrews, "Jesus . . . learned obedience through what he suffered" (5:7–8). Does this imply that our Lord was ever disobedient, that he ever sinned? No. This same epistle plainly states that in those days Jesus was tempted in every respect as we are, "yet without sin" (Heb. 4:15). God the Son experientially grasped what it meant to render utter obedience to his Father in our flesh, in our *actual* state of human existence east of Eden. He took for himself our corrupted humanity, decisively bent toward sin, and, being battered and buffeted by ever-stiffening headwinds

---

[39] John Webster, "Incarnation," in *BCMT*, 220 (emphasis original).
[40] Allen, *The Christ's Faith*, 130–31.
[41] Ibid.

of opposition, he bent it back toward God. Our Lord was not glorified at conception. Rather, he was glorified after being made "perfect through suffering" (Heb. 2:10; 5:8–9), after fully, completely, spotlessly obeying his Father within the very realm of our fallen existence. Sinlessly bearing our sinful flesh, Jesus Christ became the light shining in our darkness. Calvin thus remarks:

> How has Christ abolished sin, banished the separation between us and God, and acquired righteousness to render God favorable and kindly toward us? To this we can in general reply that he has achieved this for us by the whole course of his obedience. . . . In short, from the time when he took on the form of a servant, he began to pay the price of liberation in order to redeem us.[42]

Refining and punctuating Calvin's point, Cranfield adds:

> [Christ's obedience] was not just a standing where unfallen Adam had stood without yielding to the temptation to which Adam succumbed, but a matter of starting from where we start, subjected to all the evil pressures which we inherit, and using the altogether unpromising and unsuitable material of our corrupt nature to work out a perfect, sinless obedience.[43]

5. In the words of the sixteenth-century English Reformer Richard Hooker, there can be "no union of God with man, without that mean between both which is both."[44] Truer and sweeter words could scarcely be uttered. So let us turn Hooker's negation into an affirmation, saying the same thing in yet another way. There can be union of God with man only because Jesus Christ unites God with man by participating unreservedly in the being and life of both God and man as the God-man.

Thus, we must take great care to resist the tendency to dichotomize either God from Christ or Christ from us. Either way, God's saving acts and benefits are ripped from their rightful mooring in the humanity of our Savior, robbing the incarnation of its immense soteriological, mediatorial significance. Cranfield should surely be heard and heeded, therefore,

---

[42] *Inst.*, 2.16.5.
[43] Cranfield, *The Epistle to the Romans*, ICC, 1:383n2.
[44] Richard Hooker, *Laws of Ecclesiastical Polity*, in *The Works of That Learned and Judicious Divine Mr. Richard Hooker* (Oxford: Clarendon Press, 1865), 50:3.

when he declares that the Word did not become flesh to merely stand where unfallen Adam had stood. If that were the case, Christ would have come among us only to stand apart from us—only to perform saving acts outside of himself, and bestow saving benefits other than himself.

We confess, then, that the saving acts of Christ secured reconciliation, or "at-one-ment," between God and the redeemed because those acts took place within the being and life of our Mediator, within the incarnate constitution of him who unites God with man in one person. God the Son did not become man to stand where unfallen Adam had stood, leaving our corrupted, estranged humanity unassumed and unhealed. On the contrary, God the Son became man in our sinful flesh, in our fallen nature. He penetrated the depths of our darkness to seize our ruined, wrecked humanity and make it his own, to re-create and reorient our humanity by taking it to himself—by taking it into the very life of God in the God-man. In this way, our Lord restores the ruptured relationship between God and the redeemed.

Let us make this point plainly: modern Christians tend to proclaim a gospel of extrinsic and abstract relations because we have long undervalued or overlooked the reality that reconciliation between God and man occurs within Christ, not outside of him. Our Lord secured atonement between God and the redeemed by working out our salvation within his own incarnate constitution. God the Son has done nothing less or other than heal and save the humanity he assumed from us. Were this not so, Christ would not be the Mediator of our salvation, for mediators most certainly cannot mediate what they do not possess. Precisely because he indeed has healed and saved the humanity he assumed from us, the incarnate Christ is the ground and source of every aspect of our salvation, a salvation he mediates to us in the giving of himself.[45]

---

[45] Torrance, *The Trinitarian Faith*, 155, 161; Colyer, "The Incarnate Saviour," 38, 44.

5

Christ for Us, Christ in Us

THE MEDIATION OF OUR

INCARNATE SAVIOR

The incarnation is a monumental rebuke of our misguided aspirations, for it accomplishes the severe mercy of rendering absurd any notion that rapprochement between God and humanity is accomplished from the side of humanity. We do not seek and find a reclusive God; he pursues and overtakes us in our rebellion. We do not perforate his unapproachable light; he penetrates our unsearchable darkness. We do not interrogate the Jesus of history to excavate the God of eternity; that infinite and eternal God storms space and time to confront us face to face in the face of Christ. The incarnation scandalizes our desire for heroism without humility, for glory without grace, for human ascent without divine descent. That is because the incarnation sets before us the unsettling yet liberating reality that rapprochement between God and humanity is accomplished only and ever from the side of God.

"God has done the impossible, the incredible thing in Jesus Christ," announces T. F. Torrance, "but it is only now that he has done it that we see how utterly impossible it actually is, impossible for us to accomplish from the side of humanity."[1] Indeed, God is fond of shattering the puny notions we

---

[1] Thomas F. Torrance, *Incarnation: The Person and Life of Christ*, ed. Robert T. Walker (Downers Grove, IL: IVP Academic, 2008), 10.

harbor about him, as well as the grand delusions we cherish about ourselves. He shatters both simultaneously in his incarnation. In ironic and astonishing fashion, God brings about reconciliation between himself and humanity from his side, not by repudiating our humanity but by assuming it. From the moment of Christ's conception in Mary's womb, the infinite and eternal Son of God has deigned to live out his divine life forevermore in our human nature. Accordingly, John Calvin wisely warns that "if you want to have anything in common with Christ you must especially take care not to despise His flesh."[2]

Calvin's point is that anything and everything Christ shares with us results from the humanity we share with him. This is simply to say, with the apostle Paul, that "there is one God, and there is one mediator between God and men, the man Christ Jesus" (1 Tim. 2:5). The implications of these words from Calvin and Paul warrant pause: God and man, long alienated, have been brought together, reconciled, in the person of Christ. God has made the body of our Lord the place where God and men meet. God gives himself and all his saving benefits to us in and as man in our incarnate Savior. God draws near to us, and we no less draw near to God, in and through the God-man.

We concluded the previous chapter by stating that the saving acts of Christ secure "at-one-ment" between God and the redeemed because those acts occur within the being and life of our Mediator, within the incarnate constitution of the One who unites God with man as the God-man. God the Son healed and saved the corrupted, estranged humanity he assumed from us so the incarnate Christ might be the ground and source of every aspect of our salvation—so the one Mediator of salvation might mediate the salvation that is his alone to give in and through the very humanity he healed and saved. We will develop this theme in this chapter, discussing the atonement that our Lord secured for us and mediates to us by working out our salvation within his incarnate constitution from birth to ascension.

Substitution and Incorporation: The Vicarious Humanity of Christ

Christian orthodoxy, as articulated by the Nicene Creed, confesses "one Lord Jesus Christ, the Son of God . . . God from God, Light from Light, true

---

[2] Calvin on John 6:56, CNTC, 4:171.

God from true God . . . of the same essence [*homoousion*] as the Father, through whom all things came into being, both in heaven and in earth."[3] Jesus of Nazareth is not similar to but identical with the eternal Word, God the Son, the second person of the Trinity. His coming in our flesh was the unprecedented and radical inbreaking of God himself into the universe he created. What is more, his coming in our flesh was the taking of our humanity into his own divine life, that he might humanly mediate the very life of God to us in and as man. It is crucial to grasp that God the Son did not merely become man *in* a human being, as if his assumption of our humanity were in any sense less than true and full. The church's confession allows for neither a deistic disjunction between God and creation nor a Nestorian disjunction between the divine and human natures of her Lord. Rather, God the Son became man not just *in* a human being, but *as* a human being. The incarnation is thus internally, necessarily, and dynamically related to salvation, inasmuch as the incarnate Christ is himself the very substance and sum of that salvation.[4] Athanasius exquisitely expresses the relationship between Christ's incarnation and our salvation as follows:

> For if the Word were in the Body putatively, as they say, and by putatively is meant imaginary, it follows that both the salvation and the resurrection of man is apparent only. . . . But truly our salvation is not merely apparent, nor does it extend to the body only, but the whole man, body and soul alike, has truly obtained salvation in the Word Himself. That then which was born of Mary was according to the divine Scriptures human by nature, and the Body of the Lord was a true one; but it was this, because it was the same as our body, for Mary was our sister inasmuch as we all are from Adam.[5]

We must now hasten to add that mediation, by definition, cannot be only one-directional. The very purpose and point of the incarnation is such that the mediation of the God-man is always and ever bidirectional. As Paul tells us, that mediation is not merely *from* God *to* men, but *between* God *and* men (1 Tim. 2:5). Just as surely as Christ humanly mediates God to men in and as man, therefore, he humanly mediates men to God in like

---

[3] "The Creed of Nicaea (325)," in *CC*, 30–31.

[4] Christian D. Kettler, *The Vicarious Humanity of Christ and the Reality of Salvation* (Eugene, OR: Wipf & Stock, 2010), 127–28.

[5] Athanasius, "To Epictetus," *Letters of Athanasius*, no. 59, in *NPNF*, 4:572–73.

manner. Assuming our humanity, body and soul alike, the man Christ Jesus personally lives and acts in our place and on our behalf. All Christ is and does as our incarnate Savior he is and does for us—that is, in solidarity with us as one of us. Consequently, all that he renders to the Father in our humanity as our Mediator he renders as ours. Stating the matter clearly and concisely, Christ works out our salvation within the constitution of his own vicarious humanity. Of Latin origin, the adjective *vicarious* describes the nature of a substitute or representative, one who is and acts for others. To speak of the vicarious humanity of Christ is thus to say that he assumed our humanity and made it his own in order to be for us whom we could not and would not be, and to do for us what we could not and would not do.

Most modern evangelicals understand Christ's crucifixion in vicarious terms—that is, as an act of penal substitution whereby Christ died in our place and on our behalf. Yet many modern evangelicals fail to understand that Christ's assumption of our humanity was the grand and glorious reality whereby he became the One who is and acts vicariously for us from his incarnation thereafter, undertaking one comprehensive work of redemption that includes his birth, baptism, life, death, resurrection, ascension, and his ongoing ministry at the Father's right hand.[6] Grasping the immense soteriological significance of the vicarious humanity of Christ, therefore, cannot help but deepen and broaden common notions of what it means for us to be reconciled to God by every aspect of our incarnate Savior's embodied existence. Of this reality, our evangelical forebears were well aware, as this rich and impassioned flourish from Calvin displays:

> We see that our whole salvation and all its parts are comprehended in Christ [Acts 4:12]. We should therefore take care not to derive the least portion of it from anywhere else. If we seek salvation, we are taught by the very name of Jesus that it is "of him" [1 Cor. 1:30]. If we seek any other gifts of the Spirit, they will be found in his anointing. If we seek strength, it lies in his dominion; if purity, in his conception; if gentleness, it appears in his birth. For by his birth he was made like us in all respects [Heb. 2:17] that he might learn to feel our pain [cf. Heb. 5:2]. If we seek redemption, it lies in his passion; if acquittal, in his condemnation; if remission of the curse, in his cross [Gal. 3:13]; if satisfaction, in

---

[6] Oliver D. Crisp, "By His Birth We Are Healed: Our Redemption, It Turns Out, Began Long Before Calvary," *Christianity Today* 56, no. 3 (March 2012): 32.

his sacrifice; if purification, in his blood; if reconciliation, in his descent into hell; if mortification of the flesh, in his tomb; if newness of life, in his resurrection; if immortality, in the same; if inheritance of the Heavenly Kingdom, in his entrance into heaven; if protection, if security, if abundant supply of all blessings, in his Kingdom; if untroubled expectation of judgment, in the power given to him to judge. In short, since rich store of every kind of good abounds in him, let us drink our fill from this fountain, and from no other.[7]

The vicarious humanity of Christ brings to expression the representative character of his person and work, underscoring that our incarnate Lord is never other than the One who is and acts for us—in our stead, as our Substitute. It does not follow from Christ's substitution *for us*, however, that our Savior and Mediator is remote or absent *from us*.

We must also hasten to add, then, that the vicarious humanity of Christ brings to expression not merely one but two internally related facets—thus, twin or dual facets—of his person and work: substitution/representation *and* incorporation/participation.[8] Here, too, Calvin helps us understand why we must take special care not to despise the humanity of our Lord:

Christ, having been made ours, makes us sharers with him in the gifts with which he has been endowed. We do not, therefore, contemplate him outside ourselves from afar in order that his righteousness may be imputed to us but because we put on Christ and are engrafted into his body—in short, because he deigns to make us one with him. For this reason, we glory that we have fellowship of righteousness with him.[9]

The gifts of God that Christ humanly mediates are surely imputed (credited to us and reckoned ours), declares Calvin—but not while our Savior and Mediator is remote or absent from us. Only as we are made one with Christ does his righteousness overwhelm our unrighteousness, because only by being engrafted—incorporated—into his body do we come to share what is his. As such, the Reformer tells the redeemed that *we must not contemplate Christ outside ourselves from afar*. That would be tantamount to nullifying the incarnation and mediation of our Lord. Christ did not make our humanity his own to be our Substitute in isolation from us, but to in-

---

[7] *Inst.*, 2.16.19.
[8] Kettler, *The Vicarious Humanity of Christ*, 128.
[9] *Inst.*, 3.11.10.

clude us in the humanity he re-created and reoriented to God. Christ works out our salvation within the constitution of his own vicarious humanity so he might mediate salvation to us by our sharing in that humanity. In other words, just as surely as the incarnation means Christ's incorporation into our humanity that needed healing and saving, our redemption and reconciliation with God means our incorporation into the new humanity of our Mediator—the humanity that Christ has indeed healed and saved. If we are not to see ourselves as afar from the One who has joined himself to us in the bond of body and soul, therefore, we must grasp that salvation means nothing less than participation in our Savior's vicarious humanity—nothing less than incorporation in our incarnate Substitute.

The Vicarious Birth of Christ

The Word became our human flesh and dwelt among us (John 1:14). To those who deem this too implausible and ignoble to countenance, Tertullian quips: "For which is more unworthy of God, which is more likely to raise a blush of shame, that *God* should be born, or that He should die? That He should bear the flesh, or the cross?"[10] This third-century saint provides a pointed and timely reminder to his twenty-first-century counterparts about the birth of Christ, one that is no less true about all theologizing on the incarnation and all Christian theologizing in general: the triune God of the gospel is not beholden to self-designated masters. He cannot be domesticated, tamed, managed, or controlled. When discussing the birth of our Lord, then, let us not seek to validate, vindicate, or even articulate this utterly unique creative act of God in his coming from beyond into human life by demanding its conformity to standards that are necessarily alien to it. Further, let us not seek to suppress this scandal or veil our flushed faces by reducing the virginal nature of this birth to a mere proof for the deity of Christ or to a mere theory that makes possible God the Son's becoming man. In so doing, we do not succeed in authenticating who or how God is; he alone can do that! Rather, we give reason to suspect that we know neither the Scriptures nor the power of God.

The vicarious nature of Christ's birth is manifestly confessed in the Nicene Creed, which proclaims that "for us men and for our salvation [he]

---

[10] Tertullian, *On the Flesh of Christ*, in ANF, 3:525.

came down and was incarnate, becoming human."[11] Just as surely as Christ is our incarnate Savior and the one Mediator between God and men, he lives and acts in our place and on our behalf in all things; his birth is no exception to this rule, but the very basis and condition for it. As we discussed at length in chapter 4, however, many Christians, particularly modern Christians, attempt to isolate, dissociate, and segregate our Lord from sin and sinners at the point of his birth. Yet this is *not* the aim of Scripture, which instead uses the birth of Christ to *identify* him with sin and sinners. The genealogy in Matthew's Gospel tells us that Jesus is "the son of David, the son of Abraham" (Matt. 1:1). And the genealogy in Luke's Gospel concludes by joining Jesus to the very fountainhead of fallen humanity, naming him "the son of Adam" (Luke 3:38). Both genealogies, moreover, include several notorious people without the slightest attempt to evade or explain away their relation to Christ. On the sordid lineage of our Lord, Thomas Weinandy notes:

> Jesus' ancestors were more than common sinners; they were often a despicable lot. Far from hiding this fact, the Gospel writers appear to glory in it. It was from these ancestors that Jesus took his flesh. He was one of them, and thus he was deeply woven within the defiled but common fabric of man.[12]

Martin Luther focuses on one such ancestor, Judah, to drive this point home:

> For it was necessary for [a] lapse to take place in the very line in which the Son of God was to be born. Judah, the very eminent patriarch, a father of Christ, committed [an] unspeakable act of incest in order that Christ might be born from a flesh outstandingly sinful and contaminated by a most disgraceful sin. For he begets twins by an incestuous harlot, his own daughter-in-law, and from this source the line of the Savior is later derived. Here Christ must become a sinner in His flesh, as disgraceful as He ever can become. The flesh of Christ comes forth from an incestuous union; likewise, the flesh of the Virgin, His mother, and of all the descendants of Judah, in such a way that the ineffable plan of

---

11 "The Creed of Nicaea (325)," in CC, 31.
12 Thomas Weinandy, *In the Likeness of Sinful Flesh: An Essay on the Humanity of Christ* (Edinburgh: T&T Clark, 1993), 128–29.

God's mercy may be pointed out, because He assumed the flesh or the human nature from flesh that was contaminated and horribly polluted.[13]

Indeed, the genealogies in Matthew and Luke aim to herald that Christ's birth marks his incorporation into the generations of Israel and Adam—the generations of fallen humanity that our Lord, the second Adam, summed up in himself for us and our salvation.[14]

The birth of our incarnate Savior, his incorporation into the generations of Israel and Adam, was graciously accomplished from the side of God by the omnipotent freedom of God. Without human provocation or solicitation, and apart from normative human reproductive action, Christ was conceived in the womb of the virgin Mary by the creative act of the life-giving Spirit (Matt. 1:18–21; Luke 1:30–35). Thus, Calvin rightly observes that Christ "is the bright mirror of God's wonderful and singular grace; for he has attained an honor that, in so far as he is man, he could not have deserved."[15] The fruit of Mary's womb, the man Christ Jesus, does not remotely facilitate and transmit some "thing," about which he knows nothing firsthand, in bestowing *our* gracious birth from above by the power of the Spirit, for his birth signals that *he himself* was graciously born from above by the power of the Spirit. This should duly stun us, but not unduly surprise us, for this is simply what it means to confess that our Lord truly is the one Mediator between God and men as man—namely, that he humanly mediates what he humanly possesses, and that we humanly participate in what is his to share.

At the same time, the creative act of the Spirit in the birth of Christ was not a creation from nothing, but a creation from the virgin womb of Mary. It was a creative act in which the Spirit seized upon the existing old creation and fashioned not only from it but within it a new creation, the humanity of the second Adam. The birth of Christ is routinely idealized, sentimentalized, and even romanticized. Insistent that we not trivialize the divine humility and profound humanity of this re-creative act, however, Tertullian reminds us that God the Son made our flesh his own amidst "the uncleanness of the generative elements within the womb, the filthy concre-

---

[13] "Lecture on Genesis 38:1–5," in *LW*, 7:12.
[14] Thomas F. Torrance, *The Mediation of Christ*, rev. ed. (Colorado Springs, CO: Helmers & Howard, 1992), 41.
[15] *Inst.*, 2.14.7.

tion of fluid and blood, of the growth of the flesh for nine months long out of that very mire."[16]

When the fullness of time had come, God sent forth his Son to become flesh in our flesh, to be incorporated unreservedly into our Adamic existence, "born of woman, born under the law" (Gal. 4:4). True God from true God in eternal union with the Father, the Son made what is ours his own, joining himself to us. The living Truth of God has thus become the living Way to the Father (John 14:6), for he has penetrated our nature to perform a redemptive, re-creative work from within it, opening a way within that old humanity into the new, "that he might be the firstborn among many brothers" (Rom. 8:29). Our regeneration or rebirth, then, results from our sharing in the birth of Christ, from our participation in the birth of our incarnate Substitute. The singular occurrence of Christ's being born from above by the Spirit occurs in each and every instance of rebirth, when one is made a new creation in Christ by being born from above by the Spirit into Christ. Never does this result from natural human generation or self-will; it is always accomplished from the side of God, not humanity. All who receive Jesus Christ, all who believe in his name, are graciously made to share in his birth, to participate in the new creation in him (John 1:12–13).[17] As attested in Charles Wesley's hymn for the ages, the mystery of Christmas is indeed the meaning and message of the gospel:

> Hark! the herald Angels sing,
> glory to the new-born King;
> Peace on earth and mercy mild,
> God and sinners reconciled. . . .
> Hail the heaven-born Prince of Peace!
> Hail the Sun of Righteousness!
> Light and life to all he brings,
> risen with healing in his wings;
> Mild he lays his glory by,
> born that man no more may die;
> Born to raise the sons of earth,
> born to give them second birth.[18]

---

[16] Tertullian, *On the Flesh of Christ*, in ANF, 3:524.
[17] Torrance, *Incarnation*, 94, 101.
[18] Charles Wesley, "Hark, the Herald Angels Sing," no. 24 in *The English Hymnal* (London: Oxford University Press, 1933), 43.

THE VICARIOUS BAPTISM OF CHRIST

The baptism of Christ is recorded in all three Synoptic Gospels and is referenced in John's Gospel (Matt. 3:13–17; Mark 1:9–11; Luke 3:21–22; John 1:29–34). Its significance is difficult to overstate. Jesus's wading into the waters of the Jordan marked the beginning of his public ministry. From this paradigmatic turning point, the headwinds of satanic temptation and human opposition blew with ever-increasing force against the face of our Lord, and from there he set his course steadfastly toward Golgotha. There in the River Jordan, the Spirit of God descended on Christ to anoint him for the ministry at hand, that he might be the One who both bears and bestows the Spirit. And there the self-presentation of Jesus to John the Baptist prompted his Father to rend the heavens and exuberantly exclaim, "This is my beloved Son, with whom I am well pleased" (Matt. 3:17). The Gospel writers record the *birth* of Christ in a manner that highlights his true and full humanity, his identity as the Son of David, Abraham, and Adam. But the Gospel writers employ the *baptism* of Christ to bear unambiguous witness, in the words of God the Father and then John the Baptist, "that this is the Son of God" (John 1:34).

The paradox is palpable, for our incarnate Savior is emphatically identified as the Son of God precisely as he stands in the Jordan presenting himself for what Scripture tells us is a baptism of repentance for the forgiveness of sin (Matt. 3:6, 11; Mark 1:4; Acts 13:24; 19:4). Is this biblical grounds to deem Christ a sinner? Surely not (John 8:46; Heb. 4:15; 9:14; 1 Pet. 2:22; 1 John 3:5). Should we then conclude that Christ received this baptism in merely an illustrative fashion, providing a piece of theatre as an object lesson on repentance for us even though it was empty and extraneous for him? Every bit as surely not. Rather, the baptism of Christ occasioned *his self-attestation* to the reality of his identification with sin and sinners—that is, the reality of his incorporation into our humanity. His wading into the Jordan was a gripping affirmation that he, the Son of God, truly, not seemingly, had assumed what is ours and made it his own; that he truly had entered our actual state of human existence east of Eden; that he truly had summed up in himself the generations of Israel and Adam; that he truly is and acts in solidarity with us as one of us; that he truly came in our place and in our flesh to render a truly authentic human response to the Father; and that he truly renders that response ours.

The baptism of Christ was a vicarious baptism in which he rendered authentic confession and repentance of sin for us as one of us. This was no perfunctory ritual our Lord performed to initiate his march to Golgotha. In fact, Jordan has as much to do with our salvation as Golgotha, and is inextricable from it. Jesus showed this by tying his baptism in the Jordan to his death on the cross, calling the latter his "baptism" as well (Mark 10:38–39; Luke 12:50). Jordan at one end of Christ's public ministry and Golgotha at the other constitute two aspects of one comprehensive baptism, two facets of one complete fulfilling of all righteousness within the realm of our unrighteousness (Matt. 3:15; John 19:28–30). When discussing the self-presentation of Christ for baptism at both Jordan and Golgotha, then, we must bear in mind that "baptism" is a transliteration of the Greek word βάπτισμα, or *baptisma*, which means "immersion, submersion." The baptism of Christ at the Jordan was a sign and seal of his being *immersed into* the reality of confession and repentance of sin, offering for us the perfect human response to our existence east of Eden. Likewise, the baptism of Christ at Golgotha was a sign and seal of his being *immersed into* the reality of divine judgment, bringing to completion for us God's condemnation of sin in the very flesh our Lord assumed from us (Rom. 8:3).

Let us recall that the vicarious humanity of Christ brings to expression two internally related facets of his person and work: substitution/representation and incorporation/participation. What does this have to do with the baptism of Christ? And what does his baptism have to do with our own? Everything! Our baptism is a sign and seal of our being *immersed into Christ*. Our baptism, in other words, signifies and seals the reality of our incorporation into the incarnate Savior crucified and resurrected for us, and thus the reality of our participation in the sonship of the One who rendered his perfect filial righteousness to the Father for us as ours.[19] Jesus hinted at this, albeit cryptically, when he told James and John that "with the baptism with which I am baptized, you will be baptized" (Mark 10:39). Yet the apostle Paul brings this plainly to view, declaring: "Do you not know that all of us who have been baptized into Christ Jesus were baptized into his death? We were buried therefore with him by baptism into death, in order that, just as Christ was raised from the dead by the glory of the Father, we too might walk in newness of life" (Rom. 6:3–4). Elsewhere, Paul reiter-

---

[19] Kettler, *The Vicarious Humanity of Christ*, 146–47.

ates that "the body of the flesh" has been put off, for we have "been buried with [Christ] in baptism, in which you were also raised with him through faith in the powerful working of God, who raised him from the dead" (Col. 2:11–12). When we are baptized in the name of the Father, the Son, and the Spirit (Matt. 28:19), we testify to the reality of our sharing in the baptism of the Son, who was verified in his sonship by the Father and anointed for his ministry by the Spirit while he stood in the Jordan receiving a baptism of repentance for the forgiveness of sin. Since the fourth century, orthodox Christians of every sort have declared with one voice, "We confess one baptism for the remission of sins."[20] That one baptism is the baptism of Christ. It is his baptism that provides the context and efficacy for our baptism into him. And just as surely as there is only one Lord, there is only one baptism (Eph. 4:5): the baptism *of* the Lord, in which his living members are made to participate.

THE VICARIOUS LIFE OF CHRIST

Throughout the whole of his life—not just from Jordan to Golgotha, but from Bethlehem to Golgotha—Christ reoriented our humanity, justifying and sanctifying our condemned and corrupted existence within his own righteous and holy life. To confess that the life of our Lord was a vicarious life is to say much more than that his life was merely exemplary, even if it was most certainly that. It is to say that his life—the faithful, obedient, holy life he lived before God the Father—was a life he lived in our place and on our behalf. So, in union with Christ, we come to share, to participate, in the life he lived for us and for our salvation. Jesus is the second and last Adam, the One who has made our humanity his own to remake us in God's image, given that he is the full and exact image of God *as man* (Col. 1:15, 19; Heb. 1:3). To that end, he had to undo all the ruin and wreckage, all the perversion and distortion, that resulted from the first Adam's fall into sin. Our Lord needed to be faithful where we are not; he needed to obey his Father where we do not; he needed to pray when we will not; he needed to be holy where we are not; he needed to worship where we will not; he needed to fully love

---

[20] "The Constantinopolitan Creed (381)," in CC, 33. The Council of Constantinople is recognized as the Second Ecumenical Council by Christian orthodoxy, following the First Ecumenical Council of Nicaea (325). The Council of Constantinople received the Creed of 325 in its entirety and slightly expanded it (this confession concerning baptism is one such expansion); thus, the Constantinopolitan Creed is widely known and used as the Nicene Creed. All references to the Nicene Creed in this book are from the original Creed of 325.

and trust God where we cannot. He needed, in other words, to save us from us in and as one of us, bending us back to God after we had become bent in upon ourselves in self-righteousness, self-lordship, and self-worship.

Viewed from this perspective, the life of our incarnate Savior, lived in full trust and obedience before God his Father, is supremely good news for sinners, for he accomplished *for* humanity, *within* our humanity, what we would not and could not. The redemption and restoration of our fallen selves cost Christ much, ensuring that his life was characterized by enormous inner and outer pain and suffering—loss, grief, rejection, contempt, betrayal, temptation, loneliness, shame—as he endured our brokenness with unfathomable love. That is to say, Christ resolved to bear the full force and weight of our distorted condition to consecrate us to the Father in his own self-consecration. From manger to cross, in anguish and heartbreak, with obedience and endurance, our incarnate Savior undertook our human condition east of Eden so as to perfect it before God. He and only he could and did set our humanity to rights from every way it had gone horribly wrong, thereby becoming the source and ground, the substance and sum, of the salvation that is his alone to share. The epistle to the Hebrews thus reads:

> In the days of his flesh, Jesus offered up prayers and supplications, with loud cries and tears, to him who was able to save him from death, and he was heard because of his reverence. Although he was a son, he learned obedience through what he suffered. And being made perfect, he became the source of eternal salvation to all who obey him. (5:7–9)

The entire earthly life of Christ was vicarious, an awful and merciful substitution to which Scripture naturally bears ample testimony. One example of particular poignancy is our Lord's temptation in the desert, in which the echoes of unfaithful Israel and unfaithful Adam resound. Bearing the flesh of Israel and Adam, Christ underwent the temptation common to us all—the temptation to live as if God is not God. Jesus entered the desert, the scene of Israel's temptation, the crucible of unbelief and disobedience. And there, weary, parched, and famished, our Lord heard those refrains familiar to every descendant of Adam: Did God really say . . . ? Can God really be trusted? Where is your Father now? Does he not care for you? How could this be his will? Are you not entitled to just a little self-pity? Are you not able to be self-sufficient? In a grand reversal of our insolence and arrogance, Jesus answered for Israel, for Adam, and for all of us: "Man shall not live by bread alone, but by every word that comes from the mouth of God. . . . You shall not put the Lord your God to the test. . . . You shall worship the Lord your God and him only shall you serve" (Matt. 4:4, 7, 10). From within our unbelief, Jesus believed. From within our self-reliance, Jesus reposed fully upon God. From within our disobedience, Jesus obeyed his Father. From within our refusal to believe that God really loves us, Jesus took his only comfort in that very love. All this our incarnate Substitute did for us and *as* us, that he might render his life ours!

The vicarious life of Christ was a recovery mission for lost humanity, a mission in which our Lord constantly and consistently offered his Father an authentic humanity in the place and on the behalf of ours. This last and life-giving Adam confronted and bested temptation as we did not (Luke 4:1–13); he fulfilled the law as we did not (Matt. 5:17); he loved his enemies as we did not (Luke 22:50–51); he trusted the Father as we did not (John 11:40–42); and in abject affliction, he submitted his will to the Father as we did not and do not (Luke 22:39–45). We could continue at length. But the point is that the Word became flesh to "fulfill all righteousness" (Matt. 3:15), righteousness that we duly owed God but did not, could not, and most certainly would not attain. We would do well to confess with Irenaeus of Lyons, then, that our incarnate Savior summed up humanity, remaking us into God's image throughout the course of the redemptive life he lived for us:

> [The eternal Word of God] was in these last days, according to the time appointed by the Father, united to His own workmanship, inasmuch as He became a man liable to suffering. . . . When He became incarnate, and was made man, He commenced afresh the long line of human beings, and furnished us, in a brief, comprehensive manner, with salvation; so that what we had lost in Adam—namely, to be according to the image and likeness of God—that we might recover in Christ Jesus.[21]

Jesus did all of this not primarily to provide us an example to follow, thereby throwing us back upon ourselves so that we might feebly attempt

---

[21] Irenaeus, *Against Heresies* 3.18.1, in *ANF*, 1:446. The phrase "He commenced afresh" reads *in seipso recapitulavit* in Latin. This phrase is best translated "He summed up in himself" and has come to represent what is often called Irenaeus's "recapitulation" theory of atonement.

to emulate him out of our own resources and resolve. Imitation of Christ as such can never attain the righteousness of God, and cannot even suffice as a technique for enriching human life in and of itself, for humans have no life in and of themselves. East of Eden and apart from Christ, human existence takes the form of *living death*—that is, biological life amidst relational death, estrangement and alienation from the God who is life, so that we are dead in sin and trespasses (Gen. 2:17; Eph. 2:1–3; Col. 2:13). The rich and robust life of which Scripture speaks goes far beyond naturalistic reductionisms; it is neither a human entitlement nor a human achievement, but a divine attribute and a divine gift. God the Son came to live out his divine life in our human nature that he might humanly mediate the life that is his to us, that we might come to participate in all our incarnate Substitute has accomplished for us in and as man (John 1:4; 11:25; 14:6).

The life of the Christian can be an imitation *of* Christ (*imitatio Christi*) only because it is first a participation *in* Christ (*participatio Christi*). Through such participation in the vicarious life of Christ, the benefits to his church abound! As we share in his life, his righteousness is imputed to us, resulting in our being justified in him. With Paul, we are to deem our pedigrees, privileges, and moral achievements "rubbish," taking comfort instead that we are "found in him," sharing in the righteousness that is only our Mediator's to grant (Phil. 3:4–9). We are justified, in other words, by being incorporated into the incarnate Savior who is himself our righteousness (1 Cor. 1:30).

But there is much, much more! Sharing in the vicarious life of Christ, the church *actively* shares in the holiness, obedience, prayer, worship, and faith of her Mediator. What Christ fully accomplished in our flesh and blood he *images* in those who belong to him. God, after all, predestined us "to be conformed to the image of his Son" (Rom. 8:29). Our holiness is a participation in his own; our obedience to the Father a participation in his own; our prayers a participation in his own; our worship a participation in the worship he renders to the Father, rendering it ours. Even our faith is a sharing in his faith. There is nothing we are asked to be or do that the One who lives and acts in our place and on our behalf has not already accomplished for us—and is not delighted to share with us. Christ is the one Mediator of our salvation, in every way and at every point. Our Lord humanly mediates his life to us that we may participate in the fullness thereof: "For my flesh is true food, and my blood is true drink. Whoever feeds on my flesh and drinks my blood abides in me, and I in him. As the living Father sent me, and I live because of the Father, so whoever feeds on me, he also will live because of me" (John 6:55–57).

We need Jesus, the whole of who he is for us and in us. We need him not only to mediate God to us, but also to mediate us to God. And so he came not only to save us as God, but to save us as human—to save us from our floundering faith, our halfhearted obedience, our reluctant prayer, our self-involved worship, and our self-styled righteousness. Sanctifying it all in himself, he offers his Father the holiness and wholeness of his humanity for ours in and as ours. When we would not believe, would not obey, would not worship, even when we *would* seek to crucify him, Jesus loved us. How has our salvation come about? Helmut Thielicke answers:

> It happened thus—God came down to you and searched for you. It happened thus—he became your brother. It happened thus—he planted himself in the abyss which yawned between you and him, which you had torn open in defiance. It happened thus—he placed himself in the same rank as you, he was found to be in the likeness of man (Phil. 2:7), he is tempted as you and I (Heb. 4:15), and endures the Evil One with you, and at your side. It happened thus—he takes your loneliness upon his shoulders (Mark 15:34), dies your death, tastes your fear (Mark 14:33), has endured captivity (Luke 22:47ff.) and taken it captive (Eph. 4:8).[22]

Jesus lived our life so that we may share in his. He asks nothing from us that he has not already done for and in us, and that we cannot now do with joyous freedom as we participate in the vicarious life that our incarnate Savior presently lives at the Father's right hand.

THE VICARIOUS DEATH OF CHRIST

The vicarious baptism and life of Christ found their proper end in the vicarious death of Christ, at least insofar as the filial obedience learned by the Son in the days of his flesh was made perfect—brought to completeness, fullness, and wholeness—at the cross. But in no sense does the cross eclipse the incarnation. In fact, the cross is seen aright only in light of the incarnation. It cannot be otherwise, because the incarnation is inherently atoning,

---

[22] Helmut Thielicke, *Between God and Satan*, trans. C. C. Barber (Grand Rapids: Eerdmans, 1962), 71.

and atonement is inherently incarnational. The incarnation is atoning in that the hypostatic, or personal, union of the divine and human natures in Christ is a profound reconciliation of God and man within the very person of our Lord. God the Son, the eternal Word, the second person of the Trinity, has taken our humanity into himself, and thus into the very life of God, banishing the separation between God and man within himself, the God-man. While the incarnation is not the totality of Christ's atoning activity, then, it is the basic condition and comprehensive context in which that atoning activity is brought to full and glorious fruition. Further, the very nature of the incarnation gives impetus and a sense of inevitability to the cross; for when Christ assumed our humanity and made it his own, he also made his own all that that entailed, namely, the inevitable experience and end of all human existence east of Eden. That is to say, when Christ was incorporated into our humanity and entered the state of our *actual existence*, he made his own the *experience* and *end* that inevitably attended the reality of his identification with sin and sinners—the penalty of divine judgment, condemnation, and death.

Whenever the cross is not seen in light of the incarnation, the cross is sure to be deformed. When this occurs among evangelicals, for instance, the deformation usually takes the shape of Christ's standing between God and men as an *inter*mediary, a third party accomplishing a mere transaction that has no intrinsic relation to or bearing upon either God or men. But when the cross is seen in light of the fact that our incarnate Mediator is *homoousion* with God and man, that he participates truly and fully in the being and life of both God and man as the God-man, the cross is a horrible, magnificent reality.

On the one hand, we find that not merely half of Christ but the whole Christ—God and man—became a curse for us. To save us, in other words, God cursed our fallen humanity and himself underwent that curse. In this sense, the cross is a self-malediction, the self-imprecation of God. It was not just a man who suffered and died for us, but the Lord as man; not just the life of a man that was offered to save us, but the life of God as man. On the other hand, we find the notion that Christ died for sinners so they do not need to die themselves to be utterly fallacious. Such a notion does not take seriously the justice of God, the direness of our fallen predicament, or the divinely intended effect of Christ's death within the believer. In truth, then,

Christ died for sinners so that, in and with him, they too could die. That is our only hope, for the design of our Lord's death is not to forgive sin in the abstract, but to judge and destroy sin in its concrete human expression in the lives of sinners. The cross is the most penetrating judgment on humanity that could ever be made, the full and final exposure of sin for what it really is: contempt for and violence against God. Even though he sought us in our suicidal flight into the far country, still we seized upon *him*, spat in his face, and slew him on a tree.[23] Yet, in our slaying of him, he slew us—that we might have life in him. For these reasons and more, we proclaim with Calvin, "This is the foolishness of the cross and the wonder of angels, which not only exceeds but swallows up all the wisdom of the world."[24]

The vicarious death of Christ was penal and substitutionary. He offered himself as a perfect sacrifice to his Father and was judged in our place and on our behalf, bearing in his body and soul our guilt and shame, the full force of our alienation, condemnation, and death. Our Lord thereby satisfied without remainder the demands of God's holiness, that we might be justly and freely forgiven. Attesting to the vicarious nature of Christ's death, Paul announces, "Christ redeemed us from the curse of the law by becoming a curse for us" (Gal. 3:13). Luther thus observes:

> Paul guarded his words carefully and spoke precisely. And here again a distinction must be made; Paul's words clearly show this. For he does not say that Christ became a curse on His own account, but that He became a curse "for us." Thus the whole emphasis is on the phrase "for us." . . . Surely these words of Paul are not without purpose: "Christ became a curse for us" and "For our sake God made Christ to be sin, who knew no sin, so that in Him we might become the righteousness of God" (2 Cor. 5:21). . . . Whatever sins I, you, and all of us have committed or may commit in the future, they are as much Christ's own as if He Himself had committed them. In short, our sin must be Christ's own sin, or we shall perish eternally.[25]

At the same time, Luther saw the cross in the only way the cross may be seen aright: in light of the incarnation. Accordingly, he did not confine to the cross alone Christ's being made sin for us and in us, as if this were

---

[23] Torrance, *Incarnation*, 246.
[24] Calvin on Gal. 3:13, *CNTC*, 11:55.
[25] *Lectures on Galatians* (1535), in *LW*, 26:277–78.

an anomalous exception within, or an unprecedented departure from, our Lord's redemptive activity to that point. Rather, Luther viewed Christ's being made sin for us and in us at the cross as the inevitable culmination and completion of what commenced at Christ's conception in the womb of Mary. It was then and there that God the Son made our humanity and all that that entailed his own, so that he might act upon sin from the inside, so that he might destroy sin from within the realm of sin. Regarding Galatians 3:13 and Christ's becoming a curse for us, therefore, Luther adds:

> He attached Himself to those who were accursed, assuming their flesh and blood; and thus He interposed Himself as the Mediator between God and men. He said: "Although I am flesh and blood and live among those who are accursed, nevertheless I am the blessed One through whom all men are to be blessed." Thus He joined God and man in one Person. And being joined with us who were accursed, He became a curse for us; and He concealed His blessing in our sin, death, and curse, which condemned and killed Him.[26]

Jesus is our incarnate Savior all the way down indeed, for having entered the state of our actual existence in assuming our flesh and blood, he proceeded to press ever more deeply into that existence, pursuing it all the way to its nadir at the cross. Christ suffered our fallen human experience with progressive profundity, in other words, bearing but never perpetuating our sin in his body and soul; and this he did until he plumbed the depths of Golgotha, plumbed the depths of our unholy corruption, guilt, and shame, and obliterated our sin at its very root. When we confess the Apostles' Creed, we proclaim our faith in Jesus Christ, the Son of God, who "suffered under Pontius Pilate, was crucified, dead and buried."[27] That Christ is the Son of God, and that he died for us, is, after all, the manifold witness of the apostles themselves.

Even so, many Christians try to mitigate the mystery and gravity of Christ's death by claiming that only his humanity died, not his deity. This we cannot and must not do. Christian orthodoxy flatly rejects any Nestorian disjunction between the divine and human natures of our Lord that would posit that the man Jesus died independently from God the Son; this

---

[26] Ibid., 26:289–90.
[27] "The Apostles' Creed, Textus Receptus (c. 700)," in *CC*, 24.

is to deny the hypostatic union of God with man in the person of the God-man, and thus to deny the incarnation. Far from undermining the cross, the incarnation interprets the cross. So let us not shrink back from making this breathtaking affirmation: the person who died for us at Golgotha was none other than God the Son incarnate.[28]

Does this affirmation that the whole Christ died for us mean that God the Son ceased to exist, even temporarily? Of course not. Scripture does not equate even the death of mere humans with the cessation of their existence, much less the death of God the Son, who has life in himself. Then what sort of death did Christ die at Golgotha? His was a vicarious death, undertaken in our place and on our behalf; this means he died the death to which sinners are subject: physical and spiritual death. Christ suffered physical death in the separation of his soul from his body, that decreational judgment whereby God pulls apart what he put together when he breathed the breath of life into the man he formed from the dust of the ground, making him a living creature (Gen. 2:7). More startling still, Christ suffered spiritual death in the form of excruciating estrangement within the Trinitarian fellowship, as heard in his destitute cry, "My God, my God, why have you forsaken me?" (Matt. 27:46; Mark 15:34; cf. Psalm 22).[29] The vicarious death of Christ means that he drank our cup of judgment to its last and bitterest dregs, descending body and soul into the depths of death, into the yawning abyss of divine condemnation upon sinners. God the Son died at Golgotha, and God the Father suffered the death of his dear Son. Rightly understood, as Michael Reeves notes, confessing the death of God is not the end of faith, but the beginning of true faith: "For, on the cross, Christ the Glory puts to death all false ideas of God; and as he cries out to his Father and offers himself up by the Spirit (Heb. 9:14), breathing out his last, he reveals a God beyond our dreams."[30]

Christ presented himself for both aspects of his one comprehensive baptism, the first at Jordan and the second at Golgotha; and in both instances, he prevailed upon those who sought to prevent his purposes (Matt. 3:13–15;

---

[28] Donald Fairbairn, *Life in the Trinity: An Introduction to Theology with the Help of the Church Fathers* (Downers Grove, IL: IVP, 2009), 168–69. The Second Council of Constantinople declares in no uncertain terms: "If anyone does not confess that our Lord Jesus Christ who was crucified in the flesh is true God and the Lord of Glory and one of the Holy Trinity; let him be anathema." See "The Second Council of Constantinople, Anathema X (553)," in *CC*, 50.

[29] Fairbairn, *Life in the Trinity*, 174–76.

[30] Michael Reeves, *Delighting in the Trinity: An Introduction to the Christian Faith* (Downers Grove, IL: IVP Academic, 2012), 127–28.

16:21–23). Far from resigning himself to the cross with a posture of passive nonresistance, then, our Lord actively pursued and owned our condemnation. Seizing our sin-wracked humanity for himself, in other words, Christ sinlessly marched that humanity to Golgotha to procure our only hope: the dissolution and destruction of our flesh. Peter tells us that while Christ committed no sin, "He himself bore our sins in his body on the tree, that we might die to sin" (1 Pet. 2:22, 24). Yet Christ did not bear our sins in his body to simply settle a score in our stead any more than we die to sin by merely emulating his example of self-mortification. Our incarnate Savior did not suffer a death that has no intrinsic relation to us or bearing upon us. Rather, he died for us to mediate the saving benefits of his death to us as we share in his vicarious humanity. Christ did not die to exempt sinners from dying themselves; his death saves us from sin precisely because it kills our sinful self!

Paul teaches that all "who have been baptized into Christ Jesus were baptized into his death" (Rom. 6:3). To be immersed into the crucified One is to be immersed into his crucifixion. We share the grave of our incarnate Substitute because we participate in his death. Or, as Paul proclaims, we were "buried . . . with him" because we were "united with him in a death like his" (vv. 4–5). What Christ accomplished within the constitution of his own vicarious humanity at Golgotha is thus what he humanly mediates to those who have been incorporated into him.

So just what did the vicarious death of Christ accomplish? Paul tells us "our old self" was crucified with Christ, that "the body of sin," or "the body of the flesh," might be put off and brought to nothing (Rom. 6:6; Col. 2:11). The death Christ died "he died to sin, once for all," to the end that those who share his grave must also consider themselves "dead to sin" (Rom. 6:10–11). That is to say, Christ bore our sinful self, the whole of our fallen human nature, in his body on the cross. As the altogether sinless One who altogether identified himself with sinners, he died to sin once for all in that our sin was condemned definitively and without remainder in the flesh he assumed from us. Whether it be realized liberation from the enslavement of sin or ongoing mortification of the arrears of sin, therefore, the only source of our death to sin is our participation in the death of Christ.[31]

---

[31] C. E. B. Cranfield, *The Epistle to the Romans*, ICC (Edinburgh: T&T Clark, 1998), 1:308–10, 314; *Inst.*, 2.16.7.

The Vicarious Resurrection of Christ

Christ took the place of sinners in every respect in his death, such that nothing about his death, as death, mitigates its severity and horror. His death was nothing less or other than the wages of the sin he became for us (2 Cor. 5:21; cf. Rom. 6:23). First and foremost, then, as Richard Gaffin so ably contends, "It is . . . not only meaningful but necessary to speak of the resurrection as the redemption of Christ."[32] The resurrection of Christ is nothing if not the Father's remission of the guilt and penalty of sin that our Lord bore as he went to the grave, condemned; it is nothing if not the Father's deliverance of our Lord from the power and curse of death, which had dominion over him until he was raised in newness of life (Rom. 6:9); and it is nothing if not the Father's acquittal and acceptance of the One from whom he turned in judgment as our Lord descended into that abyss, crying, "My God, my God, why have you forsaken me?" (Matt. 27:46).[33]

Even so, many Christians are not accustomed to viewing the resurrection of Christ as his redemption, and some, confronted yet again by the unremitting offense that is the incarnation, will no doubt be inclined to demur, deeming it beneath our Lord to speak of him in any sense as the recipient of redemption. Here again we find ourselves at the heart of what it means for Christ to be our incarnate Substitute, Savior, and Mediator. Let us be clear, then, about the implications at hand. To deny that the resurrection of Christ is his redemption is to negate that he is *truly* our incarnate Substitute, the One who personally lives and acts for us as one of us. But if Christ has not *truly* taken our sin, guilt, judgment, condemnation, and death as his own, all these frightful realities can only and ever remain our own. Further, to deny that the resurrection of Christ is his redemption is to deny that the incarnate Savior's humanity *actually* touches ours, to negate that he saves us by *actually* becoming sin in us. But if we negate that Christ actually became sin in us, we forfeit any reason to believe that we have actually become the righteousness of God in him (2 Cor. 5:21).[34] Finally, to deny that the resurrection of Christ

---

[32] Richard B. Gaffin Jr., *Resurrection and Redemption: A Study in Paul's Soteriology*, 2nd ed. (Phillipsburg, NJ: P&R, 1987), 116.

[33] Ibid.; I. Howard Marshall, *Aspects of the Atonement: Cross and Resurrection in the Reconciling of God and Humanity* (Bletchley, Milton Keynes, U.K.: Paternoster, 2007), 86–87.

[34] Jesus Christ was set forth as a propitiation—a sin-bearing, wrath-assuaging sacrifice—that God might "show his righteousness . . . that he might be just and the justifier of the one who has faith in Jesus" (Rom. 3:25–26). Yet if Christ did not actually become sin in us—if this is only a *virtual* reality, *as if* Christ became sin in us while in fact he did not—then the cross is anything but a demonstration of God's justice with respect to Christ. Likewise, if believers have not actually become the righteousness of God in Christ—if this is only another *virtual* reality,

is his redemption is to negate that he is *really* our incarnate Mediator, the One in whom every aspect of our salvation is to be sought and found. Christ cannot mediate redemption if he is not *really* possessed of redemption, nor can we participate in a redemption that is not his to share (1 Cor. 1:30). We are beneficiaries, proclaims the apostle Paul, of "the redemption that is in Christ Jesus" (Rom. 3:24), as he is "the firstborn from the dead" (Col. 1:18; cf. Rev. 1:5). He is the singular representative in whom we receive remission of sin and guilt, freedom from condemnation, deliverance from the power of death, newness of life, and acceptance by the Father. Thus, Gaffin observes that any soteriology that moves directly from Christ's death to the bestowal upon others of the benefits Christ accomplished by his own obedience unto death seriously short-circuits Paul's soteriology. We can experience redemption only because that redemption was first applied to Christ himself by the Father through the Spirit.[35] What is true here is indeed true everywhere: the scandal of the incarnation is the glory of the gospel.

The Word became flesh in a womb from which no one had ever yet been born, and he came forth from a tomb "where no one had ever yet been laid" (Luke 1:26–35; 23:53). The virgin birth of Christ marked the commencement of his earthly life and the resurrection marked its consummation. Together, then, the virgin birth and the resurrection mark the mystery of the incarnation, attesting to the continuity and discontinuity between Christ and our fallen humanity. In both events, God came from beyond in his omnipotent freedom to act redemptively and re-creatively upon our humanity from within it. He acted in continuity with our fallen humanity so we might share in the divine life that God the Son lives out within our humanity, and in discontinuity so we might be freed from the ruin and wreckage of our old humanity east of Eden into new life in the new humanity. God the Son entered the virgin *womb* to penetrate our nature and perform a redemptive, re-creative act from within it, opening a way within that old humanity into the new; that way broke wide open when Christ put our flesh to death in his death and was raised the first of the new humanity (1 Cor. 15:21–22). Consequently, his exit from the virgin *tomb* marks that redemptive, re-creative act of God from within our humanity in which Christ was resurrected out

---

as if we are the righteousness of God in Christ while in fact remaining our otherwise unrighteous selves—then our justification is anything but a demonstration of God's justice with respect to us.

35 Gaffin, *Resurrection and Redemption*, 117.

of "the body of sin," out of "the body of the flesh," which he put off and brought to nothing at Golgotha (Rom. 6:6; Col. 2:11; cf. Rom. 8:3).[36]

"Even though we once regarded Christ according to the flesh," heralds Paul, "we regard him thus no longer. . . . The old has passed away; behold, the new has come" (2 Cor. 5:16–17). To be sure, Paul does not mean that the resurrected Christ is no longer to be regarded as human or as embodied—God in and as man. Quite the contrary, Paul is at pains to establish in 1 Corinthians 15 that if our Lord was not raised bodily from the dead, then Christian faith and hope are not just futile but positively pitiful. The point Paul pressed upon first-century Christians in Corinth must not be wasted upon us, their twenty-first-century counterparts. As C. S. Lewis noted, "We also, in our heart of hearts, tend to slur over the risen *manhood* of Jesus, to conceive Him, after death, simply returning into Deity, so that the Resurrection would be no more than the reversal or undoing of the Incarnation."[37] Human existence is embodied, not least the human existence of the embodied God. Far from being subverted or superseded, therefore, the personhood of our incarnate Savior is forever preserved in his resurrection from the dead. And unlike the temporary resuscitations of Lazarus and others (John 11:38–44; cf. Matt. 9:18–26; Luke 7:11–17), the resurrection of Christ can never be undone. His empty tomb signals that sin, death, and evil have been definitively upended; and though they continue to molest Christ's members as we eagerly anticipate our future bodily resurrection, sin, death, and evil can never gain the upper hand on those whose life is hidden with Christ in God (Col. 3:1–3).

Christ's vicarious resurrection is the pattern for ours, precisely because our resurrection is a participation in his. "From now on, therefore," declares Paul, speaking of believers from the very inception of their Christian existence, "we regard no one according to the flesh. . . . If anyone is in Christ, he is a new creation" (2 Cor. 5:16–17). All who have been incorporated into Christ, in other words, have been not figuratively but truly, actually, really incorporated into his dying and rising to newness of life. Christ subjected the flesh he assumed from us to crucifixion, destroying "the body of sin," "the body of the flesh," the whole of our nature we bring from the womb east of Eden, showing that the death of the "old self" is our only hope

---

[36] Torrance, *Incarnation*, 96–97.
[37] C. S. Lewis, *Miracles* (1947; repr., New York: Touchstone, 1996), 193.

for life (Rom. 6:6). Yet Christ's death and resurrection are two inseparable aspects of one redemption, such that "if we have been united with him in a death like his, we shall certainly be united with him in a resurrection like his" (v. 5). The life that the resurrected Christ lives to God renders the death he died a true dying to sin (v. 10). Thus, our Lord can no more bestow justification without sanctification—righteousness without holiness, or remission of sin without newness of life—than he can be torn asunder.[38] We have been changed, not quantitatively but qualitatively. Crucified with Christ, it is no longer we who live, but the resurrected Christ who lives in us (Gal. 2:20), restoring and preserving our authentic personhood and humanity. Consequently, we "put off [the] old self . . . and . . . put on the new self, created after the likeness of God in true righteousness and holiness" (Eph. 4:22–24). Calvin comments:

> As the graft has the same life or death as the tree into which it is ingrafted, so it is reasonable that we should be as much partakers of the life as of the death of Christ. If we are ingrafted into the likeness (*in similitudinem*) of Christ's death, and His death is inseparable from His resurrection, our death will therefore be followed by our resurrection. . . . The apostle desired to point quite simply to the efficacy of the death of Christ, which manifested itself in putting to death our flesh, and also the efficacy of His resurrection in renewing within us the better nature of the Spirit.[39]

The Vicarious Ascension of Christ

In his very body that was resurrected to newness of life, Christ ascended to heaven, undertaking there, as a true and authentic human, the mediation that constitutes his ever-faithful, never-failing high priesthood, and presenting his living members in and with himself to the Father, who now receives us with paternal eagerness and delight.[40] Paul joyously exclaims:

> God, being rich in mercy, because of the great love with which he loved us, even when we were dead in our trespasses, made us alive together

---

38 Gaffin, *Resurrection and Redemption*, 119–26.
39 Calvin on Rom. 6:5, *CNTC*, 8:124.
40 This discussion on the vicarious ascension of Christ draws significantly from John C. Clark, "Satisfaction, Intercession, Participation: John Calvin on Receiving Christ and Enjoying the Benefits of His Priesthood," in *Between the Lectern and the Pulpit: Essays in Honour of Victor A. Shepherd*, ed. Rob Clements and Dennis Ngien (Vancouver, BC: Regent College Publishing, 2014), 81–83.

with Christ—by grace you have been saved—and raised us up with him and seated us with him in the heavenly places in Christ Jesus, so that in the coming ages he might show the immeasurable riches of his grace in kindness toward us in Christ Jesus. (Eph. 2:4–7)

"Christ did not ascend to heaven privately for Himself, to dwell there alone," notes Calvin.[41] Rather, as Paul makes altogether clear, our Lord's ascension was vicarious. He entered heaven in the redeemed humanity into which we have been incorporated, securing a common inheritance for Head and members alike.[42] The bodily ascension of Christ thus established our participation in his return to the Father. This means that the reconciliation Christ won for us in his body is appropriated only as the body of Christ shares in the body of her ascended Substitute, now and forever. In other words, the incarnation can no more be reserved for the earthly life of Christ than our salvation can be relegated to a past event or reduced to that which is merely static. The incarnation is, quite simply, the basis for the dynamic reality of Christian existence, both present and future, given that the eternal Son of God assumed our humanity so we may forevermore share in his even now in the heavenlies.[43]

Modern evangelicals often view salvation as synonymous with or totalized by Christ's paying the penalty for our sins. When this view holds sway, the cross is routinely—albeit erroneously—identified as the apex of our salvation, the end to which all Christ's redemptive activity moved; in effect, then, the cross often overshadows, even eclipses, the ascension. In point of fact, however, Christ's paying the penalty for our sins served the end of our life-giving, life-transforming reconciliation with God, the end of our living before the Father in and with Christ, and this means the cross served the ascension. Our salvation is thus neither synonymous with nor totalized by Christ's self-sacrifice, because it follows from the efficacy of Christ's once-for-all self-sacrifice that he is our everlasting intercessor, the everlasting Mediator between God and men. Having entered heaven in our redeemed humanity, forevermore the embodied God, Christ's mediation is bidirectional; in and as man, he humanly mediates God to us, just as in and as man, he humanly mediates us to God.

---

[41] Calvin on John 14:2, *CNTC*, 5:75.
[42] *Inst.*, 2.16.16; Calvin on Eph. 2:6, *CNTC*, 11:143.
[43] Kettler, *The Vicarious Humanity of Christ*, 209, 224–29.

In both aspects of our Lord's bidirectional mediation, his heavenly ascent and exaltation exhibit the indelible impress of his earthly descent and humiliation, as opposed to a decisive break from them. On the one hand, mediating God to us, the ascended and exalted Christ does not overpower and repel us with a naked majesty. Christ unites God with man by participating unreservedly in the being and life of both God and man as the God-man; thus, the God we meet face to face in the face of Christ has *first-hand experiential knowledge* of being buffeted by, and learning obedience amidst, the harshness of human existence under the conditions of sin. He touched our humanity at its deepest point of alienation and estrangement. Consequently, we have a Mediator at the right hand of the Father who is profoundly acquainted with suffering and temptation, whose sympathy for our weakness magnifies divine mercy, inducing us to draw near to God with well-founded confidence (Heb. 2:14–18; 4:14–16). On the other hand, mediating us to God, the ascended and exalted Christ does not advocate for us by pleading before the Father like a common suppliant; this would not only diminish the majesty of the Son, but also deny the unity of the Godhead. Rather, Christ's advocacy for us consists of his continual appearance before the Father adorned in the unfading splendor of his death and resurrection—the unremitting assertion of sin-bearing victory by the One who was raised glorified yet wounded (John 20:24–29; Revelation 5). What Christ accomplished in his earthly descent and humiliation is thus realized in his heavenly ascent and exaltation, where his high-priestly mediation brings to fruition the reconciliation of God and man in his very person— where, in his body, of which we are members, he forges a new and living way of access for us to the Father (Heb. 10:19–20).

The Son's return to the Father does not render the church Christless, and thus Fatherless. Quite the contrary! Prior to our Lord's ascension, he issued an extravagant promise: "I will not leave you as orphans; I will come to you. . . . Because I live, you also will live. In that day [inaugurated by the bestowal of the Spirit at Pentecost] you will know that I am in my Father, and you in me, and I in you" (John 14:18–20). The Spirit is the personal agent of Christ's ongoing presence and power, the One in whom Christ even now draws us upward to himself. The Spirit is no mere proxy or surrogate, some non-perichoretic modality of a remote or absent Christ; the Spirit is the third person of the Trinity, who indwells us while simultaneously coinhering the Son and the Father, joining us to our embodied Mediator at the Father's right hand. As such, the mediation of the ascended Son has the stunning effect of incorporating us into his relationship with the Father, meaning that the Father receives us with *precisely the same* paternal acceptance and affection as he does his eternally beloved, only begotten Son! The South African churchman Andrew Murray superbly writes:

> And how is this effected?—In virtue of His union with us, and our union with Him. Jesus is the Second Adam; the new Head of the race. He is it in virtue of His real humanity, having in it the power of true divinity that filleth all. Just as Adam was our forerunner into death, and we have all the power of his sin and death working in us and drawing us on, so we have Jesus as our Forerunner into God's presence, with all the power of His death and His resurrection-life working in us, and drawing and lifting us with divine energy into the Father's presence. Yes, Jesus with His divine, His heavenly life, in the power of the throne on which He is seated, has entered into the deepest ground of our being, where Adam, where sin, do their work, and is there unceasingly carrying out His work of lifting us heavenward into God's presence, and of making God's heavenly presence here on earth our portion.[44]

The vicarious ascension of Christ establishes our true knowledge and pure worship of God, which means that our response to the Father, resulting from our incorporation into the Father-Son relationship, finds its basis in the Son's own response to the Father; for no human truly knows or rightly relates to the Father except the Son—and anyone included in the Son. This is simply to confess that our Lord's mediation is not one-directional, that he does not mediate God to us only to stop short of mediating us to God. We have not been redeemed only to be thrust back upon our own resources and resolve. The nature of our redemption should mercifully dismantle any semblance of the grand delusion that rapprochement between God and humanity is accomplished from the side of humanity. In Christ, God achieves this rapprochement from the side of God—not by repudiating our humanity, but by assuming it. The Word became flesh to live and act personally on our behalf. He trusted and obeyed the Father perfectly on our behalf. He perfectly confessed and repented of our sins on our behalf,

---

[44] Andrew Murray, *The Holiest of All* (1921; repr., Springdale, PA: Whitaker House, 1996), 366–67.

and on our behalf received the verdict of guilty. He perfectly thanked and praised the Father on our behalf; and he lives and acts now and forevermore on our behalf—not remotely, but with us as one of us, so that all he renders to the Father as our incarnate Mediator he renders ours! Accordingly, our response to the Father's acceptance of us in the Son can only and ever be rendered in Christ's name as his living members, since our trust, obedience, confession, repentance, and praise can never be less or other than our partaking in his. Let us stress, then, that Christian worship is the believer's participation through the Spirit in the Son's communion with the Father—that is, the worship of the church is her participation in and with Christ in his vicarious life of worship and intercession.[45]

Because we have been consecrated in body and soul by Christ's consecration of his body and soul for us, we are to render what Calvin called the "finest worship of God." This worship entails prayer, praise, faith, obedience, service to our neighbor, and mutual love, care, and intercession for fellow believers—a comprehensive self-offering in grateful response for Christ's once-for-all self-offering for us. Calvin rightly deems this worship the only possible alternative to false worship—to idolatry—inasmuch as all true worship of God depends "solely upon Christ's intercession." Since the only Mediator between God and men is the man Christ Jesus, "he is the only way, and the one access, by which it is granted us to come to God . . . to those who turn aside from this way and forsake this access, no way and no access to God remain."[46] We are not a plurality of individuals whose worship is but an offering to the Father based on Christ's work for us. Rather, we are a corporate priesthood of believers, made one body by our participation in the singular and utterly unique mediation of our embodied, ascended High Priest. Worship is our response to the Father's reception of us in Christ; and this response is shaped by and reflective of our participation in Christ's priesthood, as the only way we can or do worship the Father is in and through Christ, who gathers up the worship of his members, cleanses it, and presents it together with his own.[47]

---

[45] James B. Torrance, *Worship, Community, and the Triune God of Grace* (Downers Grove, IL: IVP Academic, 1996), 15, 46–50.

[46] *Inst.*, 2.15.6; 3.20.19; Calvin on John 17:19, *CNTC*, 5:146, Rom. 12:1, *CNTC*, 8:262–65, Heb. 13:15, *CNTC*, 12:210–11; 1 Pet. 2:5, *CNTC*, 12:258–60.

[47] J. B. Torrance, "The Vicarious Humanity and Priesthood of Christ in the Theology of John Calvin," in *Calvinus Ecclesiae Doctor*, ed. W. H. Neuser (Kampen: J. H. Kok, 1979), 71–73.

6

The Abundant Blessings
of Salvation

OUR UNION WITH THE
INCARNATE SAVIOR

The eternal Son of God took for himself our flesh and blood, reaching
into the depths of our human existence in alienation from God in order to
bring about "at-one-ment."[1] This means that *everything* he has done, and
now does, as the incarnate Lord Jesus Christ was and is atoning. His birth,
baptism, life, death, resurrection, and ascension were atoning events, and
these events have ongoing effects. But they are by no means to be separated
from who he is, for he himself is the reconciliation between God and humanity. Jesus Christ simply *is* our atonement—our salvation, our peace, our
redemption—because in him alone our flesh and blood have been savingly
united to God. "The theme of reconciliation," Andrew Purves writes, "is
woven into the fabric of the gospel because it is woven into the being of the
Savior and takes place within his incarnate person, not outside or adjacent
to him in an instrumental way."[2] The Son of God became incarnate that
he might rebirth our humanity into his humanity, secure our life in his life,

[1] Portions of this chapter have been adapted from material in Marcus Peter Johnson, *One with Christ: An Evangelical Theology of Salvation* (Wheaton, IL: Crossway, 2013).
[2] Andrew Purves, *Reconstructing Pastoral Theology: A Christological Foundation* (Louisville, KY: Westminster
John Knox Press, 2004), 24.

baptize us into his baptism, heal and rectify us in his crucifixion and resurrection, and ascend with us into his fellowship with his Father. Thus, the salvation accomplished *by* Jesus Christ has actually taken place *in* Jesus Christ, in the union of God and man in his person. Our christology is not meant to function as an outward apparatus for a preconceived theory of salvation; rather, the person of Christ is himself the substance and sum of the salvation he secures. Salvation, in other words, is identical with Jesus Christ.

Jesus does not, indeed cannot, give us salvation apart from giving us himself. Salvation cannot be objectified or "thingified," because Jesus Christ is the salvation that he gives—there is no salvation anywhere else than in the humanity that Christ has assumed and restored to fellowship with God. This sheds light on perhaps the most enigmatic and momentous utterance of our Lord:

> Truly, truly, I say to you, unless you eat the flesh of the Son of Man and drink his blood, you have no life in you. Whoever feeds on my flesh and drinks my blood has eternal life, and I will raise him up on the last day. For my flesh is true food, and my blood is true drink. Whoever feeds on my flesh and drinks my blood abides in me, and I in him. (John 6:53–56)

These words caused offense, bewilderment, and desertion among those who heard them, swiftly thinning out the throng that followed Jesus, even depleting the ranks of his disciples.[3] These words are indeed the most provocative way of stating what Jesus so often pressed upon his audience, then and now—that he himself, in the fullness of his person, is the living essence of our salvation: "*I am* the living water. . . . *I am* the bread of life. . . . *I am* the temple of God. . . . *I am* the light of the World. . . . *I am* the way, and the truth, and the life. . . . *I am* the resurrection and the life" (see John 2:19; 4:10; 6:35; 8:12; 11:25; 14:6). *He is* all of this as the Son of God, who, by joining himself to us, sanctified and justified our flesh and blood, restoring us to communion with his Father. His crucified, resurrected flesh constitutes our eternal life just as surely as our fallen flesh constitutes our death. The most basic need of fallen, corrupted, condemned humanity is

---

[3] This "hard saying," as the disciples referred to it (John 6:60), still bewilders modern evangelical commentators who do not see union with the crucified, resurrected, ascended humanity of Jesus Christ as necessary to salvation. In such a case, Jesus's words are often reduced to little more than a metaphor for our faith in his impending death.

the re-created, sanctified, justified humanity of the Son of God. Thus, "Unless you eat the flesh of the Son of Man and drink his blood, you have no life in you."[4] Eternal life is not available to us—in fact, there are no saving benefits whatever available to us—apart from our participation in the God who comes to us clothed in our flesh. John Calvin puts it this way:

> First, we must understand that as long as Christ remains outside of us, and we are separated from him, all that he has suffered and done for the salvation of the human race remains useless and of no value to us. Therefore, to share in what he has received from the Father, he had to become ours and to dwell within us . . . for, as I have said, all that he possesses is nothing to us until we grow into one body with him.[5]

Calvin insists that the whole of Christ's saving work on our behalf—his birth, baptism, life, death, resurrection, and ascension—is "useless" unless he "dwells within us . . . until we grow into one body with him." There is, quite simply, no "work" of Christ that can be accessed apart from union with his person—salvation does not exist anywhere else. Calvin's emphasis here simply echoes the rich and pervasive teaching on union with the incarnate Jesus Christ found throughout the New Testament, which teaching subsequently found prominence in the writing and preaching of the church fathers and Protestant Reformers.[6] Calvin thought the gospel was neatly summed up by 1 Corinthians 1:30: "And because of [God] you are in Christ Jesus, who became to us wisdom from God, righteousness and sanctification and redemption." Jesus Christ is the fountain of all God's blessings to us, and so we enjoy those blessings only as God places us *in him*. "For this is the design of the gospel," Calvin writes, "that Christ may become ours and that we may be ingrafted into his body."[7] And the reason we not only *must* be in Christ, but *are able* to be in Christ, is that he has come and made our flesh and blood his own.

---

[4] Let us be altogether clear about the point at hand. Throughout chapters 4 and 5, we discussed "flesh" largely in terms of the human constitution as ruined and wrecked by sin. Christ came in the likeness of this sinful *sarx* (Rom. 8:3) precisely in order to sanctify and justify it, healing our sinful flesh of its manifold maladies. Thus, when the church echoes Scripture in speaking of the life-giving flesh (and blood) of Christ, the proper reference, of course, is not the sinful *sarx* that he subjected to crucifixion, but rather the resurrected humanity of our ascended and glorified Lord. As Paul declares, the church participates in the body and blood of the *risen* Christ (1 Cor. 10:16).

[5] *Inst.*, 3.1.1.

[6] Johnson, *One with Christ*, 19–24. Cf. Constantine Campbell, *Paul and Union with Christ: An Exegetical and Theological Study* (Grand Rapids Zondervan, 2012).

[7] Calvin on 1 Cor. 1:19, *Comm.*, 20/1:60.

To be joined to the incarnate Christ is what it means to be saved. When we are so joined to him, we receive all the benefits he accrued for us in his birth, baptism, life, death, resurrection, and ascension: the gifts and the Giver cannot be separated. This chapter seeks to highlight the way in which the incarnation is indispensable for how we view the glorious gifts of our Savior, how the enfleshing of God the Son provides the inner "theo-logic" of his saving benefits. Seeing that these benefits are more than we can include in one chapter, we have selected three that we feel are particularly imperative for understanding salvation in Christ: justification, sanctification, and adoptive sonship. But before we explore these gifts, we must attempt to articulate the mystery of our union with Jesus Christ, giving voice to the grand reality that we are really and truly joined to the incarnate Son of God.

The Nature of Our Union with Jesus Christ

Because the believer's union with Christ is the defining reality of salvation, it is important that the nature and characteristics of that union be defined. It is inevitable that the way in which one conceives of the nature of this union will determine how one conceives of its benefits. Of course, this is most obviously true when the gospel is conceived of altogether apart from union with Jesus Christ. But it is still immensely significant for those who may admit the fact of the union but consider that union in abstract and impersonal ways—for instance, as a mere mechanism or delivery system for the transmission of Christ's gifts. In both cases, there is a more or less subtle dichotomizing of the person and work of Christ. From the outset, then, we want to be clear to distinguish the stark ontological reality of union with Christ from reductionistic understandings of it that rely heavily on sentimentalism, metaphors, and legal contracts. Each of these reductions leads into rather static and impersonal understandings of the gospel, seeing that none of them necessarily requires an *incarnate* Savior! So let us offer a definition of the astounding mystery before us, which finds elaboration below: *To be united to Christ means that we are truly joined to the incarnate person of Christ himself, who is present in his gospel by the power of the Holy Spirit and received through faith, and by this union we are brought to participate in the very life and love of the Trinity.*

Our Union with Christ Is a Profound Mystery

The significance of mystery needs to be recovered by modern evangelicals.[8] After all, the most profound gospel realities are rooted in mystery. The creation of the world *ex nihilo*; God's triune being; the incarnation; and the death, resurrection, and ascension of Christ, to name just a few, are all impenetrable, irreducible mysteries that are not only most real, but in fact provide the structure and meaning of reality. Given that God is the object of the church's theology and worship, it should come as no surprise to us that in our encounters with him, our understanding is transcended. Confronted by the transcendent mystery of God, we are led to confession, adoration, and awe. Such is the importance of mystery, which is necessary in our theology to enable us to rightly behold the reality of God's mighty being and acts. Instead of keeping mystery—and its twin sister, paradox—"hidden from sight like a deformed imbecile of whom we are ashamed," Vernon Grounds writes, we should "welcome it proudly into the throne-room of theology—a kind of Cinderella at long last discovered and exalted to her rightful place."[9] For generations, modernist Christians have been given over to the unholy excesses of rationalism; thus, we do well to remember that our understanding of the reality of God and his creative, redemptive acts is not diminished, but rather illumined and magnified, by their mysterious nature. The litmus test for what is true and real for the Christian is not naïve self-reliance on one's empirical and logical powers, but the truth and reality of God's self-revelation.[10]

Divine gospel mysteries are realities that we believe, confess, and adore rather than explain away or, worse, attempt to solve. Among these great gospel mysteries is what the apostle Paul calls "Christ in you, the hope of glory" (Col. 1:27). Indeed, for Paul, the mystery of Christ's union with his bride is elemental to the preaching of the gospel, and it is a mystery for which he was willing to suffer and die (Col. 4:3; Eph. 6:19–20). The proper response to such glorious good news is captured well by the eighteenth-century Scottish churchman Thomas Boston:

> The Gospel is a doctrine of mysteries. O what mysteries are here! The
> Head in heaven, the members on earth, yet really united! Christ in the

---

[8] See Christopher A. Hall and Steven D. Boyer, *The Mystery of God: Theology for Knowing the Unknowable* (Grand Rapids: Baker, 2012).

[9] Vernon C. Grounds, "The Postulate of Paradox," *BETS* 7, no. 1 (Winter 1964): 3.

[10] According to Calvin, "everything that is announced concerning Christ seems very paradoxical to human judgment." Calvin on Rom. 6:1, *Comm.*, 19/2:218.

believer, living in him, walking in him: and the believer dwelling in God, putting on the Lord Jesus, eating his flesh and drinking his blood! This makes the saints a mystery to the world, yea, a mystery to themselves.[11]

To say that the depth of the mystery of our union with Christ lies beyond our comprehension means neither that this union is somehow less than real nor that there is finally nothing we can say positively about it. As we will see below, Scripture is rich with language and images that help us articulate and imagine the intimacy and beauty of our oneness with the God-man. In the end, however, these biblical portrayals intend to lead us to trust and adoration. Paul's confession of the mystery of the union between Christ and his bride leads Calvin to exclaim:

> For my own part, I am overwhelmed by the depth of this mystery, and am not ashamed to join Paul in acknowledging at once my ignorance and my admiration. How much more satisfactory would this be than to follow my carnal judgment, in undervaluing what Paul declares to be a deep mystery! Reason itself teaches how we ought to act in such matters; for whatever is supernatural is clearly beyond our own comprehension. Let us therefore labor more to feel Christ living in us, than to discover the nature of that intercourse.[12]

Union with the Incarnate Christ

The church's union with Christ cannot be reduced to a union with his benefits, to a union that occurs only in our thoughts or sentiments, or even to a contractual or legal union, though it surely has elements of all these. Christ gives himself to us for our salvation, and does so as none other than the crucified, resurrected, ascended, glorified, and still incarnate Savior. Indeed, that is the goal of the incarnation: that having taken upon himself our humanity, Christ might reconstitute us in the humanity he restored. He joined himself to our humanity that we might be joined to his. Any union with Christ that did not include his incarnate person would not be redeeming, as our humanity has not been redeemed anywhere else! This helps us to see why the nature of our union with Christ is described in Scripture in such intensely intimate and even bodily terms. This union extends into

---

[11] Thomas Boston, *Human Nature in Its Fourfold State* (1720; repr., Carlisle, PA: Banner of Truth Trust, 1964, 1989), 257.
[12] Calvin on Eph. 5:32, *Comm.*, 21/1:325.

the depths of our existence as humans because such were the depths that Christ entered to heal us. Jesus's startling insistence that we must eat his flesh and drink his blood exemplifies this intimacy. But no less startling is Paul's description of the same reality:

> For no one ever hated his own flesh, but nourishes and cherishes it, just as Christ does the church, because we are members of his body. "Therefore a man shall leave his father and mother and hold fast to his wife, and the two shall become one flesh." This mystery is profound, and I am saying that it refers to Christ and the church. (Eph. 5:29–32)

Accustomed as we are to reading this passage primarily as a treatise on human marriage, we risk losing what lies at the root of this "profound mystery," namely, that we are members, limbs and organs, of Christ's body, one flesh with him. The intimate and mysterious joining of male and female that characterizes marriage is here said to be quintessentially fulfilled in Christ and his church. And just as the intimacy between male and female in marriage never includes less than the joining of their bodies, so it is with the union between Christ and his bride. Indeed, failure to understand the physical reality of this union is what drives Paul's exasperation with the Corinthians, who thought it permissible to unite their bodies with prostitutes: "Do you not know that your bodies are members of Christ? Shall I then take the members of Christ and make them members of a prostitute? Never! Or do you not know that he who is joined to a prostitute becomes one body with her? For, as it is written, 'The two will become one flesh'" (1 Cor. 6:15–16). Paul contends that bodily union with a prostitute is shamefully unholy *because believers are already in a union with Jesus Christ that includes their bodies.* Unless our bodies are really joined to Christ's body, Paul's admonition here rings hollow.

Imagine the alternatives. What if our union with Christ were something less or other than union with his incarnate person? What would salvation consist of in such a case? Would not the tendency arise to begin thinking of salvation in rather abstract, depersonalized ways? To ask it pointedly, would our soteriology be characterized by impersonal mechanisms or transactions in which salvation is understood primarily as a reception of this or that benefit—whether forgiveness, righteousness, holiness, eternal life, heaven— rather than a sharing in the One who includes *within himself* all of his benefits? Such reductions and more are near at hand whenever we lose sight of the internal relation between the incarnation and the atonement—in other words, whenever we separate the Giver from his gifts. The gospel mystery of the incarnation shows us in a most astonishing way that God has come to bring us the greatest gift there is: himself. The riches of his life and love have been opened up to us in the humanity of his beloved Son. There is no salvation anywhere else, as Calvin was fond of pointing out: "For the Lord Jesus, to communicate the gift of salvation which he has purchased for us, must first be made ours, and his flesh be our meat and nourishment, seeing that it is from it that we derive life."[13]

Sharing in the Life of the Trinity

Because Jesus is truly, fully, and unreservedly one with the Father and truly, fully, and unreservedly one with us, the incarnate One is the Mediator between God and man: "For there is one God, and there is one mediator between God and men, the man Christ Jesus" (1 Tim. 2:5). Just as Jesus gives us his gifts precisely by giving us himself, so in giving us himself, he brings us to share in what makes him who he is—his relationship with the Father and the Spirit. By becoming incarnate, the Son of God extended his relationship with his Father and the Spirit into our human existence so that we come to know and experience God as he really is. Our union with Christ is a fully Trinitarian reality, a gospel truth he pressed upon his disciples on his way to the cross:

> And I will ask the Father, and he will give you another Helper, to be with you forever, even the Spirit of truth, whom the world cannot receive, because it neither sees him nor knows him. You know him, for he dwells with you and will be in you. I will not leave you as orphans; I will come to you. Yet a little while and the world will see me no more, but you will see me. Because I live, you also will live. In that day you will know that I am in my Father, and you in me, and I in you. (John 14:16–20)

Consider the sublime Trinitarian shape of salvation on display in Jesus's words: (1) because God is intrinsically, fundamentally, and eternally the life-giving communion of Father, Son, and Spirit, (2) our redemption is ac-

---

[13] John Calvin, "John Calvin, to the Pastors of the Town and Territory of Zurich . . . ," *Tracts and Letters*, vol. 2, trans. and ed. Henry Beveridge (Carlisle, PA: Banner of Truth Trust, 2009), 207–208.

complished only as the Father sends the Son, conceived by the power of the Holy Spirit, in order that (3) the Spirit may in turn join us to the incarnate Son, who brings us into his own communion with his Father. Because God is none other than the communion of Father, Son, and Spirit, salvation is Trinitarian coming down and Trinitarian going up. To put it another way, God loves us with the very love that God is. T. F. Torrance writes:

> The Love of God revealed to us in the economic Trinity [who God is in his external relations] is identical with the Love of God in the ontological Trinity [who God is his inner being]; but the Love of God revealed to us in the economic manifestation of the Father, the Son and the Holy Spirit in the history of our salvation, tells us that God loves us with the very same love with which he loves himself.[14]

Just as the love of God is literally penetrating—the Father, Son, and Spirit mutually indwell one another—so the love he extends to us is the same: through the indwelling of the Spirit, we are in the Son, who is in the Father. We are brought into the life of the Trinity. For those of us who are accustomed to thinking of God as inaccessibly remote, the fact that we share in the union between the Father, Son, and Spirit is indeed, as D. A. Carson calls it, "breathtakingly extravagant."[15]

The extravagance is the result of the mystery of Christ's person and our saving union with him. Because we are united to the person of Christ, who is fully man *and* fully God, we are united to God through his humanity.[16] As such, we are redeemed from inauthentic human existence to authentic human existence—creaturely humanity in communion with God. The "theo-logic" of salvation is the mystery of the incarnation, which tells us in the most tangible way that it is God's intention to join us to himself through his Son by the Spirit. Robert Letham explains:

> The Trinity created us with a capacity to live *in him*, as creatures in and with our Creator. The incarnation proves it. If it were not so and

---

[14] T. F. Torrance, *The Christian Doctrine of God: One Being Three Persons* (Edinburgh: T&T Clark, 1996; repr., 2006), 165 (bracketed notes added).

[15] D. A. Carson, *The Gospel According to John*, Pillar New Testament Commentary (Grand Rapids: Eerdmans, 1991), 569.

[16] As Robert Letham points out, "Strictly speaking, we are united to [Christ's] humanity, but his humanity is inseparable from his deity, due to the hypostatic union . . . this does not mean any blurring of the Creator-creature distinction, any more than the assumption of humanity by the Son in the incarnation does. His humanity remains humanity (without confusion, without mixture). So, we remain human, creatures." *The Holy Trinity: In Scripture, History, Theology, and Worship* (Phillipsburg, NJ: P&R, 2004), 268.

could not be so, then Jesus Christ—God and man—could not be one person, for the difference between Creator and creature would be so great that incarnation would not be possible. But now our humanity in Jesus Christ is in full and personal union with God, and so in union with Christ we are brought into union with God.[17]

The Presence of Christ in the Gospel and through Faith

Now that we have briefly laid out the nature of our union with Christ, we turn to consider another crucial question: *How* do we come to be united to him? Or, what are the means through which Christ is truly present to us? After all, if salvation depends on being joined to him, surely he must be present to us to be received! On this question, we feel an important Latin phrase may prove especially helpful: *distinctio sed non separatio,* "distinct but not separate." It is helpful because it brings clarity to the way we think and speak about salvation, keeping our thought and speech about the gospel from dissolving into impersonal or static concepts.

Take, for instance, the common expressions "saved by the gospel," "saved by faith alone," or even "the saving power of the cross." These are biblically and historically faithful ways of expressing something significant about salvation. But they may be taken to imply that the Savior himself is tangential to salvation. Surely, apart from the presence of the living Christ, neither the gospel nor faith can save us any more than could a piece of carrot cake! But if that is so, we are right to ask what Paul means when he writes, "For I am not ashamed of the gospel, for it is the power of God for salvation to everyone who believes" (Rom. 1:16).

Here is where our Latin phrase—*distinctio sed non separatio*—becomes crucial. The gospel and faith are both *means* through which Christ is present to us, but it is Christ himself who is the *object and end* of both. Because Jesus Christ alone is our salvation, we must be able to make a distinction between Christ and his gospel without thereby separating Christ from his gospel. Likewise, because Jesus Christ alone is our salvation, we must also be able to make a distinction between Christ and our act of faith without thereby separating them. Without this careful delineation, the vital connection between the gospel, faith, and Jesus Christ may be lost.

Let us begin with the true presence of Christ in the gospel. Christ or-

---

[17] Ibid., 470.

dained the apostolic witness to himself as the means by which he dwells in us and we in him. The preaching and teaching of the gospel, the written and inspired testimony to Christ in Scripture, is the arena in which Christ is redemptively present:

> I do not ask for these only, but also for those who will believe in me through their word, that they may all be one, just as you, Father, are in me, and I in you, that they also may be in us, so that the world may believe that you have sent me. The glory that you have given me I have given to them, that they may be one even as we are one, I in them and you in me, that they may become perfectly one, so that the world may know that you sent me and loved them even as you loved me. (John 17:20–23)

Earlier, Jesus had said that he would send the Spirit so that he would be in us as he is in the Father (John 14). Here, he disclosed the means by which this would occur—through the apostolic testimony to him. The faithful reception of this testimony results in union with the incarnate Son and thus with the Father: in other words, salvation. It is not, therefore, the mere propositional, factual content of the gospel that saves, but rather Christ "clothed with his gospel," as Calvin puts it.[18] While the gospel certainly does include knowledge *about* Christ, it is only our experiential knowing *of* Christ that is redemptive. The reception of the apostolic testimony to Christ is thus the Spirit-vivified vehicle of Christ's self-bestowal. "To preach the gospel," Martin Luther writes, "is nothing else than Christ's coming to us or bringing us to him."[19] The living Word and Son of God is the substance of the preached and written word of God.[20]

The apostles knew this well. John sums up his Gospel by writing, "Now Jesus did many other signs in the presence of the disciples, which are not written in this book; but these are written so that you may believe that Jesus is the Christ, the Son of God, and that by believing *you may have life in his name*" (John 20:30–31). Christ is the living reality of his word. Paul writes similarly about the power of the gospel for salvation: "And you also *were included in Christ* when you heard the word of truth, the gospel of your salvation" (Eph. 1:13 NIV). To these passages, we may add many others (Rom.

---

[18] *Inst.*, 3.2.6.
[19] Martin Luther, *The Marburg Colloquy and The Marburg Articles, 1529*, in LW, 38:41, cited in Paul D. L. Avis, *The Church in the Theology of the Reformers* (1981; repr., Eugene, OR: Wipf & Stock, 2002), 89.
[20] Christ is also the living substance of the tangible words of God, baptism and the Lord's Supper, a topic we will explore in chapter 7.

10:14; 2 Cor. 13:3; Gal. 3:1; Eph. 4:21) that bear sufficient testimony to the fact that Christ himself is present to be heard and received in the apostolic word.[21] Christ should never be separated or sundered from his word, and neither should he be confused or conflated with it—much less replaced by it.

A similar confusion of means for ends often occurs in the way Christians understand the role of faith in salvation. Evangelical Protestant doctrine has long been marked by its allegiance to the five *solas* of the Reformation, one of which is *sola fide* (the assertion that we are saved "by faith alone"). However, the Reformers never meant that faith is saving *because* one believes, but rather that faith is saving *because of whom faith receives*. We are saved, in other words, not because of some intrinsic merit or efficacy in our faith, but because faith grasps and lays hold of Christ himself. This is a constant refrain from the Reformers and their heirs. Luther writes that faith "unites the soul with Christ as a bride is united with her bridegroom. By this mystery, as the Apostle teaches, Christ and the soul become one flesh."[22] Jonathan Edwards concurs: "Now it is by faith that the soul is united unto Christ; faith is this bride's reception of Christ as a bridegroom."[23] Calvin also agrees:

> What a remarkable commendation is here bestowed on *faith*, that, by means of it, the Son of God becomes our own, and "makes his abode with us!" (John 14:23) By faith we not only acknowledge that Christ suffered and rose from the dead on our account, but, accepting the offers which he makes of himself, we possess and enjoy him as our Saviour.[24]

If Christ is not truly present to be apprehended in faith, then what does it mean to say that we are "saved by faith"? If we do not make a careful distinction here, we are at great risk of collapsing salvation back into our human experience of faith, implying that faith is a religious disposition that God finds worthy of salvation. Thus, we must not confuse faith with

---

[21] Rom. 10:14 and Eph. 4:21 are especially instructive examples. Many scholars feel that Romans 10:14b is often mistranslated. The phrase, they think, should be translated, "And how are they to believe in him *whom* they have never heard?" indicating that Christ himself speaks through the gospel preached. See J. D. G. Dunn, *Romans 9–16*, Word Biblical Commentary, vol. 38b (Dallas, TX: Word Books, 1988), 620; C. E. B. Cranfield, *The Epistle to the Romans*, ICC (Edinburgh: T&T Clark, 1998), 2:534; John R. W. Stott, *The Message of Romans* (Downers Grove, IL: IVP, 1994), 286. The same may apply to Eph. 4:21. The NIV reads, "you heard *about Christ*," while the ESV reads, "assuming that you have heard *about him*." Ernst Best is among those who say that this cannot be the meaning of the Greek. Rather, it is Christ *himself* who is heard. *Ephesians* (Edinburgh: T&T Clark, 1998), 427.
[22] *Explanations of the Ninety-Five Theses, 1518 LW*, 31:151.
[23] Jonathan Edwards, *Miscellanies* (No. 271), in *The Works of Jonathan Edwards*, ed. Thomas A. Schafer (New Haven, CT: Yale University Press, 1994), 13:220.
[24] Calvin on Eph. 3:17, *Comm.*, 21/1:262.

the object of our faith. Saving intimacy with Christ is not the *same thing* as faith; rather, our saving union with him is the *result of faith*. The insight here, of apostolic origin (John 1:12; 17:21, 26; 20:31; 2 Cor. 13:5; Gal. 3:26; Eph. 1:13; 3:17; Col. 2:6–7, 12), is that while faith is surely saving, faith is not our Savior—Christ alone saves us. Faith should never be separated from salvation in Christ, but faith surely needs to be distinguished from the Christ whom faith receives. Strictly speaking, the "theo-logic" of the Reformation slogan *sola fide* is not that we are saved "*on account of* our faith alone," but that we are saved "*in Christ* through faith alone." So by all means, let us insist that sinners are saved through faith alone. But let us insist all the more that it is not faith that saves, but rather Christ present through faith who saves.[25]

THE GOSPEL BLESSINGS OF THE INCARNATE CHRIST

Calvin was adamant that his readers must exercise care in how they thought about salvation and the flesh of Jesus Christ. We can find life in Christ, he insisted, only when we seek that life in his flesh. Jesus *cannot* be our source of life apart from his humanity. "Therefore," he writes, "if you wish to have any interest in Christ, you must take care, above all things, that you do not disdain his flesh."[26] The reason Calvin gave for this insistence is important for what follows in this chapter. He writes:

[In the flesh of Christ] was accomplished the redemption of man, in it a sacrifice was offered to atone for sins, and an obedience yielded to God, to reconcile him to us; it was also filled with the sanctification of the Spirit, and at length, having vanquished death, it was received into the heavenly glory. *It follows, therefore, that all the parts of life have been placed in it*, that no man may have reason to complain that he is deprived of life, as if it were placed in concealment, or at a distance.[27]

Redemption, sacrifice, atonement, obedience, reconciliation, sanctification, heavenly glory: all in the flesh of Jesus Christ. It is no wonder that Calvin was careful never to separate the person of Christ from his work,

---

[25] The pastoral benefit of this insight from our evangelical forebears is enormous, given that most who struggle with assurance of their salvation tend to go "navel-gazing" (examining the strength of their faith) rather than Christ-gazing (examining the utter trustworthiness of Christ).

[26] Calvin on John 6:56, *Comm.*, 17/2:268.

[27] Calvin on John 6:51, *Comm.*, 17/2:263 (emphasis added).

for there is no salvation except *in Christ*. The remainder of this chapter is a brief foray into three of the glorious blessings we receive from the life-giving flesh of Christ.

Justification in Christ

The doctrine of justification has been a hallmark of evangelical Protestant soteriology since the time of the Reformation, when Luther and Calvin, among others, gave powerful and lucid expression to the biblical teaching that sinners are "declared in the right" before God on account of the person and work of Jesus Christ alone.[28] Our evangelical forebears believed that a proper understanding of justification was indispensable for a right understanding of the gospel, highlighting as it does that salvation is truly, wholly, and perfectly the unmerited free gift of God's grace in Christ Jesus (*sola gratia*). So important is the doctrine of justification that Luther refers to it as "the one article that preserves the church of Christ; when it is lost, Christ and the church are lost,"[29] and Calvin as the "main hinge on which religion turns."[30] The great import of justification can be seen when we consider Calvin's definition, which has found wide acceptance in the Protestant tradition:

> We explain justification simply as the acceptance with which God receives us into his favour as righteous men. And we say that it consists in the remission of sins and the imputation of Christ's righteousness.[31]

Following Luther, Calvin was giving expression to the teaching of Scripture that, by virtue of the atoning death and resurrection of Christ, and through faith in him, our sins are wholly forgiven and his righteousness is accounted ours: we are declared righteous. Our justification in Christ is the gospel we receive in answer to one of the tragedies of the fall. In Adam, all humanity exists in a state of sin and condemnation: declared unrighteous.

---

[28] We often hear it said that Luther "discovered" the doctrine of justification. Luther no more discovered justification than Neil Armstrong discovered the moon. He simply experienced and gave articulation to it in an unparalleled way in the history of the church.

[29] Cited in Bernhard Lohse, *Martin Luther's Theology: Its Historical and Systematic Development* (Minneapolis: Fortress, 1999), 258–59. This quote approximates the famous Reformation slogan, usually attributed to Luther, that justification is "the article by which the church stands or falls." Luther does not actually say this exact phrase, even if he comes rather close. For the origin of the slogan, see Justin Taylor, "6 Quotes That Luther Didn't Actually Say," http://www.thegospelcoalition.org/blogs/justintaylor/2014/02/20/5-quotes-that-luther-didnt-actually-say/, accessed Nov. 15, 2014.

[30] *Inst.*, 3.11.1.

[31] *Inst.*, 3.11.2.

In Christ alone, the second and last Adam, humanity exists in a state of forgiveness and acquittal: declared righteous.

The doctrine of justification has traditionally been formulated in judicial, forensic terms in recognition that the apostle Paul's teaching often reflects the language of the divine courtroom in which God acts as the sovereign Judge, acquitting those guilty of transgressing his law (forgiveness) and granting them the representative righteousness of Christ's law-fulfilling obedience (imputation). Following the Reformers, evangelical Protestants have rightly emphasized the forensic element of justification, the fact that God *declares* us forgiven and righteous in Christ alone, thus stripping away any pretense that we could somehow merit God's saving grace by way of our good works or disposition of heart (a concern so dear to Luther). This salutary emphasis, however, has often led where the Reformers never went—into merely, or one-sidedly, forensic formulations that take no account of the prior necessity of union with the incarnate Christ.[32] When this happens, justification loses its moorings in the concrete reality of our participation in the justified flesh and blood of Christ—through which we really do share in his righteousness—and so runs every risk of dissolving into a legal fiction, a forensic illusion.

What difference does the incarnation of the Son of God make to the doctrine of justification? It tells us that he assumed our humanity in its unjustified state—exactly the kind of humanity that is in need of justification—in order that, by living a life of pure obedience before God his Father, by taking upon himself the inevitable suffering and death that accompany sin, and by triumphing over sin and death in his resurrection, he might justify our humanity. In his life, death, and resurrection, Jesus overcame in himself and in our flesh the sin, guilt, and condemnation due us. Thus, strictly speaking, Jesus experiences our justification in the humanity he assumed from us *so that* we might participate in that primal justification through union with him. God does not, indeed cannot, justify us apart from joining us to his Son, because Christ is himself our justification (1 Cor. 1:30; 2 Cor. 5:21). There is no justification available to us apart from the justified humanity of Christ, because he cannot mediate what is not already his.

---

[32] A contemporary example from Wayne Grudem's popular and influential work on systematic theology: "Justification is an instantaneous legal act of God in which he (1) thinks of our sins as forgiven and Christ's righteousness as belonging to us, and (2) declares us to be righteous in his sight." *Systematic Theology: An Introduction to Biblical Doctrine* (Grand Rapids: Zondervan, 2000), 723.

It is common to find justification treated only, or primarily, in connection with the death of Christ. But doing so seriously distorts the nature of our justification, which rests upon the life, death, and resurrection of Christ taken together. Christ's entire earthly existence was continually and comprehensively "putting us in the right" before God. He lived his entire life before God his Father in perfect fulfillment of his holy will in faithfulness, obedience, prayer, praise, holiness, love, self-giving, and humility (and much more besides) for us and for our justification. As the last and life-giving Adam, Jesus was recapitulating and reclothing humanity in righteousness. This aspect of Christ's ministry is referred to as his *active obedience*, and it forms the ground for what Calvin, above, calls "the imputation of Christ's righteousness." United to Christ, we share in the perfectly righteous life he lived for us and in us—his perfect righteousness becomes ours (Phil. 3:8–9).

But our unrighteousness, condemnation, and death had to become his. This is why it is crucial to speak also of Christ's *passive obedience*, in which he submitted himself to the divine verdict upon our humanity in atonement for our sin. In becoming sin for us, he subjected himself to rejection (Isa. 53:3), humiliation (Luke 22:63–65), and, climactically, crucifixion (Phil. 2:8; 1 Pet. 2:24), in which he bore the wrath of God against sin (Rom. 5:8–9) and the condemnation of death (Rom. 8:1–3; Gal. 3:13). He did all of this so that our sins would be removed "as far as the east is from the west" (Ps. 103:12). Jesus did this in our place and as our Substitute; he alone is the propitiation for our sins (1 John 2:2). Yet this should never lead us to suppose that Christ is our atonement *apart* from us, for he bore us in himself as he subjected himself to the suffering, death, and burial of his high-priestly sacrifice. This is why we read over and over again in the New Testament that, united to Christ, we participate in his crucifixion, death, and burial (e.g., Rom. 6:3–6; Gal. 2:20; Col. 2:12, 20). Christ's passive obedience was representative, to be sure, but it was a representation in which he assumed, crucified, and buried our humanity that was subject to the conditions of sin, condemnation, and death.

His life was a justifying life, and his death a justifying death, but we must not stop there, for his resurrection was a justifying resurrection—he was "raised for our justification" (Rom. 4:25). What does Jesus's resurrection have to do with our justification? As Richard B. Gaffin Jr. points out, the resurrection of Christ was the vindication of his righteous life and death.

Christ identified himself with us in order to bear the guilt of our sin. He became a curse and was made subject to the condemnation of the law unto death, so that "consequently, his being raised on account of our justification identified him with us in the justifying verdict inevitably attendant on the righteousness which he established for us (better, which he established for himself as he was one with us) by his obedience unto death."[33] Another way to put this is that our justification is a participation in Christ's own resurrection-justification, in which he was released from the verdict of condemnation and his righteous obedience was supremely vindicated. In our union with the resurrected Jesus, we share in the vindication and affirmation of his life and death.

The active and passive obedience of Christ, the whole of his life, death, and resurrection taken together, constitute our justification. In other words, as Torrance writes:

> Justification means not simply the non-imputation of our sins through the pardon of Christ, but positive sharing in his divine-human righteousness. We are saved, therefore, not only by the death of Christ which he suffered for our sakes, but by his life which he lived in our flesh for our sakes and which God raised from the dead that we may share in it through the power of the Spirit. It is in that light, of his atoning and justifying life, that we are to understand the Incarnation of the Son in the whole course of his obedience from his birth to his resurrection.[34]

Our justification, therefore, can take place only as we are included in the One who was justified for us: "There is therefore now no condemnation for those who are in Christ Jesus" (Rom. 8:1). The difference that the incarnation makes to the doctrine of justification is that justification has taken place in the flesh of the Son of God exclusively. Our justification thus depends upon our being joined to the One who joined himself to us. Although this is often ignored or obscured in contemporary evangelical theology, it is something our evangelical fathers Luther and Calvin knew very well:

> But so far as justification is concerned, Christ and I must be so closely attached that He lives in me and I in Him. What a marvelous way of

---

[33] Richard B. Gaffin Jr., *Resurrection and Redemption: A Study in Paul's Soteriology*, 2nd ed. (Phillipsburg, NJ: P&R, 1987), 123.
[34] Thomas F. Torrance, *Theology in Reconstruction* (Eugene, OR: Wipf & Stock, 1996), 155; idem, *Incarnation: The Person and Life of Christ* (Downers Grove, IL: IVP Academic, 2008), 81.

speaking! Because He lives in me, whatever grace, righteousness, life, peace, and salvation there is in me is all Christ's; nevertheless it is mine as well, by the cementing and attachment that are through faith, by which we become as one body in the Spirit.[35]

Therefore, that joining together of Head and members, that indwelling of Christ in our hearts—in short, that mystical union—are accorded by us the highest degree of importance, so that Christ, having been made ours, makes us sharers with him in the gifts with which he has been endowed. We do not, therefore, contemplate him outside ourselves from afar in order that his righteousness may be imputed to us *but because we put on Christ and are engrafted into his body*—in short, because he deigns to make us one with him. For this reason, we glory that we have fellowship of righteousness with him.[36]

To be sure, Luther and Calvin affirm imputation, but they establish it on a personal/participatory ground, such that justification is no mere external transaction. Justification is only and ever real because our union with Christ is real.

Sanctification in Christ

The guardians of the Roman Catholic magisterium were horrified and incredulous when they heard how the Reformers spoke about justification. Surely if such a doctrine were promulgated among the faithful, Rome protested, it would obviate the need for holiness and good works, leading to moral laxity and even licentiousness. Therefore, they cursed such teaching.[37] As Calvin puts it, the Roman church gravely misread the situation by assuming that the Reformers had conflated justification in Christ with the whole of salvation, as if justification exhausts the gospel. Calvin's retort to such a misunderstanding is telling:

---

[35] *Lectures on Galatians* (1535), in *LW*, 26:167–68. See also, ibid., 130, 132.

[36] *Inst.*, 3.11.10 (emphasis added). For more on the relationship between justification and union with Christ in the Reformers, see Paul Louis Metzger, "Mystical Union with Christ: An Alternative to Blood Transfusions and Legal Fictions," in *Westminster Theological Journal* 65, no. 2 (2003), 201–13; Marcus Johnson, "Luther and Calvin on Union with Christ," in *Fides et Historia* 39, no. 2 (2007), 59–77; idem, *One with Christ*, chapter 3; Richard B. Gaffin Jr., "Justification and Union with Christ," in *A Theological Guide to Calvin's Institutes: Essays and Analysis*, ed. David Hall (Phillipsburg, NJ: P&R, 2008), 248–69.

[37] Literally accursed at the Council of Trent, as stated in the council's article 11: "If anyone says that men are justified either by the sole imputation of the justice of Christ or by the sole remission of sins, to the exclusion of the grace and the charity which is poured forth in their hearts by the Holy Ghost, and remains in them, or also that the grace by which we are justified is only the good will of God, let him be anathema." "The Canons and Decrees of the Council of Trent (1563)," in *CC*, 421

Although we may distinguish between [justification and sanctification], Christ contains both of them *inseparably in himself*. Do you wish, then, to attain righteousness in Christ? You must first possess Christ; but you cannot possess him without being made partaker in his sanctification, because *he cannot be divided into pieces*. . . . Since, therefore, it is *solely by expending himself* that the Lord gives us these benefits to enjoy, he bestows both of them at the same time, the one never without the other. Thus it is clear how we are justified not without works yet not through works, since in our sharing in Christ, which justifies us, sanctification is just as much included as righteousness.[38]

Calvin paints a graphic word picture intended to communicate the depth of our participation in Jesus Christ: "he cannot be divided into pieces." One can no more be justified without being sanctified than Christ can be dismembered. In union with Christ, we share in *all* that he is for us. Jesus Christ is himself our "righteousness *and* sanctification and redemption" (1 Cor. 1:30).[39] Rome had seriously misunderstood what it means to be united to Christ.

Apparently, so had the Romans before them. Calvin's defense of the inseparable relationship between justification and sanctification was a fifteen hundred-year-old echo of the first attempt at dividing Christ into pieces, which was answered by the apostle Paul:

Are we to continue in sin that grace may abound? By no means! How can we who died to sin still live in it? Do you not know that all of us who have been baptized into Christ Jesus were baptized into his death? We were buried therefore with him by baptism into death, in order that, just as Christ was raised from the dead by the glory of the Father, we too might walk in newness of life. (Rom. 6:1–4)

In other words, so the thought goes, does not the free grace of God in justification furnish the occasion for my continual sinning? The way in which Paul does *not* answer this question is as revealing as how he does. Notice that Paul does not say, "Do you not know that we all owe God a debt of gratitude for the fact that he has justified us freely in Christ?" Neither does he say, "Do you not know that our justification produces in us the effect of

---

[38] *Inst.*, 3.16.1 (emphasis added).
[39] As Anthony Hoekema has aptly and succinctly put it, "If Christ is indeed our sanctification, we can only be sanctified through being one with him." *Saved by Grace* (Grand Rapids: Eerdmans, 1989), 62.

sanctification?" Nor, finally, does he say, "Do you not know that God will eventually send his Spirit to sanctify you?" No, Paul's answer stretches back to the all-encompassing reality of salvation: our participation in the death, burial, and resurrection of Christ.

Just as the Son of God justified our guilty and condemned flesh in his life, death, and resurrection in order that we might be justified in him, so too he sanctified our depraved and polluted flesh in his life, death, and resurrection in order that we might be sanctified in him: "For them I sanctify myself, that they too may be truly sanctified" (John 17:19 NIV). By becoming incarnate, the Son entered incorruptibly into the depths of our corruption to heal and liberate us from our unholiness. His earthly life was a constant encounter with, and sanctifying of, the maladies common to our depraved human nature: disease, self-justification, fear, hatred, idolatry, nakedness, and shame, to name several. His sanctifying death marked the crucifixion and burial of the sinful nature he assumed from us, putting to death our "body of sin" so that we might be free from its bondage (Rom. 6:6). In his sanctifying resurrection, he raised us up to participation in the newness of his holy life, that we might be finally "alive to God" and "slaves to righteousness" (vv. 4, 11, 18). Jesus Christ accomplished our sanctification *within* our humanity; thus, sanctification is possible only in union with the incarnate, crucified, resurrected Word of God: "The holiness of the church is derived from God through Jesus Christ, through his self-sanctification or self-consecration in life and death on our behalf. He sanctified himself in the human nature he took from us, that we might be sanctified through the Word and truth of God incarnated in him."[40]

Because Jesus simply *is* our righteousness and holiness, apart from incorporation into him we can no more achieve our sanctification than we can our justification. As Luther knew well, sanctification is just as much *sola gratia* and *sola fide* as justification:

> My holiness, righteousness and purity do not stem from me, nor do they depend on me. They come solely from Christ and are based only in Him, in whom I am rooted by faith, just as sap flows from the stalk into the branches. Now I am like Him and of His kind. Both He and I

---

[40] Thomas F. Torrance, *Atonement: The Person and Work of Christ*, ed. Robert T. Walker (Downers Grove, IL: IVP Academic, 2009), 386.

are of one nature and essence, and I bear fruit in Him and through Him. The fruit is not mine; it is the Vine's.[41]

Several important implications for the doctrine of sanctification follow the confession that Christ *is* our holiness. The first is that sanctification should never be thought of as our moral response *to* the gospel, but rather as a constitutive reality *of* the gospel. Integral to our salvation is the wonderfully good news that we have been chosen in Christ "before the foundation of the world, that we should be holy and blameless before him" (Eph. 1:4), then re-created in Christ for good works (2:10). God has predestined us to be conformed to his Son (Rom. 8:29), and our gradual transformation into his image is gloriously *good news*—Calvin calls it "the design of the gospel"[42]—without which we would not be saved, and without which the gospel would be truncated.

Second, Jesus's self-sanctification spells the crucifixion of our "knowing good and evil" (Gen. 3:22 NIV) and the resurrection of its replacement: true knowledge of God's holiness. Because holiness is a divine attribute[43]—"Only thou art holy, there is none beside thee"[44]—the creature in alienation from God can achieve only self-styled goodness, what we might call moral rectitude, which falls under the decisive judgment of Jesus. The union of God and man in Christ is exactly the watershed difference between morality and sanctification, for in Christ we share in the enfleshed holiness of God himself—a blessing we could never achieve through moral ascendancy. Sainthood, therefore, is not an honor reserved for those we judge to have earned the title by right of an exemplary holiness. The designation "holy one," or saint, is conferred upon every last person united to the holy Christ:

> He sanctifies because as the one who assumes our human nature he is in our place, and acts in our place, making us—not merely potentially, but actually—holy, consecrated to God. God made him our sanctification; to be a saint is to have one's holiness in Christ Jesus.[45]

---

41 "Sermon on the Gospel of St. John 15:5," in *LW*, 24, 226. We hope against hope that the caricature that Luther had no doctrine of sanctification is recognized as just that.

42 Calvin on 2 Cor. 3:18, *Comm.*, 20/2:187.

43 See John Webster, *Holy Scripture: A Dogmatic Sketch* (Cambridge: Cambridge University Press, 2003), 27.

44 Reginald Heber, "Holy, Holy, Holy!" no. 162 in *The English Hymnal* (London: Oxford University Press, 1933), 234.

45 John Webster, *Holiness* (Grand Rapids: Eerdmans, 2003), 82–83.

Third, because holiness can be found only in the One who unites God and man in himself, doctrines of sanctification grounded in any other reality than our initial and ongoing communion with Christ are wholly inadequate. For instance, it is a customary doctrinal refrain to speak of Jesus as Savior and the Holy Spirit as sanctifier. This is a reflection of the nonchristological, and therefore non-Trinitarian, pneumatology we discussed in chapter 2. We simply reiterate here the implications for the doctrine of sanctification: Jesus does not send the Spirit to the church so that she might become holy in his absence; rather, he sends the Spirit *that he may indwell the church as her holiness*. Only Christ can sanctify his bride, and he does so through the Spirit. Loosed from the self-giving of Jesus Christ, the beauty and mystery of sanctification all too easily degenerates into technique and methodology— "seven steps to spiritual growth" and the like—that are often little more than self-help programs designed to motivate the *human* spirit. On the contrary, the *Spirit*ual life of the Christian is none other than a baptism by the Spirit into Jesus Christ, who crucifies and resurrects us into the power and freedom of his living, sanctifying presence. That is why John Williamson Nevin writes:

> The Christian is not called, either before or *after* his conversion, to *form an independent holiness for himself*; but only to receive continuously the stream of life that flows upon him from Christ. . . . And still this absolute *passivity* is at the same time the highest *activity*; since Christ works, not *without* the man, but in the *very inmost depths of his being*, infusing into the will itself the active force of his own life.[46]

In other words, "Whoever abides in me and I in him, he it is that bears much fruit, for apart from me you can do nothing" (John 15:5). The question of sanctification is therefore the question of Christ's presence to his church. As such, any answer that does not begin with the preached word and sacraments (see chapter 7) cannot be other than anemic, bereft as it is of the primary means of Christ's holy, nourishing presence.

Children of God in Christ

Justification and sanctification are two magnificent and inseparable blessings we receive in union with the incarnate Son of God. However, neither

---

[46] John Williamson Nevin, *The Mystical Presence: A Vindication of the Reformed or Calvinistic Doctrine of the Holy Eucharist*, American Religious Thought of the 18th and 19th Centuries, vol. 20 (New York: Garland, 1987), 235 (emphasis original).

one by itself, nor both taken together, would exhaust the riches of the salvation that he is. As astonishing as it ought to seem, Jesus came to do even more than secure our forgiveness, righteousness, and holiness. Indeed, these blessings are oriented around another blessing so exceedingly lavish and indescribably full of wonder that it taxes our credulity and even our imagination: the Son of God became human to share with us what is most precious to him—life-giving intimacy with his Father.

Of all the blessings we receive in union with the incarnate Son of God, this one is perhaps the most staggering of all. Jesus means to share with us his own sonship. By this we do not mean that Christ merely shares with us the *benefits* of his relationship with God his Father, which is most certainly true. We mean the more radical consequence of the incarnation—namely, that the eternal Son of God, without ever ceasing to be who he is, became human and thus brought our humanity into his existence with the Father through the Spirit. To be joined to Jesus Christ by the power of the Spirit and through faith means that we then participate, by way of his humanity, in the life and love he shares with the Father in the unity of the Spirit.

As inexplicable and impossible as this seems, this is precisely what Jesus promised time and again: "In that day you will know that I am in my Father, and you in me, and I in you" (John 14:20; cf., 14:2, 6–7, 10, 23). It is important to stress that Jesus was not referring to a generic unity or love, but rather the very same oneness and love that he has always had with his Father, to whom he prays, "The glory that you have given me I have given to them, that they may be one *even as we are one*, I in them and you in me, that they may become perfectly one, so that the world may know that you sent me and loved them *even as you loved me*" (John 17:22–23; cf., 15:9; 16:14–15, 27; 17:11, 21, 26). Of all the promises held out to us in Christ, should not these words inspire in us the *deepest* sense of delight and wonder?

These living words of Jesus made a forceful impression on the apostle John, who would proceed to make much of our being the children of God in Christ, of dwelling in the Father through the Son.[47] In fact, the whole meaning of eternal life is summed up by our sharing in the Father's gift of his Son: "And this is the testimony, that God gave us eternal life, and this life is in his Son. Whoever has the Son has life; whoever does not have the

---

[47] In concert with his Gospel, John's first epistle is characterized by its emphasis on the relationship we share with the Father through the Son: 1 John 1:1–3; 2:23–25; 3:1–3, 9–10, 24; 4:7–17; 5:1–4, 13, 18, 20.

Son of God does not have life" (1 John 5:11–12). The life we have in the Son is none other than the life he has always shared with his Father. That life is accessible to us only through his incarnation, which marks not only the mystery of the union of God and man, but, as such, the entrance into our humanity of the Son's relationship with the Father.[48] To be united to Christ is to be made a participant in his righteousness and holiness, *but also in his sonship.*[49] Edwards writes of those united to Christ, "For being members of God's own natural Son, they are in a sort partakers of his relation to the Father: they are not only sons of God by regeneration, but by a kind of communion in the sonship of the eternal Son."[50]

The apostle Paul also frames much of his understanding of the gospel in terms of sharing in Christ's sonship. The beautiful doxology that opens the letter to the Ephesians is instructive for our understanding:

> Blessed be the God and Father of our Lord Jesus Christ, who has blessed us *in Christ* with every spiritual blessing in the heavenly places, even as he chose us *in him* before the foundation of the world, that we should be holy and blameless before him. *In love he predestined us for adoption as sons through Jesus Christ,* according to the purpose of his will, to the praise of his glorious grace, with which he has blessed us *in the Beloved.* (Eph. 1:3–6)

Paul uses a term here that is unique to his letters, the Greek word *huiothesia*, which is often translated "adoption." The word is a compound of *huios* ("son") and *thesis* ("placing"), and could be rendered literally as "placed as sons" or "son-placed," although there is some disagreement among biblical scholars about how best to translate it.[51] Although it is commonplace to assume that Paul's use of *huiothesia* is indebted to the practice of adoption in the Roman culture in which he wrote, and so is to be understood on those terms, we believe there is a more tantalizing

---

[48] This is perhaps the most important reason why John identifies the spirit of the antichrist with those who deny that Christ has come *in the flesh* (1 John 2:22; 4:2–3).

[49] By the grace of adoptive sonship, we thus share in what Christ is naturally. Or, as Calvin writes, "We must hold therefore that Christ, being the eternal Son of God, and of the same essence and glory with the Father, assumed our flesh, to communicate to us by right of adoption that which he possessed by nature, namely, to make us sons of God." "John Calvin, to the Pastors of the Town and Territory of Zurich . . . ," *Tracts and Letters*, 2:213.

[50] Edwards, "The Excellency of Christ," *Works*, 19:593, cited in Robert W. Caldwell, *Communion in the Spirit: The Holy Spirit as the Bond of Union in the Theology of Jonathan Edwards*, Studies in Evangelical History and Thought (Eugene, OR: Wipf & Stock, 2007), 132.

[51] See J. M. Scott, "Adoption, Sonship," in *Dictionary of Paul and His Letters*, ed. Gerald F. Hawthorne, Ralph P. Martin, Daniel G. Reid (Downers Grove, IL: IVP, 1993), 15–18 (hereafter *DPHL*).

and theologically salient point at hand. Whether or not Paul was thinking of the prevailing cultural practice, we cannot know for sure. What we do know is that his understanding of adoption is thoroughly Trinitarian and christological; indeed, we might do better to refer to it as adoptive sonship through the Spirit. We are adopted as sons and daughters because we have been incorporated into the Son through the Spirit. The following passage from Galatians is especially telling:

> For in Christ Jesus you are all sons of God, through faith. For as many of you as were baptized into Christ have put on Christ. . . . But when the fullness of time had come, God sent forth his Son, born of woman, born under the law, to redeem those who were under the law, so that we might receive adoption as sons [*huiothesian*]. And because you are sons, God has sent the Spirit of his Son into our hearts, crying, "Abba! Father!" (Gal. 3:26–27; 4:4–6)

The Spirit, whom Paul elsewhere calls the "Spirit of Christ" and the "Spirit of adoption as sons" (Rom. 8:9, 15), is the One who brings us into fellowship with God's Son. In other words, when Paul speaks of Christians as "placed as sons," he has at the forefront of his mind our being placed in *the* Son, Jesus Christ, by the Spirit.[52] This is a clear echo of Jesus's promise about his sending of the Spirit from the Father (John 14), in the fulfillment of which our hearts echo forth the cry of Jesus himself: "*Abba, Father*" (Mark 14:36). Baptized into the Son by the Spirit, we participate in the eternal love that grounds every other love and the eternal life that grounds all other life—the love and life of the Father and the Son in the unity of the Spirit.

Given the tremendous gravity of the blessing of sharing in Christ's sonship, we find it lamentable that, despite its prominence in Scripture and in the history of Christian thought, it has largely disappeared from our soteriological consciousness. This is due, in part, to the prominence in modern evangelical theology of the doctrine of justification, which has become practically synonymous with salvation. When the gift of adoptive sonship is treated in theology texts, which is not a given, it is more often than not

---

[52] Douglas Moo attributes the source of Paul's notion of sonship to the "unique sonship of Christ." *The Epistle to the Romans*, New International Commentary on the New Testament (Grand Rapids: Eerdmans, 1996), 499. He adds, "We, 'the sons of God,' are such by virtue of our belonging to *the* Son of God." Ibid., 505. For an extended discussion of this point, see Johnson, *One with Christ*, chapter 5.

cast under the shadow of justification.[53] The obscuring effect this has on the doctrine of our participation in Christ's sonship is not difficult to predict. When adoption takes on the forensic and imputative character of its more celebrated doctrinal counterpart—stripping it of the utterly unique and astounding relational involvement with the Father, Son, and Spirit that it encompasses—adoption often becomes a mere soteriological appendage or afterthought. Before long, adoption becomes a side benefit of justification, a benefit that ostensibly materializes out of Christ's redemptive work, rather than an actual sharing in the filial relation between the Son of God and his Father that has *eternally* existed.

We think this is a soteriological misstep, agreeing instead with Calvin that "there are innumerable other ways, indeed, in which God daily testifies his fatherly love towards us, but the mark of adoption is justly preferred to them all."[54] We concur also with J. I. Packer, who writes of adoption as "the highest privilege that the gospel offers: higher even than justification. . . . Adoption is higher because of the richer relationship with God that it involves."[55] Perhaps a recovery of the centrality of the doctrine of adoptive sonship depends upon a recovery of the central truth of our salvation: our union with the incarnate Son of God, who is truly, fully, and unreservedly one with his Father, and truly, fully, and unreservedly one with us. Maybe then we will celebrate anew the depth and wonder of the eternal life and love we share in and through Christ: "See what kind of love the Father has given to us, that we should be called children of God; *and so we are.*"

---

[53] Louis Berkhof is representative, but by no means alone, when he refers to adoption as a "positive element of justification," devoting one page to the doctrine in his *Systematic Theology* (1932; repr., Grand Rapids: Eerdmans, 1996), 515–16.

[54] Calvin on John 17:23, *Comm.*, 18/1:185. Here Calvin simply echoes the consensus of the early church fathers, who saw as central to the gospel our sharing of adoption in the communion that the natural Son of God has with his Father. See Donald Fairbairn, *Life in the Trinity: An Introduction to Theology with the Help of the Church Fathers* (Downers Grove, IL: IVP, 2009), 10.

[55] J. I. Packer, *Knowing God*, 20th anniversary ed. (Downers Grove, IL: IVP, 1993), 228.

7

Christ's Body and the Body of Christ

THE INCARNATION AND THE CHURCH

We have argued throughout this book that the incarnation is determinative for all authentically and robustly Christian thought and speech about God. The incarnate Son of God properly constitutes the nexus for all our theological understanding because he is the Way, Truth, and Life of God in our humanity. The full reality of God and the full reality of man intersect in his one person, and so he is the Alpha and Omega of our knowledge of God, the one Mediator between the self-revelation of God and our human words about him. In other words, Jesus Christ is the context and content—the Lord and Savior—of our theology, apart from whom our thinking and speaking about God are reduced to nothing more than the projection of religious fantasies. In short, we have attempted to retrieve and revive the reality that the incarnation of God is *internally and intrinsically* related to the great doctrines of the Christian faith because in Christ alone has our theologizing been reconciled to the truth about God. Further, by holding together the person and work of Christ, we have endeavored to dissolve many of the abstractions and dichotomies that regularly attend contemporary evangelical theology. Any endeavor to reorient theology around the incarnation would be profoundly incomplete, however, if it did not address that most important of internal and intrinsic relations: the relationship between Jesus Christ and his precious bride, the church.

Whenever a fissure appears in the unity of the person and work of Christ, the divide typically extends into our understanding of salvation in such a way that salvation becomes a gift we receive *from* Christ rather than the gift *who is* Christ; gift and Giver are put asunder. This soteriological divide leads to depersonalized objectifications of the gospel in which the person of Christ becomes merely instrumental for his saving work. Before long, we find ourselves clinging to a cross, not to the crucified One himself.

Sadly, these divisions, and the objectifications and abstractions that follow, do not stop there, extending as they usually do into our ecclesiology. One's understanding of the nature of the church is more or less a direct reflection of one's understanding of the nature of salvation. In other words, to speak explicitly about salvation is to speak implicitly about the church. The reverse is also true: to speak explicitly about the church is to speak implicitly about salvation. Ecclesiology is the only context in which soteriology is ultimately intelligible, as salvation makes no sense outside the church. What kind of soteriology do we reflect, then, when we do not posit a direct and internal connection between the church and salvation? What do we reflect about our understanding of salvation when we view the church as "theologically secondary" to, or an "artificial appendage" of, the gospel, rather than in direct relation to that gospel?[1] Perhaps the anemic understanding of the church, and the corresponding apathy for the church, that is prevalent among far too many contemporary evangelicals is the product of a gospel that is functionally non-Trinitarian and nonincarnational, dominated by individualistic, extrinsic, and merely transactional notions of salvation. If modern evangelicalism is not typically known for its robust and vital ecclesiology, it may just be because our soteriology has led us there.

A recurring theme throughout this book has been the assertion that the person of Christ cannot be divorced from his work. Jesus Christ is our salvation because only in him has our humanity been reconciled and joined to God, and so there is no salvation if we are not joined to the One who justified and sanctified our flesh in his life, death, resurrection, and

---

[1] Gary D. Badcock, "The Church as 'Sacrament,'" in *The Community of the Word: Toward an Evangelical Ecclesiology*, ed. Mark Husbands and Daniel J. Treier (Downers Grove, IL: IVP, 2005), 199.

ascension, restoring us to communion with the Father through the Spirit. This understanding of salvation, deeply embedded in the historic Protestant tradition, seamlessly holds together the gospel of Jesus Christ and his necessary counterpart, the church. When we speak thus about salvation, we cannot help but simultaneously speak about the church, for they are one and the same reality. Our union with the incarnate, crucified, resurrected, ascended Son of God is the central fact of our salvation, and it is simultaneously the central fact of the church. To be saved is to belong to Jesus Christ, and to belong to Jesus Christ is to be among the living limbs and organs—members!—of his body. Any divorcing of these two realities can only be artificial. The following passage from T. F. Torrance poignantly illustrates this point:

> Through union with Jesus Christ the church shares in his life and in all that he has done for mankind. Through his birth its members have a new birth and are made members of the new humanity. Through his obedient life and death their sins are forgiven and they are clothed with a new righteousness. Through his resurrection and triumph over the powers of darkness they are freed from the dominion of evil and are made one body with him. Through his ascension the kingdom of heaven is opened to all believers and the church waits for his coming again to fulfill in all humanity the new creation which he has already begun in it. Thus the church finds its life and being not in itself but in Jesus Christ alone, for not only is he the head of the church but he includes the church within his own fullness.[2]

What is striking about this passage is that, although strictly speaking the subject is the church, the subject could just as easily be salvation, because Jesus Christ is the personal reality of both at the same time. The being and life of Christ constitute the being and life of the church. Although for pedagogical purposes we may make a distinction between soteriology and ecclesiology, they are inseparable in the person of Christ. Outside of our participation in the embodied Son of God, we are neither saved nor the body of Christ. Having been included in him, however, we are both. In recognition of this reality, this chapter first explores the ontology of the church—the being of the church in relation to the being of

---

[2] Thomas F. Torrance, *Atonement: The Person and Work of Christ*, ed. Robert T. Walker (Downers Grove, IL: IVP Academic, 2009), 361.

Christ—and upon that foundation, proceeds to give an account of the dominically ordained means by which the church enjoys the living presence of her living Lord.

CHRIST'S BODY AND THE BODY OF CHRIST

The incarnate Son of God is the actual living reality of the church. This is so not because the church is composed of those who, sharing a similar faith, voluntarily gather together to perpetuate his memory, follow his teachings, and continue his mission in his absence. Jesus Christ is the present and living foundation of the church because we have been incorporated into him by faith—that is, united to his body. We are the recipients of his saving blessings and his communion with the Father through the Spirit, continually drawing our life and nourishment from his resurrected and glorified humanity, and thus participating in *his* mission of re-creating and reconciling the world to God.[3] Because the church inheres in him as his body and bride, she participates not only in all that he is as Savior, but also in his active presence to the world: "Thus the church has no independent existence, as if it were anything at all or had any life or power of its own, apart from what is unceasingly communicated to it through its union and communion with Christ who dwells in it by the power of the Spirit and fills it with the eternal life and love of God himself."[4] As with salvation, the existence of the church is not a blessing Christ bestows to us apart from himself, but the blessing of participating in who he is and what he does.

So intimate is this participation that the church is referred to in the most astonishing way, namely, as the body of Jesus Christ. It is greatly regrettable that this phrase has been largely emptied of significance, reduced as it so often is to a figure of speech or illustrative analogy. As the common and peculiarly modern hermeneutical wisdom has it, the phrase "body of Christ" is not much more than a linguistic or poetic device drawn from the realm of physical anatomy, one that the apostle Paul uses to illustrate the cohesiveness and ideal social functioning of the church. The church, in other words, is the body of Christ "so to speak." To put it another way, the

---

[3] The church is not called to do "missions work" for an absent Christ. Rather, as Andrew Purves rightly observes, the church is called to share in the ongoing mission of Jesus Christ, who "is in his own person the mission of God to and for the world, and any sense in which some person or movement might subsequently become identified with the mission of God is possible only on the basis of sharing in Christ's mission." *Reconstructing Pastoral Theology: A Christological Foundation* (Louisville, KY: Westminster John Knox Press, 2004), 23.

[4] Thomas F. Torrance, *Theology in Reconstruction* (Eugene, OR: Wipf & Stock, 1996), 205.

church is to function "as if" she is one physiological or sociopolitical body. The underinterpretation at play here evidences a jettisoning or obscuring of the very meaning of *incarnation*: "to be made into flesh, to be embodied." The whole goal of the Son's enfleshment was the reconstituting of our humanity through his life, death, resurrection, and ascension. The Son of God took our *bodily* existence into union with himself so that through Spirit-wrought faith we might be brought into union with the only Savior there is—the incarnate One. Any union with him that did not include his body and ours would not be redeeming. So unless we wish to succumb to an implicitly docetic soteriology—in which case our saving union with Jesus Christ would be merely *meta*physical—we would do well to delight in what Paul calls the profound mystery of the church's *one-flesh* union with her bridegroom (Eph. 5:31–32).

Recalling what we said in the previous chapter, the mysteries that are uncovered in God's self-revelation in the Son and Word of God are not meant to be explained by imposing a logic alien to that revelation. They are meant to provide the ground for creaturely apprehension and adoration of the transcendent *realities* of God's mighty redemptive acts. In the case of the mystery of the church's union with Christ, this means that we confess and delight in the reality that we are indeed the body of Christ, yet in a way that transcends mere physiological, philosophical, or social explanation. While figures of speech and illustrations are never profound mysteries, and in any case are hardly worth delighting in, the mystery of our bodily participation in Christ is certainly both. It was the confession of this profound and mysterious reality that drove Paul to one of the most breath-taking utterances in Holy Writ: "And [God] put all things under [Christ's] feet and gave him as head over all things to the church, *which is his body, the fullness of him who fills all in all*" (Eph. 1:22–23). Aside from the fact that this passage does not read in any straightforward way as an analogy or illustration, the Greek in this verse is emphatic: *hētis estin to sōma autou*—the church, "which is [indeed, or in truth,] his body."[5]

In 1 Corinthians 6, furthermore, Paul precludes nonbodily interpretations of the church's union with Christ. Incredulous that some in the church

---

[5] See Frank Thielman, *Ephesians*, Baker Exegetical Commentary on the New Testament (Grand Rapids: Baker, 2010), 112. See also Harold Hoehner, *Ephesians: An Exegetical Commentary* (Grand Rapids: Baker Academic, 2002), 290.

were uniting their flesh to prostitutes, Paul directs them to the one-flesh union in which they *already* exist: "Do you not know that your *bodies* are members of Christ?" (v. 15). The Corinthians, it seems, were the historical archetype for all who would spiritualize, sentimentalize, or otherwise underinterpret what it means that the church is indeed the body of Christ. Paul puts an abrupt end to all such interpretive reductions, insisting that the church really is the body of Christ, for no less a reason than that our bodies are joined to his.

Having grasped this, how differently might we interpret what Paul writes just six chapters later? "For just as the body is one and has many members, and all the members of the body, though many, are one body, *so it is with Christ*" (1 Cor. 12:12). Accustomed as we are to reading this as an illustrative analogy that Paul constructed from human anatomy to foster church unity, we badly miss his point. Notice that Paul does not say "so it is with the *church*," which is how an analogy might begin, but rather, "so it is with *Christ*." Christ himself—and his body, which includes ours—is the ground for our unity.[6] Paul is not inventing a convenient analogy for pedagogical purposes, for which purposes some other analogy might have been just as fitting. On the contrary, he is driving home the momentous reality of our bodily union with Jesus Christ, *and from that fundamental reality, he calls the church to function as she really is: his body*. He thus concludes and punctuates his point: "Now you are the body of Christ and individually members of it" (v. 27). Taken as an empty metaphor or pedagogical device, the church as the body of Christ becomes just another sentimentalizing abstraction, a cute yet ultimately vapid phrase that blinds us to the fundamental reality of the church, which is her union with the incarnate Son of God. "The expression *body of Christ*," insists Simon Chan, "is more than a metaphor for some intimate social dynamic between Christ and his church. It is an ontological reality, as Christ is ontologically real."[7] To say that the church is the body of Christ denotes the reality that Christ is not who he is

---

[6] The mystery of Christ's human body transcends our categories, since his body is capable of including our bodies within it without ever ceasing to have its own spatio-temporal existence, and is always infinitely greater than the sum of its churchly parts. As Paul J. Griffiths reminds us, Christian discourse about bodies should begin not with *our* bodies, but with *Christ's* body: "Christ's body is, first, the most real of all bodies: it belongs to the second person of the Holy Trinity. . . . Among other bodies, it is this one that for Christians is of primary and unsurpassable significance, this one in terms of which all other bodies must be thought about and understood." "Christians and the Church," in *Oxford Handbook of Theological Ethics*, ed. Gilbert Meilaender and William Werpehowski (Oxford: Oxford University Press, 2005), 400.

[7] Simon Chan, *Liturgical Theology: The Church as Worshipping Community* (Downers Grove, IL: IVP, 2006), 27.

apart from his church, "which is his body, the fullness of him who fills all in all" (Eph. 1:23). That Christ would so identify himself with his church, John Calvin writes, is our exceedingly great consolation and comfort:

> This is the highest honour of the church, that, until he is united to us, the Son of God reckons himself in some measure imperfect. What consolation is it for us to learn, that, not until we are along with him, does he possess all his parts, or wish to be regarded as complete.[8]

JESUS CHRIST: THE SACRAMENT OF SACRAMENTS

We have so far attempted to show that the incarnation of the Son of God is internally rather than externally related to the existence of the church, which is to say that the being and life of the church derive from the being and life of Jesus Christ. He does not merely provide the conditions under which the church can exist in response to his work and in his absence. The person of Christ is himself the living reality of his church, apart from whom the church would be but a lifeless carcass. The reality of the church is constituted by her union and communion with the incarnate, crucified, resurrected, and ascended Christ. The church, then, is a participant in the glorious mystery of the incarnation, in which the Son of God joined himself to us that we may be joined to him. Christ's body has a direct and internal relation to the body of Christ, and whenever the church has embraced this relation, she has been unmistakably sacramental.

The one, holy, catholic, and apostolic church has been indelibly marked by her sacramental nature precisely because she has embraced the mystery (Greek: *mustērion*; Latin: *sacramentum*) of Jesus Christ. At root, the mystery of Christ is that in him heaven and earth have been joined together; God and man, Creator and creature have been united; the infinite and the finite, the immaterial and the material, the invisible and the visible have become one. A sacrament, as famously defined by Augustine, is a "visible sign of an invisible reality." If there ever was a *sacramentum*, it is surely the incarnate Son of God, who is the ultimate visible sign (in our flesh and blood) of the ultimate invisible reality (God). God is truly present in the body and blood of Jesus. The original sacramental mystery is Jesus himself, "the image of the invisible God" (Col. 1:15). The Christian church is

---

[8] Calvin on Eph. 1:23, *Comm.*, 21/1:218.

inherently sacramental because we confess the Lord Jesus Christ, who is the one great Mystery and Sacrament of the universe, through whom all things were created and *in whom* all things hold together (Col. 1:16–17). The sacramental nature of the church is not an outmoded vestige of a premodern worldview needing the intellectual liberation that may come from bending the knee to either modern rationalism or postmodern skepticism. The church is sacramental because her life and salvation are entirely dependent upon the union in Jesus Christ of the visible and the invisible, of man and God. The sacraments, themselves ordained and given by the Lord, are the visible signs assuring us that we are joined to him, the one Sacrament and Mystery of our salvation.

To refer to Christ as the "mystery" of our salvation is no imaginative wordplay. This word is employed to reflect the biblical teaching that the revelation of the incarnate Son of God is exactly that, a *mustērion*. Paul uses this Greek term twenty-one times in his letters, and although the term is multilayered, it has as its essential reference the revelation of the person and work of Jesus Christ. For Paul, the mystery of Christ is nothing less than the content of the gospel, the gospel that he was commissioned by Christ himself to proclaim, and for which he suffered imprisonment (Col. 4:3; Eph. 6:19–20). To briefly define what Paul means by this term, we note the following. First and foremost, the mystery is Jesus Christ himself, whom Paul calls "God's mystery" (Col. 2:2). As the esteemed New Testament scholar Peter T. O'Brien notes: "Christ is the starting point for a true understanding of the notion of 'mystery' in [Ephesians], as elsewhere in Paul. There are not a number of 'mysteries' with limited applications, but one supreme 'mystery' with a number of applications."[9] So the essential reality of the mystery is none other than Jesus Christ. The applications of which O'Brien speaks necessarily include: (1) the indwelling of Christ in his people, or what Paul calls the "riches of the glory of this mystery, which is *Christ in you*, the hope of glory" (Col. 1:27); (2) the resultant mystery of those gathered together in him, the mystery of the body and bride of Christ (Eph. 3:4–7; 5:32); and (3) the mystery of God's plan to unite everything in heaven and earth in Jesus Christ (Eph. 1:9–10; Col. 1:15–20). Thus, all the applications or aspects of the one great mystery of Jesus Christ—salvation, the church, and the reconciliation of the cosmos—are brought together in

---

[9] Peter T. O'Brien, "Mystery," in *DPHL*, 623.

his person.[10] In short, Jesus is the mystery of God's comprehensive purpose to reconcile the world to himself.

When the highly influential Latin Vulgate (late fourth/early fifth centuries) translated Paul's Greek *musterion* into the Latin *sacramentum*, the use of the term *sacrament* was enshrined forevermore in Christian vocabulary. We should not allow disputes that have subsequently arisen regarding the sacraments to obscure the much more significant point here: the mystery of the gospel is woven into the scriptural narrative, and the substance of that mystery is Jesus Christ himself. Thus, the church belongs to that mystery and celebrates his mysteries. Calvin, who heartily accepted Augustine's definition of sacrament, writes the following about the sacraments:

> I say that Christ is the matter or (if you prefer) the substance of the sacraments; for in him they have all their firmness, and they do not promise anything apart from him.[11]

Christ is himself the "substance" of the sacraments because he ordained them and gave them to us to bring us to participation in *the* Sacrament, apart from whom the sacraments would be nothing but empty symbols. Jesus is both their substance and *goal*. The sacraments are, in other words, visible signs of the invisible reality of our union with Jesus Christ, of whom Leonard Vander Zee says:

> Christ is the quintessential sacrament, the visible sign of the invisible grace of God. The sacraments Christ instituted are a means God uses to unite us with him and seal all the promises of his grace to us. It is a divinely ordered way for us to share in the reality accomplished for us in Christ.[12]

Many modern evangelicals are reticent to embrace a robust sacramental theology. Regrettably, however, that reticence distances them not only from the historic Christian church but also from the historic evangelical tradition. If modern evangelicals have become largely nonsacramental in

---

[10] This strongly suggests that soteriology, ecclesiology, and cosmology are properly grounded in christology, a suggestion that most Christian theologians would not explicitly deny, though few explicitly advance.

[11] *Inst.*, 4.14.16. Martin Luther writes provocatively of Jesus Christ as the "one single sacrament" with "three sacramental signs." *Babylonian Captivity of the Church* (1520), in *LW*, 36:18. See Gary D. Badcock, *The House Where God Lives: The Doctrine of the Church* (Grand Rapids: Eerdmans, 2009), 268.

[12] Leonard J. Vander Zee, *Christ, Baptism and the Lord's Supper: Recovering the Sacraments for Evangelical Worship* (Downers Grove, IL: IVP Academic, 2004), 51.

thought and churchly practice, it may be because we have forgotten our confession of the ultimate visible sign of the ultimate invisible reality, failing to embrace the Christ-mystery behind the sacraments. The incarnation proves that God does indeed savingly join himself to us through created, physical, material means, namely, the humanity of his Son. And it is none other than the Son who gives us the holy mysteries of word, water, bread, and wine to bring us the salvation that he is. It is to these holy mysteries of the Son that we now turn.

THE PREACHED WORD AND THE INCARNATE WORD

It is common knowledge that Protestants, following Martin Luther and Calvin, have maintained that there are two Christ-ordained sacraments of the church: baptism and the Lord's Supper. What is not so commonly known is that the Reformers, without calling it a sacrament as such, believed that preaching is a deeply sacramental act in which we encounter the living Christ and receive him through faith. In the words of Luther, "To preach the gospel is nothing else than Christ's coming to us or bringing us to him."[13] The preaching of the word of God, for our Protestant forebears, was not so much preaching *about* the word of God, but, more important, it was the preaching *of* the Word himself—Christ truly present in his word. Christ is not only the object of the preaching, but also its living and speaking subject. Thus, Calvin maintains that the preaching of the gospel, indeed the whole of the church's gospel ministry, is the self-communication and reception of Jesus Christ:

> Just as God has set all fullness of life in Jesus, in order to communicate it to us by means of him, so he has ordained his Word as the instrument by which Jesus Christ, with all his benefits, is dispensed to us.[14]

> The end of the whole gospel ministry is that God, the fountain of all felicity, communicate Christ to us who are disunited by sin and hence ruined, that we may from him enjoy eternal life; that in a word all heav-

---

[13] Cited in Paul D. L. Avis, *The Church in the Theology of the Reformers* (1981; repr., Eugene, OR: Wipf & Stock, 2002), 89. Cf. Luther: "Furthermore, Christ Himself is present when I preach. . . . For Christ is present and makes my words come true." "Sermon on the Gospel of St. John 8:28," in *LW*, 23:386.

[14] John Calvin, *Calvin: Theological Treatises*, trans. with introduction and notes by J. K. S. Reid, Library of Christian Classics, vol. 22 (Philadelphia: Westminster, 1954), 143.

enly treasures be so applied to us that they be no less ours than Christ's himself.[15]

According to Calvin, God has ordained the preached word as a means through which we receive Christ. We might even say that for the Reformers, the preaching of the word is, to recall Augustine, a "visible [and audible] sign of an invisible reality [the living, speaking Christ]."

In their insistence on the sacramental nature of preaching—the real presence of Christ in his word—the Reformers were on faithful exegetical ground. As we showed in chapter 6, numerous passages in Scripture bear witness to this mystery. Especially worth recalling is the significance of Jesus's high-priestly ministration on the night of his betrayal, when he lifted his disciples in prayer before his Father, assuring them that he would be present *to and in* all those who would receive their word (John 17:20–23). Although Paul was not present on this sublime occasion, he, too, learned from Christ that the authority for, and substance of, his preaching was the living Word of God himself: "And we also thank God constantly for this, that when you received the word of God, which you heard from us, you accepted it not as the word of men, but as what it really is, the word of God, which is at work in you believers" (1 Thess. 2:13; cf. Rom. 10:14; 2 Cor. 13:3; Gal. 3:1; Eph. 1:13; 4:21).[16]

In addition to the sufficiently clear biblical testimony to the real presence of Christ in his word, there is an underlying soteriological assumption of great import, which we state as a series of questions: If Christ were not truly present in the gospel that bears witness to him, how would anyone ever be saved? In what sense could the gospel be the "power of God for salvation to everyone who believes" (Rom. 1:16) if the Savior were not truly present through that gospel? Are sinners saved through the preaching of the gospel merely because they cognitively assent to particular historic, redemptive "truths" proclaimed therein, or is the preaching of the gospel a *means* through which the living, present Christ binds us to himself? At stake here is an entire understanding of the nature of salvation. If our theology of preaching is nonsacramental—wherein preaching is understood as proclamation *about* Christ, but not the means through which he is savingly

---

[15] Ibid., 171.

[16] Even translations tend to obscure the point that Christ is the present subject who speaks through his word. For elaboration on this point, see chapter 6, fn. 21.

present—our soteriology will be only indirectly related to his person. It will inevitably reflect the ideational, abstract, and transactional modes of thought germane to it. If, on the other hand, the preaching of the word is understood as a means through which we encounter and receive the living, incarnate Word himself, then our soteriology will be directly related to his person. It will reflect the relational, concrete, and participatory modes of thought germane to it.

If evangelicals are to recover the sacramental nature of preaching, we will have to make an all-important distinction in our understanding of the word of God. That distinction is between (1) the word of God *inscripturated and proclaimed* and (2) the Word of God *incarnate*. The former refers to the written word, the Bible, and the preaching of that word. The latter refers to the eternal and living Son of God, who has existed with and as God from the very beginning, through whom all things (including the Bible and preaching) came into being, and who became flesh (John 1:1–3, 14). The distinction is crucial, not only for how we conceive of salvation and the nature of preaching, but also in order to avoid the biblicism, and perhaps even the bibliolatry, that results from a facile identification of the Bible with the Lord Jesus. To be sure, we must never separate Christ *from* his written word, from whom it derives its authority; but neither can we collapse Christ *into* his word, as if the book were itself the mediator between God and man.

Perhaps the surest and clearest way to express this point is to say that the written word of God and the preaching of that word is a means, not an end. The inscripturated word is a God-ordained *means* for which communion with the incarnate Son and Word of God is the *end*. As C. S. Lewis remarks: "It is Christ himself, not the Bible, who is the true Word of God. The Bible, read in the right spirit, and with the guidance of good teachers, will bring us to him."[17] To say this in other words, Jesus Christ is himself the living essence and Word behind and above the written and preached word that testifies to him. The function of the written and preached word—and, as we shall see, the visible words of water, bread, and wine that accompany it—is to bring us into the reality of Jesus Christ, who is its living substance. Abstracted from the true presence of Christ, the written and preached word

---

[17] C. S. Lewis, *Letters of C. S. Lewis*, ed. Walter Hooper (1993; repr., Harvest Books, 2003), 247, cited in Christian Smith, *The Bible Made Impossible: Why Biblicism Is Not a Truly Evangelical Reading of Scripture* (Grand Rapids: Brazos, 2012), 117.

would be emptied of divine, redemptive reality, relegated to merely historical and doctrinal significance. By contrast, when we mark the distinction
between the written and preached word and the Word incarnate, we allow
the former to function as intended—as divinely ordained means through
which we encounter and come to experience God in Christ. As Jesus made
clear, Scripture has no independent life, as if we might seek and know God
there apart from his living and active Word and Son: "You search the Scriptures because you think that in them you have eternal life; and it is they that
bear witness about me, yet you refuse to come *to me* that you may have life"
(John 5:39–40). The same goes for the apostolic proclamation of the Word:
"The one who hears you hears me, and the one who rejects you rejects me"
(Luke 10:16).

Because the Son of God is the living essence of the word of God *as the
Word*, Jesus is not a word of God among other words of God—as Moses
and Elijah were keenly aware (Luke 9:29–33; 24:27)[18]—but is himself the living and saving Word of God, the end to which every other word of God can
only be a means. Herein lies the ultimate authority and splendor of Scripture and its proclamation: they are divinely appointed and inspired ways in
which God makes himself known by literally communicating himself to us
through and in his Son, by the Spirit. These ways function sacramentally
in service to *the Way*, bringing us to share in the life-giving presence of the
Word of God in our flesh.[19] According to Andrew Purves, the implications
for the significance of the sermon are startling: "Through our union with
Christ, whereby we share in the life of Jesus Christ, the sermon becomes a
present form of the incarnation, an enfleshment in speech today of the once
historical and always eternal and living one Word of God. The sermon *is*
the Word of God."[20]

When the eternal Son and Word of God became incarnate, he came
preaching the good news of the reconciliation between God and man that
he is. In anticipation of his death, resurrection, and ascension, he entrusted

---

[18] The encounter between Moses and Elijah and the transfigured Christ is pregnant with bibliological significance. Here we have the Law and Prophets represented in conversation with the One to whom they bear
witness.

[19] Geoffrey Bromiley succinctly states the relationship between the forms of the word of God as follows: "The
proclaimed Word has a valid ministry . . . only insofar as it serves the incarnate Word in accordance with the
written Word and in exposition and application of it." "The Ministry of the Word of God," in *Incarnational
Ministry: The Presence of Christ in Church, Society, and Family*, ed. Christian D. Kettler and Todd H. Speidell
(1990; repr. Eugene, OR: Wipf & Stock, 2009), 90.

[20] Purves, *Reconstructing Pastoral Theology*, 157.

that preaching to the apostles and the church apostolic. He did this not so that the church might proclaim the Word in his absence, but so that, through the Spirit, he would be continuously present in and as that Word was preached. Whatever elegance, learnedness, or exegetical and technical sophistication the preaching of the word may otherwise possess, it relies ultimately on its *being possessed by Christ*. Preaching involves the preacher being mastered by the Word much more than it does him being master of the word. As Karl Barth forcefully asserts, Christ ever remains the Lord of his revelation: "He speaks for Himself whenever He is spoken of and His story is told and heard. It is not He that needs proclamation but proclamation that needs Him."[21] Absent Christ's real presence, what function could the inscripturated, proclaimed word of God have in the church other than to serve as the perpetual recollection and mental appropriation of his saving deeds, to entice hearers to sentimental reflection, or to impart exegetical insights? As we have shown, there are good reasons to insist on more than this. And insist we should, for as Dietrich Bonhoeffer proclaims, without the real presence of Christ in his word, the church is broken:

> The whole Christ is present in preaching, humiliated and exalted. His presence is not the power of the congregation or its objective spirit, out of which the preaching is made, but his existence as preaching. If this were not so, preaching could not have had that prominent place which the Reformation insisted upon. . . . It is the form of the present Christ to which we are bound and to which we must hold. If the complete Christ is not in the preaching, then the Church is broken.[22]

The Visible Words and the Incarnate Word

The incarnation of the Son of God determines and defines the sacramental nature, thinking, and practice of the church. It is a fundamental tenet of the church historic that in the person of Jesus Christ we encounter the saving mystery-sacrament of the union of God and man, of the uncreated and the created, of the invisible and visible. This is why John Williamson Nevin is certainly right to state, "The sacramental question falls back at once upon the Christological question; which again lies at the foundation

---

[21] Karl Barth, *Church Dogmatics*, IV/1, ed. G. W. Bromiley and T. F. Torrance, trans. G. W. Bromiley (Peabody, MA: Hendrickson, 2010), 227.

[22] Dietrich Bonhoeffer, *Christ the Center*, trans. Edwin H. Robertson (New York: Harper & Row, 1978), 51–52.

of the whole idea of the church, and forms the *only* basis of an earnest and truly scientific theology in any direction."[23] The implication that looms in this statement is that nonsacramental thinking is simply non-Christian, primarily because Christian thinking is governed by the mystery of God incarnate. This is, of course, the thesis that we have been advancing throughout this book, and that we have extended into this chapter on the church. It is now time to bring this thesis to bear specifically on what Protestants have always maintained are the two sacraments of the church, baptism and the Lord's Supper.

As the Reformers rightly insisted over against the medieval Roman church, these two physical and visible signs—one of water, the other of bread and wine—were alone instituted by the Word himself as the sacramental mysteries of the gospel.[24] They are, to use a double entendre, the sacraments of the Word. That is, they are sacraments for which the *primary* referent is the Word become flesh, constituting as he does the living reality of the signs; and for which the secondary referent is the apostolic witness to Christ, that is, the preached and written word. Baptism and the Lord's Supper are, in other words, grounded in the incarnate Word and informed by the inscripturated and preached word. Indeed, because it is only and ever in the gospel that Christ gives himself to be received, the Reformers maintained that the administration of water, bread, and wine are always to be accompanied by the preaching of that gospel, for apart from it they would be empty signs. The sacraments are not meant to hang in midair, as it were, but to be interpreted by, and to interpret, the nature of the gospel, which is nothing other than our union with the incarnate Savior. Alongside the audible words of the gospel stand the visible, tangible, edible words of the gospel—water, bread, and wine. They impress into our hearts and minds, and right into our bodily existence, the Word of God himself.

---

[23] John Williamson Nevin, "Dr. Hodge on the Mystical Presence," *Weekly Messenger of the German Reformed Church* 13, no. 7 (May 24, 1848), cited in *Coena Mystica: Debating Reformed Eucharistic Theology*, ed. Linden J. DeBie, The Mercersburg Theology Study Series, vol. 2 (Eugene, OR: Wipf & Stock, 2013), 6. Nevin tried unsuccessfully to convince the eminent nineteenth-century Princeton theologian Charles Hodge of this fact. His failure explains, in part, the ensuing nonsacramental cast of modern evangelicalism.

[24] The Reformers rejected the sacramental status of the additional five rites recognized by the Roman church—confirmation, penance, holy orders, marriage, and anointing of the sick. They did so on the scriptural grounds that Christ did not ordain these as sacraments of the church, *per se*, not because they did not think of them as highly significant or even possessing a sacramental nature of a kind. On marriage, for instance, see chapter 8.

Baptism

How is the water of baptism a sacrament of the gospel? It is a visible sign of the invisible reality of our immersion (Greek: *baptisma*) into Jesus Christ and his death and resurrection. Baptism is God's gift to us in which we tangibly experience what it means that we are saved. It is the initiatory sacrament of the church by which God identifies us with his Son through the Spirit; it tells us *who* we are by way of telling us *whose* we are. Baptism does this in at least three inseparably related ways.

First, baptism is performed "in the name of the Father and of the Son and of the Holy Spirit" (Matt. 28:19). There is no baptism into Christ that does not have as its consequence and end immersion into his life with the Father through the Spirit. Indeed, this is the purpose of the atoning life, death, and resurrection of Christ: our participation in the life and love he shares with the other two divine persons. Thus, baptism is a thoroughly Trinitarian affair, bringing us to share in the life of the Trinity by our sharing in Jesus Christ. Of special importance in this regard is the baptism of Christ himself, accompanied as it was by the power and presence of the Spirit and his loving Father's commendation, "This is my beloved Son, with whom I am well pleased" (Matt. 3:17). This event and these words were not for him alone, but belong to all those baptized into the Son by the Spirit. Every true Christian baptism is a sharing in the baptism Jesus underwent in the Jordan, a baptism that finally terminated in his death and resurrection; this sharing is so intimate that we too become the Father's beloved children through the Spirit. Our baptisms—or *christenings*, to use the beautiful and wise word of the church, which means "immersion into Christ"—are to be understood in the same way as the rest of our saving relations to him, in vicarious and internal relation to his person and work. Jesus underwent baptism to "fulfill all righteousness" (Matt. 3:15). This was an act in which Jesus consecrated our fallen humanity—the only kind of humanity that needs baptizing—in vicarious identification with us so that we might come to share in his once-for-all baptism by the Spirit. Thus, the relation between his baptism and ours is not to be understood in an external or exemplary way, as if our baptism could add anything to his, but by way of our direct, personal participation in his one act of sanctifying and justifying our humanity that began in the Jordan River and concluded in his death and resurrection.

Second, baptism serves as a visible and tangible sign of the reality of our incorporation into Christ's atoning death and resurrection. Commonly in Scripture, water signifies both death and life, a signification fulfilled in our baptism into Christ. Placed under the water, we are given the vivid, tangible expression of our participation in Christ's substitutionary death: the death of our old, sinful humanity. In Vander Zee's words, "The baptismal font becomes our coffin."[25] Raised out of the watery tomb, we are given the vivid, tangible expression of our participation in Christ's substitutionary resurrection: the resurrection of our new, holy humanity:

> Do you not know that all of us who have been baptized into Christ Jesus were baptized into his death? We were buried therefore with him by baptism into death, in order that, just as Christ was raised from the dead by the glory of the Father, we too might walk in newness of life. For if we have been united with him in a death like his, we shall certainly be united with him in a resurrection like his. (Rom. 6:3–5)

Baptism is the sacrament of our new crucified and resurrected identity in Christ Jesus. Baptized into his death, we share in the crucifixion and burial of our alienated, unholy, and condemned humanity. Baptized simultaneously into his resurrection, we share in the new life of his reconciled, sanctified, and justified humanity. To use once-familiar theological terminology, the waters of baptism signify the reality of our mortification and vivification in Christ—the "making dead" of our nature enslaved to sin, and the "making alive" of our new nature enslaved to righteousness. This is no doubt the reason why baptism is so closely associated with the forgiveness of sins in Scripture, the water picturing the cleansing and purifying that takes place as we are included into Christ. It is, further, the reason why baptism is also associated closely with our justification, sanctification, and adoption in him (1 Cor. 6:11; Gal. 3:26–27), for all of these benefits are the result of our immersion into the incarnate Son of God.

Third, baptism serves as the visible sign of the reality of the church, which is Christ's body. Baptism is a communal reality, not only and primarily because it signifies our participation in the communion of the Father, Son, and Spirit, but also because it identifies us with all those who participate in that same reality. As Paul writes, "For just as the body is one

---

[25] Vander Zee, *Christ, Baptism, and the Lord's Supper*, 108.

and has many members, and all the members of the body, though many, are one body, *so it is with Christ.* For in one Spirit we were all baptized into one body—Jews or Greeks, slaves or free—and all were made to drink of one Spirit" (1 Cor. 12:12–13). As a mystery of our incorporation into Christ, baptism constitutes a rejection of individualistic notions of salvation, declaring to us that salvation and the church are inseparable realities cohering in the person of Jesus Christ. There is no baptism into Christ that is not at the same time baptism into his body, the church, which is his fullness. Baptism is a sacrament of our new identity as the body and bride of Christ.

The Lord's Supper

Modern evangelicals tend to have an ambivalent relationship with the theological tradition from which they came. On the one hand, evangelicals tend to see Reformers such as Luther and Calvin as theological allies with respect to their teaching on salvation, particularly on doctrines such as the utter sufficiency of the atoning death of Christ or justification by faith alone, among others. On the other hand, many evangelicals view the Reformers with a sense of theological alienation when it comes to their teaching on the Lord's Supper. Luther's and Calvin's affirmation of the real presence of the body and blood of Christ in the sacrament of the Supper is often met with curiosity, if not bewilderment and incredulity, by their modern-day progeny. This ambivalence on the part of modern evangelicals with respect to Reformation theology carries with it a deep irony given that the Reformers viewed their teaching on salvation and the Lord's Supper as entirely harmonious and utterly inseparable. To illustrate this irony, we include an oft-quoted passage from Calvin's *Institutes of the Christian Religion,* in which he describes the saving relation believers have with Christ:

> This is the wonderful exchange which, out of his measureless benevolence, Jesus Christ has made with us; that, becoming Son of man with us, he has made us sons of God with him; that, by his descent to earth, he has prepared an ascent to heaven for us; that, by taking on our mortality, he has conferred his immortality upon us; that, accepting our weakness, he has strengthened us by his power; that, receiving our poverty unto himself, he has transferred his wealth to us; that, taking

the weight of our iniquity upon himself (which oppressed us), he has clothed us with his righteousness.[26]

What may come as a surprise to many evangelicals, who happily and rightly embrace the rich soteriology so beautifully expressed here, is that this passage is found not in Calvin's explication of the atoning death and resurrection of Christ, nor in his explication of the benefits of justification by faith. This passage is actually located in his chapter on the Lord's Supper, a chapter, we might add, in which he affirms resolutely and repeatedly the believer's sacramental participation in the true body and blood of Jesus Christ—the real presence of Christ in the Supper. Calvin held together what many of his soteriological heirs put asunder.

This apparent dilemma provokes the following questions: Is Calvin's understanding of the Lord's Supper simply a *non sequitur* in relation to his understanding of the gospel? Or, to ask it another way, what exactly is the significance of the fact that evangelicals tend to acknowledge their debt to Calvin and Luther with respect to the meaning of the gospel, yet distance themselves with respect to the meaning of the Supper?[27] Is this merely a peripheral matter? The answer, we believe, lies ultimately in how our evangelical forebears understood the relation between the gospel and the incarnation—that is, the relation between salvation and the body and blood of the Son of God.

For both Reformers, there is quite simply no salvation for sinners apart from our sharing in the humanity of God the Son. They affirmed quite literally what all evangelicals affirm more or less figuratively: there is no salvation outside of Jesus Christ. Thus, when they spoke specifically of the true presence of Christ himself in the Supper, they were affirming what they had already claimed about his presence in the gospel more generally. Just as Christ is truly present to save us in our initial reception of him in the preaching of the gospel, so he is continually present in the visible gospel of the Supper to grow us into ever-increasing intimacy with him. Because the Reformers understood the bread and wine as a sacrament of our union with the incarnate Savior, the Supper was, for them, nothing less or other than

---

[26] *Inst.*, 4.17.2.

[27] Although Luther's and Calvin's views can be differentiated as to the *manner* in which one receives the true body and blood of Christ in the sacrament of the Lord's Supper, both affirmed the *reality* of that reception. They shared a studied opposition to Ulrich Zwingli, whose views on the Lord's Supper they feared would eventually dissolve into mere memorialism.

the gospel made tangible and edible; the Supper, in other words, exegeted and internalized the gospel. The Reformers' insistence on the real presence of Christ in the Supper was simply an application of their understanding of salvation, never less and nothing more. Just as surely as Christ was present to us as we first came to know him, so he is continually present to nourish and sustain our knowing of him. The Supper is the mystery of that ongoing salvation.

But why, exactly, did the Reformers insist on the real presence of Christ's flesh and blood, whether in our initial salvation or in our ongoing salvation? As Calvin understood it, Christ's flesh and blood (his humanity) is the location of our salvation—there is no salvation available anywhere else. Thomas Davis captures well Calvin's thought on this matter:

> [W]hen Calvin spoke of partaking of Christ, full body-and-blood Communion, he literally meant participation in a real and true human body. To speak of eating the body of Christ meant for Calvin that the Christian is nourished by and gains union with a real human body. There is, literally, a fleshly body involved in the Christian's spirit feeding on Christ. . . . That is why Calvin insisted on substantial partaking of the body of Christ in the Eucharist, for it is the human body of Christ that is the accommodated instrument of God's salvation. It is the thing by which righteousness comes to believers.[28]

There is no salvation *apart* from Jesus Christ, in other words, because salvation is only and ever *in* Jesus Christ. Salvation requires our participation in his crucified and resurrected humanity, because in him our humanity is sanctified, justified, re-created, and brought into fellowship with the Father. "Unless you eat the flesh of the Son of Man and drink his blood, you have no life in you" (John 6:53). To say it another way, Jesus Christ is himself our salvation.

Calvin's understanding of the Lord's Supper provides a biblically rich, evangelically faithful resource for those willing to affirm that salvation means nothing less than being joined to the only Christ there is: the flesh-and-blood Son of God. What follows are the key elements of Calvin's understanding especially suited to this purpose:

---

[28] Thomas J. Davis, *This Is My Body: The Presence of Christ in Reformation Thought* (Grand Rapids: Baker, 2008), 87.

1. The Lord's Supper is not something other than the gospel, but rather that same gospel in physical, tangible, edible form. The visible word of the Supper has the same purpose and the same substance as the written and preached word: communion with the living Word, Jesus Christ. The bread and wine are together a material way in which God accommodates himself to our physical, creaturely existence (the supreme way being the incarnation). Because our union with Jesus Christ remains a mystery to us, Calvin avers, God employs means especially suited to impress upon our hearts and minds its reality: "For this reason, the Lord instituted for us his Supper, in order to sign and seal in our consciences *the promises contained in the gospel concerning our being made partakers of his flesh and blood.*"[29] The bread and wine bring near to us the meaning of our salvation and, because Jesus is always present in the gospel, we continue to experience the ongoing benefits of his real presence in this gospel feast.

2. In the Supper, our partaking of the life-giving flesh and blood of Jesus Christ takes place by the power of the Spirit and through faith. By insisting that we partake of Christ by the Holy Spirit, Calvin was simply emphasizing what Jesus teaches us in Scripture: the Spirit proceeds to us from the Father and the Son in order that Christ may dwell in us (John 14:16–20; 16:12–15; 17:20–26; Rom. 8:9–11). Thus, it is entirely inadequate to conceive of the gospel Supper as a merely *Spirit*ual feast, disregarding the humanity of the Savior: "I am not satisfied with those persons who, recognizing that we have some communion with Christ, when they would show what it is, make us partakers of the Spirit only, omitting mention of flesh and blood."[30] Indeed, the role of the Spirit in the Supper is identical with his role in salvation elsewhere—to mediate to us the presence of the incarnate Savior. It follows, then, that it is also unsatisfactory to conceive of the Supper as a merely *spiritual* exercise, as if its meaning terminated upon the religious sentimentality of the communicant. Far from it! Whatever sentimentality may otherwise be involved, the reality of the Supper is the present and living Lord himself. By insisting that we partake of Christ by

[29] Calvin, "Short Treatise on the Holy Supper," in *Calvin: Theological Treatises*, 144 (emphasis added). Davis explains, "Since union with Christ, union with not just his spirit but also his body, constituted the essence of the Christian life for Calvin, then it is the Sacrament of the Eucharist that most assures the believer that such a union takes place." *This Is My Body*, 88.

[30] *Inst.*, 4.17.7. In the words of Julie Canlis: "Here Calvin is not allowing the Spirit to be the scapegoat for a thoroughly unsatisfactory doctrine of presence. The Spirit is not a spiritualized mode of Christ; rather, the Spirit is the person in whom we now have access to the embodied Jesus." *Calvin's Ladder: A Spiritual Theology of Ascent and Ascension* (Grand Rapids: Eerdmans, 2010), 117.

faith, Calvin was emphasizing the scriptural axiom that faith is the means through, in, and by which we receive Jesus Christ who is our life, "that by believing you may have life in his name" (John 20:31).[31] By Spirit-wrought faith, the believer receives the object of her faith, the One who is offered to her in bread and wine. We need to studiously avoid the notion that the presence of Christ in the Supper is no more than the faith-filled recollection of Christ's work, as if he were present only to the believer's memory:

> For there are some who define the eating of Christ's flesh and the drinking of his blood as, in one word, nothing but to believe in Christ. But it seems to me that Christ meant to teach something more definite and more elevated. . . . It is that we are quickened by the true partaking of him; and he has therefore designated this partaking by the words "eating" and "drinking," in order that no one should think that the life we receive from him is received by mere knowledge.[32]

In short, the gift of the gospel—and therefore the gospel Supper—is none other than the real presence of the incarnate Son of God. Though he is truly present by the Spirit, he is by no means replaced by the Spirit (his or ours). And though he is truly present through faith, his presence cannot be reduced to our faith experience. Christ offers *himself* to us in the visible elements of bread and wine, and through Spirit-wrought faith in the promise of his flesh and blood, we truly receive what he gives.

Calvin was the first to admit that the mystery of Christ's real presence in the Supper exceeds our powers of thought and speech, derivative as it is of the mysteries that precede and define it—the Trinity, the incarnation, and the church. Thus, in consideration of the Supper, he was led neither to rational explication or philosophical speculation, but instead to doxological adoration:

> For, whenever this matter is discussed, when I have tried to say all, I feel that I have as yet said little in proportion to its worth. And although my mind can think beyond what my tongue can utter, yet even my mind is conquered and overwhelmed by the greatness of the thing. Therefore,

---

[31] The reader may consult the previous chapter for extended comment on the role of the Spirit, and of faith, in our union with Christ.
[32] *Inst.*, 4.17.5.

nothing remains but to break forth in wonder at this mystery, which plainly neither the mind is able to conceive nor the tongue to express.[33]

Calvin's account of the Supper, which is theologically rich precisely because it is biblically faithful, manifests a deep soteriological and sacramental coherence. The mystery of our union with Christ that lies at the heart of the gospel resides similarly in the mystery of his presence in the Supper. The mystery is one and the same. Calvin offers modern evangelicals a resource, deep within our rich tradition, by which we may come to believe once again that Christ is truly and really present to his church as our one source of life and salvation. As those who partake of bread and wine, we most assuredly do so "in remembrance of" Christ and his work (1 Cor. 11:24–26). But shall we then forget that what is offered there is the body and blood of Christ? "The cup of blessing that we bless, is it not a participation in the blood of Christ? The bread that we break, is it not a participation in the body of Christ?" (10:16).

THE GREAT NEED OF THE CHURCH

"There is no more urgent need in our churches today," writes J. B. Torrance, "than to recover the Trinitarian nature of grace—that it is by grace alone, through the gift of Jesus Christ in the Spirit, that we can enter into and live a life of communion with God our Father."[34] Torrance's concern was that far too many churches were becoming soteriologically and, therefore, ecclesiologically and functionally non-Trinitarian. When the church loses sight of the central reality of the gospel, that the Son of God became incarnate so that through his life, death, resurrection, and ascension we may share in his communion with the Father through the Spirit, she inevitably suffers a crisis of identity and worship. In the place of Christ's ongoing mediation between God and man in his one person—in which he continually brings us into the life and love of the Father by the Spirit through his real presence in word and sacrament—the church is tempted to substitute its own activity and mission. We may come to believe, after all, that the church exists to worship God and to carry out his mission to the world in the absence of Jesus Christ, as if the church exists merely as a *response to* his mediation and mission, rather than as a *participant*

---

[33] Ibid., 4.17.7.
[34] James B. Torrance, *Worship, Community and the Triune God of Grace* (Downers Grove, IL: IVP Academic, 1996), 59.

in the one and only mediation and mission of Christ. If we may put it so frankly, the Pelagian and semi-Pelagian notions we strenuously avoid in our soteriology may enter through a back door into our ecclesiology when the life of the church is perceived more as an *imitatio Christi* than as a *participatio Christi*. We would do well to keep in mind that Christ's mediation for, and mission to, the world did not cease with his ascension to the Father, but is in fact realized in the church through his real presence by the Spirit. Jesus did not bring the church into existence to do what he can no longer do in his absence, but so that he might be present through and in the church as her existence, mediator, and mission. Thus, it is not Jesus who needs the present church, but the church who needs Christ present.[35]

We have labored to show that the incarnation of God the Son determines and defines the nature of the church. At our theological best, Christians have recognized that our understandings of salvation and the church are predicated upon our understanding of the person of Christ—soteriology and ecclesiology are implications of christology, not the other way around. The weightiest of all theological questions—"Who do you say that I am?"—requires a biblically, historically, and theologically faithful answer before we proceed to any others. When this precedence is given to the person of Christ, we are sure to find that the answers to our questions about salvation and the church are given only in him. Who is Jesus Christ? He is none other than God the Son incarnate, the one Mediator between God and man, who, having taken residence in our flesh and blood, sanctifies and justifies our humanity in his life, death, resurrection, and ascension, so that by the Spirit we may share in his eternal life with the Father. This is the reality of who Jesus Christ is, so this is the reality of the gospel and of the church. The church is none other than his body, joined in one flesh with him as his bride by the Spirit, constituted by that union and participant in every one of its blessings. She has and draws her life from the incarnate Son and Word of God, who is alone the continual source of her life and salvation by his real presence in word and sacrament.

The *evangelion* of Jesus Christ, which is identical not merely with what he did but with who he is, is the only reality that can provide a rich and deep, not least *evangelical*, account of the essence of the church. However, our

---

[35] This phrase is adapted from Purves's advice to pastors: "It is not Jesus Christ who needs pastoral work, it is pastoral work that needs Jesus Christ." *Reconstructing Pastoral Theology*, xvi.

ecclesiology will go only as far as our christology and soteriology will allow. Superficial and rather stale ecclesiologies in which the church is defined as a voluntary association of like-minded believers, presumably bound together by no more than their common faith interests, do little justice to the meaning of the word *evangelical* either biblically or historically. The recovery of a truly evangelical ecclesiology surely requires a return to the conviction that the church is defined and bound together by her sharing through the Holy Spirit in the life of the incarnate Son of God, who restores us to intimacy with the Father. Such a recovery requires a return to the conviction that the church is the most holy gathering of persons in the universe, continually gathered together as we are to commune with the persons of our triune God. By so doing, we may begin to see again that the church is only artificially separable from salvation because the church is constituted by her union with the Savior, who is present to nourish and sanctify his body and bride gathered in his name. This seems to require, at bottom, the belief that apart from the living presence of Christ, the church is powerless to do or be anything.

8

The Gospel of Christ and His Bride

THE MEANING OF MARRIAGE AND SEX

They covered their nakedness. With eyes opened to their broken humanity, the terrible and tragic reality of their sin, the very first thing our primal parents did was cover their naked bodies. The dawn of sin had shed its first dark light on the *sexuality* of the perpetrators; from this awful new beginning, it exposed a deep rupture in what is so precious to God: male and female he created them. So the first grand cover-up began. In a feeble effort to cover up their sin and shame, to protect themselves not only from themselves but also from God, Adam and Eve attempted to fashion their own rescue—by hiding. Yet nothing sufficed. The fig leaves proved futile, as did the trees of the garden. They were acutely aware of their nakedness, but only God knew what it meant. So he sought them out in that condition, ripe as they were with the potential for sexual distortion and violence, initiating what only an incarnate God could at length complete. He exchanged their coverings with coverings of his own making and eventually exchanged their nakedness—with his own.

The second grand cover-up began many years later, east of Eden, and continues today. It too was preceded by a shame-soaked nakedness. But this time the nakedness belonged to God, hanging on a Roman gibbet, exposed to public ridicule, awash in blood, sweat, and spit. God was doing the unthinkable, plumbing the depths of our sin—all the way down. He took to himself our fallen nakedness, our sin-compromised sexuality, sanctifying and justifying our sexual perversion in his death and resurrection. He reconstituted our humanity, re-creating us as the image of God: male and female he *re-created* them.

But even though God became naked for us, we seem to prefer him covered up. As if to insist that our sexuality was not a prime casualty of the fall, and therefore not in need of salvation, we cover up our Savior. Too ashamed and too "modest" to allow God to suffer our sexual sin and shame, we clothe Jesus on the cross. In the first cover-up, God graciously clothed us; in the second, sadly, we return the favor. The irony ought to be revealing. Right at the point where we need God to both judge and redeem our unholy nakedness, we insist that he be clothed.

A crucified but clothed Jesus speaks volumes about the church's understanding of marriage and sex. If we have only a clothed Christ, how are we to understand and interpret our nakedness? If *the* Word of God did not subject himself to our nakedness and shame, can he still function as the subject of *our* words about God at this most crucial of points? When the church is theologically deaf and blind to the implications of God's self-giving in Christ regarding our sinful sexuality, our broken maleness and femaleness, the clothed Christ may be a powerful explanatory symbol. In clothing and therefore cloaking Christ, we are bound to turn elsewhere for what ought to be a specifically theological undertaking. So the church's attempts to speak to marriage and sex, and their multitudinous distortions, have too often been merely political, moral, ethical, social, or psychological—but rarely christological, Trinitarian, ecclesial, and sacramental. If the church fails to regard her deepest theological beliefs as pertaining to marriage and sex, then marriage and sex are bound to be understood in relatively trivial ways, and treated accordingly. Do we really believe that the deepest and most intimate human relations can be properly understood and addressed when detached from God's self-disclosure and self-bestowal? If not, then let us be forthright about it, for marriage and sex are fundamentally theological issues, and unless we wish to relegate our thinking about them to the relative obscurities of moral sentiments and political platitudes, we desperately need to know and say what they have to do with *God* himself.

We hear often enough about what God hates and thus opposes. From pulpit and paper, from book and blog, we hear variously that God hates divorce, adultery, premarital sex, homoeroticism, and many other sexual and relational sins. What we get far less often are theologically rich accounts as to *why* God hates and opposes distortions of marriage and sex. Do they break God's command, or even more to the point, do they break his image and break his heart? Apart from a christological and Trinitarian account of the beauty, wonder, and mystery of gender and sex, we fear that the church's teaching will be reduced to moral bromides—even if superficially adorned with biblical proof texts. Primarily, what we hope to offer in this chapter is a description of how marriage and sex are *internally and directly*, rather than externally and peripherally, related to the gospel of God's self-giving in Christ through the Spirit, why marriage and sex are thus so very precious and holy, and why that description necessitates a triune and incarnate God.

DIVINE INDWELLING: PERSONS IN INTIMATE UNION

Marriage and sex are not self-explanatory. They are beautiful and sacred mysteries that point beyond themselves to the mystery of our three-person God and to his redemptive self-giving in the incarnation. Theology is meant to found, form, and fund the church's deepest convictions and experiences, giving holy expression to the meaning of our lives, sanctifying our thought and speech against the inevitable depreciation and trivialization that occurs whenever we divorce the grandest human realities from their divine origin. Marriage and sex surely qualify as issues needing theological interpretation, not only because they exist at the center of our human experience, but also because they were given to us by God as echoes in the created world of who God is and how God loves us. Again, a failure to think theologically where we need it most—that is, at the point of our deepest, most intimate relations—is especially dangerous for the church. Such a failure forces the church to look elsewhere to explain what marriage and sex mean. Just as we cannot grasp the meaning of God's love for us apart from understanding that God *is* the very love by which he loves us, we cannot grasp the meaning of our deepest personal intimacies apart from the intimacy that God *is*. The meaning of these relations, basic and foundational to every human existence, can neither be grounded in nor exhausted by creaturely investigation. "Indeed," writes Michael Reeves, "in the triune God is the love behind all love, the life behind all life, the music behind all music, the beauty behind all beauty and the joy behind all joy."[1]

The love, life, harmony, beauty, and joy we were created to experience are echoes of a reality that transcends and interprets them. That reality is the love-creating, life-giving, harmonious, beautiful, and joyful personal communion shared by the Father, Son, and Spirit. Here again, the importance of the theological term *perichōrēsis* comes to the fore. We mentioned in chapter 2 the vast significance of this term for the church's articulation of the inner life of God in faithfulness to the witness of Jesus Christ, who opens to us the mystery of God's eternal three-person existence. This term gives sacred expression to the interrelations among the persons of the holy Trinity, asserting no less than that God has eternally been, and will eternally be, a mutually indwelling and interpenetrating communion of persons who exist in self-giving, life-giving love. Indwelling and interpenetrating personal love is *who God is*. God the Father is who he is only in union with God the Son; God the Son is who he is only in union with his Father; and the Father and Son are who they are only in the communion of God the Spirit. We noted the importance of the term *perichōrēsis* in relation to salvation, directing us to the fact that God does who he is, which is to say that in redeeming us, God the Spirit joins us to God the incarnate Son so that we may share in the life and love of God his Father. The eternal life we receive in salvation is the life shared by the Father with the Son in the Spirit. God loves us and gives us life through the love and life that he is. Without their grounding in the reality of God, life and love become mere abstractions that end up forfeiting their significance—literally, their purpose as *signs*.

The reality of the perichoretic communion that exists among the persons of the Trinity alerts us to a provocative insight that ought to give us pause: the personal and sexual intimacy that Adam and Eve experienced as they became one flesh was not the first indwelling or penetration to occur among persons. It was, of course, the first of all *human sexual* unions, but the first indwelling or penetration among persons belongs to the eter-

---

[1] Michael Reeves, *Delighting in the Trinity: An Introduction to the Christian Faith* (Downers Grove, IL: IVP Academic, 2012), 62.

nal union between Father, Son, and Spirit. God is who he is by virtue of the indwelling intimacy shared by the divine persons; apart from it, God would not be his triune self. This most sublime of all realities is reflected in our human existence, for we are who we are by virtue of the indwelling intimacy shared by human persons, apart from which we would not be ourselves.[2] The existence of every descendant of Adam and Eve depends upon a prior union of persons—necessarily male and female—who share indwelling intimacy. The fact that a human has *being* is predicated upon the existence of two others joined as one. Thus, any given human being requires two others in such a way that human existence is necessarily and fundamentally tripersonal.

Although it would be difficult to find a more obvious way in which our triune God images himself in us, we would be remiss not to mention another, perhaps less obvious, way: every human literally dwells inside another as he or she moves from that crucial point of conception to birth—another way in which humanity is defined by interpersonal indwelling.

These echoes of God's interpersonal life in our own existence might be written off as merely coincidental or forced analogies if not for the striking correspondence between our original birth and our new birth, the original creation and the new creation. In the redemption and re-creation of the world, God the Son was sent by his Father in the power of the Spirit to be birthed into our humanity. He was made one flesh with us that we might be made one flesh with him by the Spirit, and so experience new birth and eternal life in his. Our original existence and our new existence are both constituted by interpersonal indwelling. When God deigned to image himself in our humanity, both in the original creation and in the new creation (Jesus Christ), he did so in a way that is essential to who he is. A truly Christian anthropology, in other words, must be founded on christological and Trinitarian grounds:

> What is needed today is a better understanding of the person not just as an individual but as someone who finds his or her true being in communion with God and with others, the counterpart of a trinitarian doctrine of God. . . . God is love and has his true being in communion, in the mutual indwelling of Father, Son, and Holy Spirit—*perichoresis*, the

---

[2] John Zizioulas writes: "The only way for a true person to exist is for being and communion to coincide. The triune God offers in Himself the only possibility for such an identification of being with communion; He is the revelation of true personhood." *Being as Communion* (Crestwood, NY: St. Vladimir's Seminary Press, 1985), 107.

patristic word. This is the God who has created us male and female in his image to find our true humanity in perichoretic unity with him and one another, and who renews us in his image in Christ.[3]

MALE AND FEMALE HE CREATED THEM: THE *IMAGO DEI*

What we have thus far referred to as echoes or reflections of God's tri-personal unity in human existence have their scriptural origination in the first chapter of Genesis. Here we see that God spoke something about his human creatures that should leave us speechless. Among all that the Father created through and for his Son by the Spirit, God did something utterly unique with his human creatures—he created us in his *image*: "Then God said, 'Let us make man in our image, after our likeness.' . . . So God created man in his own image, in the image of God he created him; male and female he created them" (Gen. 1:26–27). The church and her theologians have wrestled with this text for two millennia, attempting to give interpretive expression to the fearful and wonderful blessing pronounced here by God. What exactly does it mean that humankind is the *imago Dei*? What is it about humans that constitutes us as God's likeness? The history of the church's interpretation on this point is far too vast to recount in the space of this chapter.[4] Suffice it to say that two strands of interpretation have been characteristic. One interprets humanity as the image of God with relation to our rational, moral, or volitional faculties—often called the *substantive* theory of the image. The other interprets the image in relation to the ensuing mandate for humanity to "rule over" or superintend the creation (Gen. 1:26, 28)—often called the *functional* theory.

Such theories are indeed helpful in attempting to delineate what marks humankind as distinctive among God's creatures, as part of an extended accounting for the ways in which we image God. However, they cannot account for something basic to a proper understanding of that image. Specifically, neither theory, as commonly or popularly understood, requires for its application that humankind be what God says we are: both male *and* female. A male does not require a female, nor does a female require a male,

---

[3] James B. Torrance, *Worship, Community, and the Triune God of Grace* (Downers Grove, IL: IVP Academic, 1996), 38. A Christian anthropology that begins with the solitary Adam as the image of God is not very Christian at all, implying as it does a unitarian understanding of God.

[4] For a skillful summary of prominent interpretations, see Anthony Hoekema, *Created in God's Image* (Grand Rapids: Eerdmans, 1986), 33–65.

in order to moralize, exercise reason and will, or exercise dominion over the earth. Such things might be done reasonably well by a single human being. But a solitary male or female most certainly cannot image God in a way that is most basic to who he is: depicting his personal, relational, and life-giving intimacy.

Recall our text: "Then God said, 'Let *us* make man in our image, after *our* likeness.' . . . So God created man in his own image, in the image of God he created him; *male and female* he created them."[5] The plurality in God's address has been a source of consternation among many modern Christian commentators, who, under the tutelage of the currently dominant mode of historical-grammatical interpretation, tend to hold the doctrine of the Trinity in hermeneutical abeyance in their exegesis of Genesis. The "us" and "our" of God's self-reference thus become problematic: Who is God talking to? This question necessarily arises for those who insist on delaying the theological, canonical, and *Christian* implications of the text in search of an interpretation that is strictly suitable to the original author and audience.[6] We believe, however, that it is incumbent upon modern Christians to recognize the Trinitarian implications of this text, as the church has done for the vast majority of her two thousand-year existence. "Indeed," writes Martin Luther, "it is the great consensus of the church that the mystery of the Trinity is set forth here."[7] Stopping short of a christological, and thus Trinitarian, interpretation of the creation account bypasses Christ's self-disclosure as the very Word of God by whom all things, including humans, were created (John 1:3; Col. 1:15–17), the One in whom alone the *imago Dei* can be properly interpreted.

The Nicene-Constantinopolitan Creed (381), to which all orthodox Christians subscribe, has us confess belief in Jesus Christ as the One "by whom all things were made," and in the Holy Spirit as "the Lord and Giver of life," so that the church may joyfully affirm that God the Father created humankind through and for God the Son by God the Spirit. What is most basic to God's inner life is wonderfully and fearfully reflected in his human

---

[5] We hasten to note that the emphasis on male and female is reiterated in a striking way in Genesis 5:1–2: "When God created man, he made him in the likeness of God. Male and female he created them, and he blessed them and named *them* Man [*adam*] when they were created."
[6] On the nature of the plural "us" in God's address, see Bruce Waltke, *An Old Testament Theology* (Grand Rapids: Zondervan, 2007), 212–13. Waltke affirms that "several strong arguments" favor the view that the plural is a reference to God's plurality as Father, Son, and Spirit, only to finally challenge that view on what he calls the "accredited grammatico-historical rules of interpretation." Accredited by whom? Historical and grammatical technicians? Or the collective pastoral wisdom of the church through the ages?
[7] "Lecture on Genesis 1:2," in *LW*, 1:9; cf. 1:58–59. John Calvin concurs: "Christians, therefore, properly contend, from this testimony, that there exists a plurality of Persons in the Godhead." Calvin on Gen. 1:26, *Comm.*, 1/1:92.

creatures, who, as male and female, and *specifically* as male and female, image the interpersonal intimacy inherent to God's inner being. Thus, the phrase "male and female he created them" functions to give specificity to the phrase "in the image of God he created [them]." Our existence as male and female is not something that God "tacks on" to the solitary human already in his image. On the contrary, our existence as male and female is *intrinsic* to that image.[8] This is not to say that being male and female *exhausts* what we may say about the *imago Dei*, but that the distinction-in-communion that characterizes humankind as male and female is absolutely basic to the *imago Dei*. As Colin Gunton writes, God "replicates" his communal being in our humanity:

> If, first, to be created in the image of God is to be made male and female, what is implied is that in this most central of all human relatedness is to be found a finite echo of the relatedness of Father, Son, and Holy Spirit. To be God, according to the doctrine of the Trinity, is to be persons in relation: to be God only as a communion of being. It is that which is replicated, at the finite level, by the polarity of the male and female: to be in the image of God is to be called to a relatedness-in-otherness that echoes the eternal relatedness-in-otherness of Father, Son and Spirit.[9]

Male cannot properly echo or image God by himself, nor can female by herself. Adam, apart from Eve, could not fulfill what it means for man to be the *imago Dei*—alone, he would have been a distorted, "not good" image: "The LORD God said, 'It is not good that the man should be alone. I will make a helper fit for him'" (Gen. 2:18). That God pronounced negatively upon his creation at the point of Adam's solitude is telling: "It is the only negative assessment in the creation narrative," observes Henri Blocher, "and it is emphatically negative."[10] Something was not right, and it apparently could not be remedied with another male or a beast, either of which might have provided Adam superior strength in tending the garden.[11] Would it not

---

[8] Karl Barth writes, "Is it not astonishing that again and again expositors have ignored the definitive explanation given by the text itself, and instead of reflecting on it pursued all kinds of arbitrarily invented interpretations of the *imago Dei*?" *Church Dogmatics*, 3/1, ed. G. W. Bromiley and T. F. Torrance, trans. G. W. Bromiley (Peabody, MA: Hendrickson, 2010), 195. Henri Blocher adds, "If we cannot find exegetical grounds for explaining 'the image of God' by the phrase 'male and female', our thoughts should turn to the undoubted analogy between the non-solitude of God and the communal structure of humanity." *In the Beginning: The Opening Chapters of Genesis* (Downers Grove, IL: IVP, 1984), 97. Blocher goes on to argue that this is more than a mere analogy.
[9] Colin E. Gunton, *Christ and Creation* (Grand Rapids: Eerdmans, 1992), 101.
[10] Blocher, *In the Beginning*, 96.
[11] We cannot help but wonder if a reticence to see Eve's existence as necessary to the image of God has had a sometimes deleterious effect on the church's view of women. If the solitary Adam was complete as that image,

be better to say that it was impossible for Adam to be the blessed *imago Dei* by himself, precisely because he could not be male *and* female—persons in communion?[12] That would certainly qualify as "not good," for it would mean that creation was bereft of God's image. "In isolation man would not have been good," writes Karl Barth. "That is, he would not have been created good . . . we might say that it would not be good because solitary man would not be man created in the image of God, who Himself is not solitary."[13] The solitary man can only and ever reflect a unitarian God.

Enter Eve. Into Adam's isolation, and out of Adam's flesh and bones, the image-fulfilling Eve was created. What a glorious event this must have been for Adam, and for his Creator! Adam sang for joy as he was joined by the one who was "bone of my bones and flesh of my flesh" (Gen. 2:23), exulting in the fulfillment of humanity, the completion of the image of God: "in the image of God he created him; male and female he created them."[14] Once Eve was present, humanity was able to reflect the personal and relational intimacy that God is. Eve's presence meant that humanity could experience life-giving interpersonal penetration and indwelling, a finite and temporal echo of God's triune, perichoretic life.

So from the time of the first male and female, every human being, every image of God, has had something extraordinary in common: each of us owes our existence to both a divine and human union of persons. We are created by, and image, God, who, as a union of persons, is one God. We are also created by, and image, our parents, who, as a union of persons, are one flesh. Personal union is the ground of all human *being*.

For the church, the sacred beauty of marriage and sex is to be maintained as a "*theo*-logical" reality whether or not it can be maintained on the level of the world's abstract ethical or political whims. The church delights

---

it is difficult to see how Eve could be much more than a creational addendum, necessary for the *continuation* of human life but not for its basic constitution.

[12] Ray S. Anderson writes: "Adam has no fundamental 'encounter of being with being' in his relationship with the other creatures such as occurs when the woman is presented to him as a 'being from and for him.' Quite clearly the *imago* is not totally present in the form of individual humanity but more completely as co-humanity." *On Being Human: Essays in Theological Anthropology* (Grand Rapids: Eerdmans, 1982), 73.

[13] Barth, *Church Dogmatics*, 3/1, 290. Helmut Thielicke observes, "The solitary Adam is not yet 'man'; he is still not the fulfillment of the creation of man." *The Ethics of Sex*, trans. John W. Doberstein (New York: Harper & Row, 1964), 4.

[14] Had Adam remained alone, Calvin avers, he would have been but "incomplete." Calvin on Gen. 1:27, *Comm.*, 1/1:97. Calvin reflects further: "[Adam] lost, therefore, one of his ribs; but, instead of it, a far richer reward was granted him, since he obtained a faithful associate of life; for he now saw himself, who had before been imperfect, rendered complete in his wife. And in this we see a true resemblance of our union with the Son of God; for he became weak that he might have members of his body endued with strength." Calvin on Gen. 2:21, *Comm.*, 1/1:33. Apparently it was not even good for Christ, the second Adam, to be alone. More on this below.

in the holy love and intimacy of male and female because the church exists as a sign of the holy love and intimacy that brought humankind into existence. This is why the church must proclaim that the differentiation between, and the union of, male and female is utterly holy and beautiful. Indeed, it is precisely the distinction of our persons that allows for the beauty and holiness of the union—as it is with God. Human persons are defined by both the distinction and the union—as it is with the Trinitarian persons. Humans are distinctly male *or* female, but neither can exist except for the life-giving union between male *and* female.[15]

To celebrate and delight in the holy marriage and sexual union of others is by no means to denigrate the status of the *imago Dei* in males and females who are themselves not married. Far from it. Every human life is living proof of having shared most intimately in the union between male and female—our existence completely depends upon it. Each of us exists as the living bond between the male and female from whom we came. We are persons, in other words, who necessarily derive our personhood from others. We are not, and cannot be, who we are except by virtue of the one-flesh union of male and female. Contrary to the modern *zeitgeist*, humans are not self-defined. It is for this reason that the church should view with proper suspicion unqualified talk of the "single" person, for in reality, there is no such person. Each of us, whether or not we are joined in holy marital union, is constituted by interpersonal communion.[16] Our lives are not only shaped by way of sexual procreation, but also by the ways in which our nonsexual relational intimacies profoundly affect who we are and how we know ourselves. We share together, and never as isolated individuals, the mystery and wonder of our existence as male and female persons.[17]

The fall of humankind into sin, however, introduced a rupture in the image. East of Eden, male and female are not how they are supposed to

---

[15] Precisely here we are reminded that gender distinction is both *created* and a *reflection*, not an exact replication. Gender distinction is not to be projected back onto God, whose personal distinctions are reflected in ours but nevertheless transcend them.

[16] The male-female relation, T. F. Torrance asserts, "extends beyond its specific form in marriage: it has to do with the inter-personal structure of human being to which all men and women belong, whether they are married or not. Those who are not married do not exist outside the inter-personal structure of human being as it came from the creative will and love of God." *The Christian Doctrine of Marriage* (Edinburgh: Scottish Academic Press, 1989), n.p.

[17] Christopher A. Hall and Steven D. Boyer write: "Do we not find here a fascinating convergence? Ultimate reality consists in divine persons perfectly united in ecstatic love—and every human person discovers an intrinsic longing for just this kind of interpersonal intimacy." *The Mystery of God: Theology for Knowing the Unknowable* (Grand Rapids: Baker, 2012), 112. Cf., Stanley J. Grenz, *The Social God and the Relational Self: A Trinitarian Theology of the* Imago Dei (Louisville, KY: Westminster John Knox Press, 2001).

be, created as they were to delight in their distinction and rejoice in their union. In fear and shame they cover themselves and hide, a feeble attempt at self-justification. The tragedy of the fall, and the corruption and condemnation that followed, manifests itself in the lives of broken images in manifold ways, but perhaps never so clearly as in our broken and distorted intimacies. The differentiation between, and the union of, male and female are utterly sacred, for they echo God's holy existence. Tragically, then, trespasses against the holy distinction, and violations of the holy union, typify the story of humanity east of Eden. Fractured images muffle and mute the holy echo in myriad ways, joining what should be divided and dividing what should be united. Cornelius Plantinga envisions the fall as entailing both the confusion and disruption of God's creation:

> According to Scripture, God's original design included patterns of distinction and union and distinction-within-union that would give creation strength and beauty. . . . Against this background of original separating and binding, we must see the fall as anti-creation, the blurring of distinctions and the rupturing of bonds, and the one as the result of the other.[18]

From this tragic "anti-creation," male and female are by no means exempt. The unraveling of creation leads to confusions and disruptions that seek to rob males and females of their God-given strength and beauty. These perversions are pervasive among God's fallen images, and are exacerbated in our attempts at sexual self-definition and self-justification, when we take pleasure in what God does not. What God has joined together, we are prone to separate, and what God has separated, we are prone to join. In either case, the image becomes rather dim. We desperately need to be re-created; we need reimaging.

THE TRUE IMAGE OF GOD: JESUS CHRIST WITH HIS BRIDE

While interpreting the meaning of the *imago Dei* in humanity must employ careful consideration of Genesis 1 and 2, it must not terminate there; the issue is a canonical one. The incarnate Son of God is the true *imago Dei*, the fully authentic human person, the fulfillment and destiny of God's crea-

---

[18] Cornelius Plantinga, *Not the Way It's Supposed to Be: A Breviary of Sin* (Grand Rapids: Eerdmans, 1995), 29.

turely images. In other words, Jesus Christ ultimately defines for us what it means to be the image of God. When we speak of Christ as the true and perfect image of God, we must avoid the temptation to collapse that image into his deity, as if it were his divine nature, *per se*, that constitutes him as that image. That would hardly be good news for *human* beings. The significance of Jesus's being the quintessential image of God lies not in his existence as the eternal Son—for whom the ascription "image" would border on blasphemy—but in the fact that the eternal Son has become *human*.[19] Prior to the incarnation, the Son did not "image" God. The *imago Dei* is a predicate of created humanity, not humanity's Creator. God the Son is the true and full image of God precisely because, without ever ceasing to be fully God, he became truly and fully human. The enfleshing of God provides us with the "theo-logic" of the *imago Dei*.

It was into the confusion and disruption of the anti-creation that this most inexplicable reality transpired. God the Son was born into our flesh. He was born into the world that had been created by him and for him, taking on the humanity he had created. The descriptions of him in Scripture are tantalizing. He is, after all, the "image of the invisible God, the firstborn of all creation" (Col. 1:15). He is the "exact imprint of [God's] nature" and the "firstborn among many brothers" (Heb. 1:3; Rom. 8:29). And he is all of this as the second and last Adam (1 Cor. 15:45, 47). In Christ, God is not only re-creating the world and reconciling it to himself, he is also *reimaging* the world in himself. Jesus Christ is the quintessential image of God, the new Adam through whom creation has begun again. He is the new creation, in whom we are re-created and reborn into the image of God we were originally created to be. In order to enact this astounding act of re-creation, rebirth, and reimaging, the last Adam came to share fully in the humanity of the first. But as with the first Adam, so with the last: to truly image God, he needs his bride. It is not good for him to be alone.

If Jesus Christ is indeed the last Adam, the true fulfillment of the image of God in our humanity, we should expect that he would fulfill what was said of humankind in the beginning: "So God created man in his own image, in the image of God he created him; male and female he created them." If, as we have argued, "male and female" is descriptive of, and basic

---

[19] This is a point on which Calvin insisted. See his notes on Col. 1:15 and 2 Cor. 4:4, *Comm.*, 21/2:149–150 and 20/2:192–197.

to, the *imago Dei*, we should expect that Jesus would satisfy that description. In a most beautiful and transcendent way, this is exactly what he does. He refuses to be who he is as the quintessential image of God without us. Indeed, the purpose of the incarnation is that Christ may have for himself an eternal bride, his holy church. In his act of unparalleled condescension and self-giving, God the Son became incarnate, joining himself to us, so that through his birth and baptism, through his faithful and obedient life, and through his death, burial, resurrection, and ascension, we might belong to him as his beloved. By the Spirit, he births us anew, baptizing us into his death and resurrection, justifying and sanctifying us, so that we may be one flesh and one body with him forever. In the beginning, Adam and Eve were united together as one flesh, the profound mystery of God's creative purpose begun. In the *new* beginning, Christ and his bride are united together as one flesh, the profound mystery of God's creative purpose fulfilled:

> For no one ever hated his own flesh, but nourishes and cherishes it, just as Christ does the church, because we are members of his body. "Therefore a man shall leave his father and mother and hold fast to his wife, and the two shall become one flesh." This mystery is profound, and I am saying that it refers to Christ and the church. (Eph. 5:29–32)

Right at the beginning of creation, God implicated the male and female in a mystery, that of the two becoming one. It was a beautiful and blessed mystery, no doubt full of rejoicing and wonder as the two came to experience each other, and thus life, as God intended it. And yet, as Paul tells us, this profound mystery was not self-defining, for it was a mystery that ultimately anticipated another. When God created humankind male and female in his image and joined them together as one flesh, he involved humanity in a mystery-sign, the fulfillment and reality of which awaited his incarnation. "The two shall become one flesh" is a mystery at the center of both creation *and* redemption, and Jesus Christ is the meaning of that mystery, because he is that mystery in himself. By assuming our flesh into union with himself— healing, sanctifying, and justifying our broken humanity in his life, death, resurrection, and ascension—we become one body and one flesh with him through Spirit-wrought faith. Thus, the mystery of creation is fulfilled in the mystery of redemption: the last Adam with and in his bride, and his bride with and in him.

Jesus Christ is the true image of God. However, he is not that image, any more than the first Adam was, as a solitary, independent being. Just as Adam would have been incomplete without Eve, Jesus would be incomplete without his bride. To echo the astounding pronouncement of Scripture, the church is none other than Christ's body, "the fullness of him who fills all in all" (Eph. 1:23). The promise that the church is the "fullness of Christ" is so extravagant as to sound blasphemous. Is not Jesus Christ complete in and of himself? Is it really true, in Calvin's words, that Christ "reckons himself in some measure imperfect" until he is joined to his bride?[20] What sounds at first like blasphemy is, in light of the incarnation, the astounding promise that Jesus will not be who he is without us. In the extravagance of his self-giving love, he has taken our humanity into union with himself so that, through his one act of atonement, we might be joined to him forever as his body and bride through the Spirit. In other words, the bridegroom "fills himself" with his bride; he becomes one flesh with his church in order to redeem, reconstitute, and re-create us as the *imago Dei*. In creation, Eve is the fullness of Adam, and together they are the image of God. In re-creation, the church is the fullness of Christ, and together they are the fulfillment of that image. In the incarnation of the Son of God, in the mystery of Jesus Christ, creation and salvation converge.

When God the Son became incarnate, he gave to marriage, and to the physical intimacy inherent to it, a meaning it could never have had on its own. This is true not merely because he upheld marriage as divinely ordained, but more importantly *because he fulfilled in himself the reality for which marriage is a sign*. The marital intimacy of the first human pair was a sign imbedded in their bodies of an intimacy to come, a marriage through which Christ would reconcile and reunite sinners to God. The union between Adam and Eve was, we might say, the *proto-protoevangelium*—the very first glimpse of the gospel recorded in Scripture, Genesis 3:15 notwithstanding. "The two shall become one flesh" (Eph. 5:31; cf. Gen. 2:24) *refers to* the saving union between Christ and the church (Eph. 5:32).[21] When God joined together the first male and female, he etched into creation a foretaste of a holy union to come, against which the gates of hell could never prevail.

---

[20] Calvin on Eph. 1:23, *Comm.*, 20/1:218.
[21] Given that Genesis 2:24 is ultimately fulfilled in Jesus Christ, we are reminded of Jesus's insistence that he is the subject of the teaching of Moses and the Prophets (John 5:39–40, 46; Luke 24:27).

This sacred marriage between Christ and the church possesses cosmic redemptive significance, for it is a blessed union that runs into eternity. God began creation with a marriage, he redeemed a fallen creation through a marriage, and he will finally consummate his unfathomable love for us in an everlasting marriage (Rev. 19:6–9). No one has expressed this as beautifully as Jonathan Edwards:

> The end of the creation of God was to provide a spouse for his Son Jesus Christ that might enjoy him and on whom he might pour forth his love. And the end of all things in providence are to make way for the exceeding expressions of Christ's close and intimate union with, and high and glorious enjoyment of, him and to bring this to pass. And therefore the last thing and the issue of all things is the marriage of the Lamb. . . . The wedding feast is eternal; and the love and joys, the songs, entertainments and glories of the wedding never will be ended. It will be an everlasting wedding day.[22]

In Jesus Christ, the marital union between male and female has been forever sanctified. Fulfilling that original creative sign in a truly majestic and transcendent way, he came to dwell with and in his bride, sharing with us who he is as the true image of God, giving new and eternal life to our flesh from his own. Regardless of how secular culture defines it, marriage, for the church, must be defined by the gospel of Jesus Christ. Marital intimacy is divinely intended to mirror the saving intimacy between God and humanity in the person of Jesus Christ. Further, because the church is one with Christ, even as he is one with his Father through the Spirit, marriage is a sacred manifestation, on a creaturely level, of the intimacy between the triune persons of God. Accordingly, the one-flesh union between male and female necessarily transcends typically abstract moral, ethical, political, and social definition. Rather, marriage is to be understood primarily in light of God's self-revelation in Christ, and so given christological and Trinitarian definition by the church. In so doing, we will delight and take courage in confessing that marriage is a sacred and beautiful sign given to us to reflect God's ineffable love. In the union between Christ and the church, God has accomplished his redemptive and re-creative purposes, making us

---

[22] Jonathan Edwards, *Miscellanies* (No. 702), in *The Works of Jonathan Edwards*, ed. Ava Chamberlain (New Haven, CT: Yale University Press, 1994), 18:298.

his beloved sons and daughters forever. In Jesus Christ, we find that God will stop at nothing to bring us into the life and love that he is. Indeed, he is willing to become what he was not—incarnate—and literally spend himself in suffering, misery, humiliation, and death to secure us as the objects of his eternal affection. As the recipient of God's love, Christ's bride comes to share in the triune family of God, forever enjoying the love that defines all love, the life that defines all life, and the personal intimacy that defines all personal intimacy. Let us heed Edwards again:

> Christ has brought it to pass, that those who the Father has given to him should be brought into the household of God, that he and his Father and they should be as it were one society, one family; that his people should be in a sort admitted into that society of the three persons in the Godhead. In this family or household God [is] the Father, Jesus Christ is his own naturally and eternally begotten Son. The saints, they also are children in the family; the church is the daughter of God, being the spouse of his Son. They all have communion in the same Spirit, the Holy Ghost.[23]

MISIMAGING GOD AND OURSELVES

When God created Adam and Eve, joining them in marital union, he established within our humanity a sacred sign of his love. The self-giving, life-giving personal intimacy and indwelling that exists in the union between male and female was intended to mirror what God is like. It was, furthermore, an anticipation of the gospel, the exceedingly good news that the incarnate Savior would become one flesh with his bride, the church, re-creating our humanity in his self-giving, life-giving "at-one-ment." The union between male and female is thus given sacred definition in Scripture; it is to be interpreted in relation to the holy marriage first established by God at creation and quintessentially fulfilled in redemption.

Between these two great marriages, however, stands a great divorce. By the rupture introduced into creation through sin, the image of God suffered distortion and division; we became alienated from God, and therefore alienated from ourselves and from one another. The image of God was broken *in* us, and therefore broken *between* us. Broken images by definition badly

---

[23] Edwards, *Miscellanies* (No. 571), in *Works*, 18:110.

reflect God, and we do so in seemingly innumerable ways, but none more serious than the ways we distort God and therefore ourselves in our fallen intimacies and longings. The ravages of sin were bound to penetrate deeply into what makes us human: "in the image of God he created him; male and female he created them." And so they have. We were created by God to mirror his self-giving, self-denying, humanizing, procreative, unconditional, and indissoluble love. Yet east of Eden, sadly, human love is all too characteristically selfish and self-gratifying, dehumanizing and objectifying, life-thwarting, conditional, and soluble. Sin has turned us inside out, as it were, leaving us curved in on ourselves. Disoriented by our self-orientation, we have become perversely proficient in unholy marital and sexual self-definition. Given the holy gravity of human sexuality, the effects on our closest personal intimacies have been devastatingly weighty. After all, distortions and confusions of marriage and sex strike deep at what makes us human, distorting and confusing not only who we were made to be, but also how God images himself.[24] For the holy bride of Jesus Christ, the implications are more severe still, for when we implicitly or explicitly condone or participate in unholy marital and sexual expressions, we obscure the very gospel we are privileged to share.

Because the stakes are so high, the distortions of which we speak demand theological assessment. This is to be distinguished from arrogant and self-protective finger-pointing, which might suggest that each of us, in various ways, was or is not subject to, or a purveyor of, the maladies we seek to assess. It is also to be distinguished from an assessment born of joyless negativity rather than deep appreciation and joyful wonder at the holiness of marriage and sex. But we must assess them theologically, for if our theology has nothing to say to us here, it ultimately has little to say at all. In what follows, we will briefly highlight several of the most important and far-reaching symptoms of our marital and sexual sickness, acutely aware that there is far more that could be said, and perhaps said far better. The intended goal, for the authors and readers alike, is the liberation and joy that comes from repentance in Christ Jesus, the embodied Lord of our sexual identity.

---

[24] This is a good time to be reminded that we tend to express ourselves—maritally, sexually, and otherwise—in accordance with who we believe God really is. Marital and sexual unholiness in the church, of the types we shall describe below, strongly suggests that we view God as unitarian rather than Trinitarian. False views of God invariably lead to false views of ourselves and others. See Reeves, *Delighting in the Trinity*, 116.

226 THE INCARNATION OF GOD

Putting Asunder What God Has Joined Together

Marital union is a sign given to humanity that lends shape and substance to human love, for it images the indivisible, immutable love that God is. Divorce is thus also a sign, a countersign, that disfigures and disintegrates human love, implying as it does that God's love is divisible and unstable. As that countersign, divorce signals a rupture in the most essential of human relations, the union between male and female. It is a sign embedded in the anti-creation, and it constitutes an attempt to do the impossible: put asunder what God has joined.[25] In the new creation—the humanity of Jesus Christ—God has issued a resounding "No!" to this false sign, establishing, once again through marriage, an unbreakable sign of his indissoluble love. When Christ united himself in one flesh with his bride, he secured that union forever in himself, anchoring it in the eternal love of his Father through the Spirit. Because of his indefatigable and everlasting faithfulness, the church lives in the comfort and security that there is absolutely nothing that can divorce us from his love (Rom. 8:35–39). Christian marriage has the sacred privilege of sharing in this sign of the new creation, the gospel, in which God overcomes our infidelities and divisions.

Understanding and rejoicing in the union between Christ and his church, we must ask ourselves very difficult questions, questions intended to lead us to the healing that can come only from our repentance in him. T. F. Torrance gives voice to these questions: "If Christian marriage is meant to reflect that union, how can the Church tolerate divorce? What would divorce mean but that Christ can and may cut off his Church, that he holds on to us only so far as we prove faithful? Where then would we fickle and faithless sinners be? . . . This must make us ask whether the current attitude to divorce in the Church is not evidence of something very wrong, in fact evidence of a serious weakness in its grasp of the Gospel."[26] As difficult as such questions might be, can we ask any less if the mystery of marriage has indeed been fulfilled and reconstituted in Christ—that is, without ripping marriage from its proper context and moorings in the gospel? In so asking, we must not tread haphazardly and insensitively over the complexities that wither or break marriages under the pain of abuse or infidelity. Christ is, and will

---

[25] It is certainly worth pointing out that when Jesus was himself questioned about divorce, he referred his interlocutors to Genesis 2, setting marriage in the context of creation (Matt. 19:4–6).
[26] Torrance, *The Christian Doctrine of Marriage*, n.p.

remain, an utterly faithful Savior despite our unfaithfulness. But we must ask these questions, just as surely as we must answer them, in the kind of humble and trusting repentance that shows that we have not grown cold toward our Bridegroom and his gospel.

Joining Together What God Has Put Asunder

It was not good for Adam to be alone. He needed Eve so that together they could be the *imago Dei*, and he needed Eve so that together they could foreshadow the life-giving union between Christ and his bride. But just as it was not good for Adam to be alone, neither was it good for Adam to be joined to another Adam, for two reasons. First, the image of God in humanity requires the male and the female: "in the image of God he created him; male and female he created them." Just as surely as solitary Adam could not image God, neither could Adam multiplied by two. Male and female are personal distinctions within our common humanity that define humanity, whereas Father, Son, and Spirit are personal distinctions within the one God that define God; where God is concerned, union *requires* distinctions among persons. Second, two Adams, or a hundred more for that matter, could not fulfill the mandate that immediately followed their creation: "And God blessed them. And God said to them, 'Be fruitful and multiply and fill the earth'" (Gen. 1:28). Fruitfulness and multiplication require that humanity be the image of God: a life-giving, fruit-bearing union of distinguishable persons. How very much like God this is! The unity of the Father and Son in the Spirit is the life behind every life, the reason for the existence of everything and everyone (John 1:1–4; Col. 1:16; Heb. 1:2). Where God is concerned, the creation of life *requires* distinctions among persons.

If the fall is anti-creation, and necessarily includes distortion of the image of God in humanity, we might expect exactly what we find east of Eden: divisions and confusions among male and female—a dividing of what God has joined, as we have seen, but also a confusing of what God has distinguished. As lamentable as it surely is, we should not be altogether surprised when we read in Scripture that fallen images, who have "exchanged the truth about God for a lie," are given to sexual confusion: "For their women exchanged natural relations for those that are contrary to nature; and the men likewise gave up natural relations with women and were consumed with passion for one another" (Rom. 1:25–27). The fact that this passage occurs in the context of Paul's teaching on idolatry is telling. The sexual manifestation of self-worship is the anomaly of same-gender sex— the attempt to unite ourselves with ourselves. If idolatry means that we are curved in on ourselves doxologically, it means that we may also be curved in on ourselves sexually. Holy worship and holy sexuality both require some-one who is "Other" than us. Blocher writes:

> Immediately we can understand why the Apostle Paul makes a close connection between idolatry and homosexuality (Rom. 1:22–27). This sexual perversion as a rejection of the other corresponds to idolatry in its relationship to God, the rejection of the Other; it is a divinization of the *same*, the creature.[27]

God sets himself against sexual idolatry, *homo*sexuality, for ontological reasons, not political or moral reasons. As the Life of the world, he is impla-cably opposed to *all* creaturely forms of self-worship, sexual and otherwise, because idols are incapable of giving life. Confused worship, like confused sexuality, signals the death of humanity.

Virtual Sex

The one-flesh union that God forged between his male and female image is the gift of personalization; the two come to experience their humanity in a uniquely intimate way in the joining of their persons. This is a gift that redounds to every human being, for each of us is a product of, and defined by, just such a union. Divorce and homoeroticism are two ways in which this gift is obscured, one an unholy separation of persons, the other an unholy confusion. Pornography is a third. Constituted by its objectification and thus dehumanizing of the other, pornography is the absurd attempt to make the gift of sexual union what it cannot be: impersonal. It is a case of sexual unreality, a voyeuristic endeavor to steal the pleasure of sexual intimacy from that which defines it. Pornography is an invitation to the contradiction of sexual autonomy.[28] Counterfeits are sham substitutes, and pornography is no exception. It substitutes the holy images of God for impersonal images

---

[27] Blocher, *In the Beginning*, 103.
[28] The contradiction of pornography is one that it shares with "casual sex" more generally. Lewis Smedes is right: "Casual sex is a contradiction in terms." *Sex for Christians* (Grand Rapids: Eerdmans, 1994), 67.

on a screen; self-giving love for self-involved lust; life-giving communion for life-sapping masturbation; and the beauty and fulfillment of personal union for the shame and regret of personal preoccupation.

Pornography promises sexual gratification, a promise impossible for it to deliver seeing that it is everything holy sexual union is not. It stands in stark contrast to holy intimacy precisely because it contradicts who God is, and who he is for us in Christ. God is, by definition, a communion of living persons who dwell with and in one another in self-giving, life-creating love—a love that always exists for the benefit of the other. By contrast, pornography is a stimulant to idolatrous intimacy, a self-preoccupied love devoid of the possibility of life, which seeks to exploit rather than give, deriving pleasure at another's expense. The contrast is exacerbated when we consider the way in which God is for us in Jesus Christ. By becoming incarnate and suffering the abasement of our fallen humanity from cradle to grave, God the Son brings us, by the Spirit, to share in the living communion of life and love he has with his Father. In so doing, he re-creates, reimages, and authenticates our humanity in his own. Pornography is salvation's polar and evil opposite. It is dehumanizing through and through, seeking selfish pleasure in the objectification and abasement of others. Whereas in salvation Jesus Christ personalizes us by joining us to himself, in pornography we depersonalize others whom we keep at a distance. Because pornography so thoroughly distorts the nature of sexual love, the results of such self-indulgence are devastating. Pornography, far from being a merely private affair, in fact functions as a demonically effective stimulant to every other sexual sin; it is a perverse gateway to a myriad of sexual adulterations and abuses, and wreaks havoc on holy marriages.

Abortion and the Meaning of Sex

God blessed and sanctified birth when he created the first male and female in his image: "Be fruitful and multiply and fill the earth." This fruitful multiplying was intended as a reflection of God's own life-giving interpersonal love. God resanctified birth forever in Jesus Christ when he was conceived in the womb of Mary by the Spirit, a conception through which our lifeless humanity would be given new birth in his. Conception and birth, no less than marriage and sex, are given their meaning in Christ. The life that proceeded from the union of Adam and his bride was a sign of the new and eternal life that would proceed from the last Adam and his bride—life and new life, procreation and re-creation, birth and rebirth. The life that comes forth from the union of male and female has a double reflection, mirroring both the procreative union of the persons of the Trinity and the procreative union of Christ and his church. The male and female union is pregnant with life, echoing who God *is* in his personal relations and what God *does* in the gospel of our salvation. In describing why human birth is so very precious to God, we must go even a trembling step further: the new birth we receive in Christ Jesus comes about because in the incarnation, God himself experiences conception and birth! The sanctification of birth has taken place in the incarnation of God.

The meaning of sexual union is thus tied inextricably to new life.[29] Herein the ignominy of abortion becomes apparent: it means that the male and female have said "No!" to the meaning of their union at the point where God has issued a resounding "Yes!" Abortion is a total misconstrual and manipulation of the meaning of sexual intimacy.[30] As such, debating about the inception of life, as important as that is, misses the larger and looming theological point: "Why do we kill approximately 4,000 unborn babies every day in the United Sates alone?" asks Christopher West. "Because we are misusing and abusing God's great gift of sex. Make no mistake: in the final analysis, the abortion debate is not about when life begins. It is about the meaning of sex."[31] If fruit-bearing is a gift *inherent* to the blessing of sexual union, then the question of whether such life actually exists is nonsensical.

Common to all sexual and marital distortions—divorce, homoeroticism, pornography, and more—is the obscuring, refusal, or termination of life, possible or actual. In abortion, the "No!" to life is issued in such a way as to beget violent and bloody repercussions, leaving personal and re-

---

[29] But the order is not unimportant, notes Alexander Schmemann: "One does not love *in order* to have children. Love needs no justification; it is not because it gives life that love is good: it is because it is good that it gives life." *For the Life of the World: Sacraments and Orthodoxy* (Crestwood, NY: St. Vladimir's Seminary Press, 1973), 87.

[30] The denial of life that characterizes abortion is a kind of sexual idolatry shared by the adulterer and fornicator. R. R. Reno writes: "The future-oriented fertility of the sexual act threatens rather than fulfills the adulterer's or fornicator's desires. Fear of the children that naturally come from sexual intercourse . . . is why sexual desire misdirected and twisted into service of present pleasures becomes the Old Testament's favored image of idolatry. The idolater is like the man who visits prostitutes. He wants to discharge his need for worship while reserving power to live as he pleases. The silence of idols is no disappointment . . . idols are charming in their convenient emptiness." *Genesis.* Brazos Theological Commentary on the Bible (Grand Rapids: Brazos Press, 2010), 57.

[31] Christopher West, *Theology of the Body for Beginners* (West Chester, PA: Ascension Press, 2004), 13.

lational devastation in its wake for all involved.[32] Like all murder, abortion is an assault on God because it is an assault on his image. It takes place, as does all hatred for God, in the shadow of Golgotha, where our contempt was exposed to its depths: nothing would satisfy our rebellion save the bloody termination—shall we say abortion?—of God's true image, his one and only begotten Son. God experiences birth, but he also experiences its violent end.

In this violent end, the incarnate God suffers his own judgment on our sinful distortions, distortions that run deep into our being—all the way down to our naked bodies and the deepest personal intimacies that require them. In the midst of our marital and sexual sin, in our nakedness and shame, in the throes of the relational devastations we wreak upon ourselves and one another, God does the unthinkable. In Jesus Christ, God hangs battered, bruised, and bloody on a cross, naked and ashamed, the supreme demonstration that his love knows no bounds. There is no condition of ours, however humiliating and shameful, that God will not suffer to bring us forgiveness, healing, and peace. When we are included in Jesus Christ, we are put to death in his death, the death of our fallen humanity, the death of our broken marital and sexual self-definitions. And just as the Father raised the corpse of his Son from the dead by the Spirit, so we are raised in his resurrection, liberated from death and brokenness to share in his holy life.

The crucified, resurrected body of Jesus Christ is the judgment *and* salvation of our broken bodies. Jesus is the Lord over our twisted marital and sexual falsifications, but always as our merciful Savior. He alone is atonement and healing for our divided, confused, objectified, and aborted relations. The nakedness, humiliation, shame, torture, death, and burial that God in Christ suffers has as its end the glorious union between the resurrected Christ and his church. The everlasting, indissoluble, humanizing, and life-giving communion he establishes with his bride is the beginning of the re-creation of humanity in his image. In Christ, the church is re-established and re-oriented as male and female in the image of God, given freedom in repentance and forgiveness to experience marital and sexual holiness. In

---

[32] This personal and relational devastation constitutes an urgent matter of ministry for the church. Her Savior, whose body was torn apart and whose life was terminated, can alone bring peace and healing to those who suffer the ravages, heartbreak, and loneliness that abortion inevitably brings.

the mystery of Christ and his church, one flesh forevermore, marriage and sex become holy signs redeemed and fulfilled. Male and female God has created us, Christ and bride he has re-created us. We would do well to put this to prayer:

> Lord Jesus Christ, as you freely give yourself to your bride the Church, grant that the mystery of the union of man and woman in marriage may reveal to the world the self-giving love which you have for your Church; and to you with the Father and the Holy Spirit be glory and honor, now and forever. Amen.[33]

[33] Post-Communion Prayer for Marriage, *Lutheran Book of Worship*, Minister's Desk Edition (Minneapolis, MN: Augsburg Fortress, 1978), 192.

Conclusion

There is an astounding mystery at the heart of the church's confession: the eternal Son of God, without ceasing to be fully God, has become fully human—he has become what he created: the Word became flesh. He entered our existence in order to restore us—and more than that, all things in heaven and earth—to himself, bringing us into communion with his Father through the Spirit. This is why it is no exaggeration when John Williamson Nevin notes:

> "*The Word became flesh!*" In this simple, but sublime enunciation, we have the whole gospel comprehended in a word. . . . The incarnation is the key that unlocks the sense of all God's revelations. It is the key that unlocks the sense of all God's works, and brings to light the true meaning of the universe. . . . The incarnation forms thus the great central fact of the world.[1]

The apparent linguistic simplicity of the enunciation "The Word became flesh" belies its theological sublimity and cosmic significance. After all, to confess that the Word became flesh is to answer the grandest and gravest question ever posed to humanity: "Who do you say that I am?" The question, like the enunciation, is also verbally modest, but the answer it demands is a confession about the One who is the Way, Truth, and Life of all created existence. Jesus Christ, the Word become flesh, is the meaning of all reality.

Any diminishing of the great central fact of the incarnation, any failure to allow this most essential phenomenon to penetrate deeply into our minds and hearts, has the potential to strip our theology of its vitality.

---

[1] John Williamson Nevin, *The Mystical Presence: A Vindication of the Reformed or Calvinistic Doctrine of the Holy Eucharist* (Philadelphia: J. B. Lippencott, 1846), 199.

When this most astounding reality begins to fade from its proper place at the center of the church's thinking, speech, and worship—when we begin to lose sight of the fact that God is re-creating and reconstituting everything in heaven and earth in the person of his Son—our theology is bound to suffer the impersonal abstractions common to such short-sightedness, devolving ever more into religious fantasy, "spiritual" sentimentality, and its accompanying moralisms. Our theology, in other words, inevitably becomes less and less *Christ*ian. This book is our attempt to demonstrate the centrality of the incarnate Word of God for the life of the church, to demonstrate why it is that Jesus Christ is the Alpha and Omega of our thought, speech, and worship. We have endeavored to show why any and all of our words *about* God must necessarily be formed and informed by the Word who *is* God. Jesus Christ, in other words, is our *theos logos* (John 1:1), our true *theology*.

Because God entered the world in and as Jesus Christ, the meaning of God and the meaning of the world are given definitive expression in him. Christ is both the Creator and the new creation. Thus, our theology must be explicitly Christocentric, not as a matter of arbitrary theological method, but as a matter of necessity, for he is the Truth of God and the Truth of the world in his one person. To quote Dietrich Bonhoeffer again:

> In Jesus Christ the reality of God entered into the reality of this world. The place where the answer is given, both to the question concerning the reality of God and to the question concerning the reality of the world, is designated solely and alone by the name Jesus Christ. . . . In Him all things consist (Col. 1:17). Henceforward one can speak neither of God nor of the world without speaking of Jesus Christ. All concepts of reality which do not take account of Him are abstractions.[2]

If it is true that *all* concepts of reality that do not take the person of Christ into account are abstractions—that is, concepts *pulled away from* reality—it is most certainly true of our theological concepts. Throughout this book, we have hinted at the kinds of tendencies that may surface when the incarnation—the great central fact of the world—recedes from the center of our theology. To be more explicit at this closing point about the dangers

---

[2] Dietrich Bonhoeffer, *Ethics*, ed. Eberhard Bethge, trans. Neville Horton Smith (1955; repr., New York: Macmillan Publishing, 1979), 194.

inherent in such tendencies, we note the often predictable shape theology assumes when our words *about* God are not designated by the Word *of* God—when they are not, as Bonhoeffer says, designated solely and alone by the name *Jesus Christ*.

1. *A minimizing of the incarnation drifts rapidly toward a minimizing of the Trinity.* We may insist that God is a triune being, yet if we are armed with a merely nominal and superficial understanding of the incarnation, our insistence is likely to become less a confession about the reality of our existence and salvation than a box to be checked off in the service of theological orthodoxy. In point of fact, it was through the incarnation that God unveiled his existence as Father, Son, and Spirit. Therefore, for the church, the doctrine of the Trinity is not a matter of idle speculation, but the result of God's self-communicative unveiling, through which he secures his ultimate purpose for humanity: to bring us to share in the Father's eternal love for the Son in the communion of the Spirit. The church is Trinitarian not primarily or simply out of dutiful obedience to biblical data, but because, in union with the incarnate Christ through the communion of the Spirit, we have come to know the love of his Father. The church's doctrine of the Trinity, from its very inception in the apostolic witness, was born from an encounter and experience of the "grace of the Lord Jesus Christ and the love of God and the fellowship of the Holy Spirit" (2 Cor. 13:14). In other words, the church's confession and worship of the triune God is born from her confession and worship of the Word become flesh. That is why theology that makes much of the incarnation of the Son makes much of his Father and the Spirit, and, sadly, why theology that makes little of the incarnation finds less and less reason to be robustly and explicitly Trinitarian.

2. *A minimizing of the incarnation necessarily devalues the significance of the* person *of Jesus Christ in relation to salvation.* His teachings, and especially his atoning work, may still be emphasized, but they rapidly come to replace his living being as the principle of salvation. The mediatorial humanity of Christ Jesus (1 Tim. 2:5) comes to be seen as effect-producing rather than life-giving, the incarnation merely serving as a divine mechanism to secure a salvation that is performed by Christ but that is ultimately external to him. With his person receding into the background, the church's christology becomes merely a predicate of her soteriology, the person of Christ serving merely as an "outward apparatus of [a] theory of redemp-

tion, the divine machinery of salvation, rather than the very substance and process of this salvation itself."[3] Jesus Christ, accordingly, may come to be viewed as the One who accomplishes salvation even if he is not himself the substance and sum of that salvation. Predictably, *salvation* is thought to be available to sinners outside of a real and living union with the incarnate, crucified, resurrected, ascended *Savior*. His work effectively replacing his person, soteriology becomes preoccupied with the exposition and description of objectified benefits won by Christ, benefits transmitted to those who have faith, but ultimately separable from him. When the incarnation is viewed in such a perfunctory or conditional way, as the mere means by which the work of atonement is accomplished, it is no longer clear why Christ's continual existence in our redeemed human flesh is necessary. Jesus's insistence—"Whoever feeds on my flesh and drinks my blood has eternal life" (John 6:54)—becomes increasingly puzzling and unnerving, dying the death of a thousand theological qualifications. The pastoral implications prove devastating.

3. *A minimizing of the incarnation leads to a minimalistic ecclesiology.* Just as our soteriology is meant to be a predicate of our christology, and not the other way around, our ecclesiology is intended to be a predicate of both. The answers to the questions "Who is Jesus Christ?" and "How is Jesus Christ our salvation?" form the basis for our understanding of the church, whether or not we are conscious of it. To answer, on the one hand, that Jesus Christ is God incarnate, who through union with us has sanctified and justified our sinful humanity in his birth, life, death, resurrection, and ascension—such that he is himself the saving mediation between God and man—is to answer that the church is constituted and defined only on the basis of her union with him through the Spirit. The church, which is Christ's body, has no existence apart from his real, self-giving, and saving presence, through which she is brought to life as his body and bride, continually sustained and nourished by him. To answer, on the other hand, that Jesus Christ took on a human nature for the purpose of securing a salvation that is available to sinners outside of union with his incarnate humanity— obviating the necessity of his real, personal presence and of his ongoing

---

[3] John Williamson Nevin, *Antichrist: or the Spirit of Sect and Schism*, in *The Anxious Bench, Antichrist and the Sermon Catholic Unity*, ed. Augustine Thompson (1848; repr., Eugene, OR: Wipf & Stock, 2000), 39. Despite its regrettably polemical title, Nevin's essay is profoundly prescient in its assessment of the dangers attending the devaluation of the mystery of Christ's person, which he believed would come to plague the church.

mediatorial humanity—is to answer that the church may be constituted and defined in his absence. The history of evangelical Protestantism, at least, has shown that this second answer quickly leads to ecclesiologies that revolve around, and founder upon, little more than the church's memorial tribute to and gratitude for the work of a Savior whose real presence is no longer necessary for her salvation. As such, preaching becomes merely the occasion for exegetical insightfulness and personal winsomeness; water, bread, and wine merely signs; and the body of Christ merely a figure of speech. The implications for the church prove devastating.

4. *When our theology is pulled away from the reality of the incarnation, and so begins to lapse into the abstractions noted above, not only does our theology become un-Christian, but so does our thinking about everything else.* To confess that the incarnate Son of God is the meaning and central fact of the world is not to trade in sentimentalizing platitudes, but simply to state the profound mystery that the world was created by, through, and for him (Col. 1:16), that the universe is upheld by him (Heb. 1:3), and that all things in heaven and earth will finally be united in him (Eph. 1:10). How, then, shall *anything* be thought of rightly except in direct relation to Jesus Christ, who is in his person the meaning of God and the meaning of the world, the One who unites heaven and earth? When the incarnate *Logos* ceases to function as the inner *logic* of the church's thinking, she is defenseless against the perpetual threat of dualistic, disintegrating patterns of thought. When Jesus Christ is pulled away from the center of our thinking, we are compelled to deal in abstractions, succumbing alternately to materialism and hyper-spiritualism, captivated by cultural fads and political ideologies rather than beholden to the Way, Truth, and Life that is Jesus Christ. It is not long before thinking and speaking from a center in Jesus Christ come to be considered—by Christians, mind you—as shallow, impertinent, and even annoyingly pietistic: What has Jesus Christ to do with sex, politics, football, food, clothing, or technology anyway? The relevancy of Christ having been exhausted by, and relegated to, "spiritual" matters, Christian thought becomes indistinguishable from secular thinking, albeit ever so thinly veiled in Christian lingo. The noetic implications prove devastating.

It is the task and privilege of theology to conform and attune our minds and hearts to God's self-revelation and self-giving in his Son and through his Spirit, that the church may ever more delight in him. Theology is meant to sing to Jesus Christ, for he alone is the Way, Truth, and Life of God—the full, final, and saving revelation of the Creator, creature, and creation. If our singing in these pages has been unfaithful to this holy task, may it suffer the withering of the grass and the fading of the flower, even as the Word of God stands forever. All praise be to him.

Bibliography

Achtemeier, Mark, and Andrew Purves. *Union in Christ: A Declaration for the Church.* Louisville, KY: Witherspoon, 1999.

Allen, R. Michael. *The Christ's Faith: A Dogmatic Account.* T&T Clark Studies in Systematic Theology. London: T&T Clark, 2009.

Anderson, Ray S. *On Being Human: Essays in Theological Anthropology.* Grand Rapids: Eerdmans, 1982.

Avis, Paul D. L. *The Church in the Theology of the Reformers.* 1981; reprint, Eugene, OR: Wipf & Stock, 2002.

Badcock, Gary D. *The House Where God Lives: The Doctrine of the Church.* Grand Rapids: Eerdmans, 2009.

Baillie, D. M. *God Was in Christ: An Essay on Incarnation and Atonement.* New York: Scribner's, 1948.

Barth, Karl. *Church Dogmatics.* Edited by G. W. Bromiley and T. F. Torrance. Translated by G. W. Bromiley. Peabody, MA: Hendrickson, 2010.

Bauckham, Richard. "'Only the Suffering God Can Help': Divine Passibility in Modern Theology." *Themelios* 9, no. 3 (April 1984): 6–12.

Berkhof, Louis. *Systematic Theology.* 1932; reprint, Grand Rapids: Eerdmans, 1996.

Best, Ernst. *Ephesians.* Edinburgh, UK: T&T Clark, 1998.

Blocher, Henri. *In the Beginning: The Opening Chapters of Genesis.* Downers Grove, IL: IVP, 1984.

Bloesch, Donald G. *Essentials of Evangelical Theology.* Peabody, MA: Prince, 1998.

Bonhoeffer, Dietrich. *Christ the Center.* Translated by Edwin H. Robertson. New York: Harper & Row, 1978.

———. *Ethics.* Edited by Eberhard Bethge. 1955; reprint, New York: Macmillan, 1979.

Boston, Thomas. *Human Nature in Its Fourfold State.* Carlisle, PA: Banner of Truth Trust, 1964; reprint, 1989.

Bray, Gerald L. *Creeds, Councils and Christ: Did the Early Christians Misrepresent Jesus?* Fearn, Ross-shire, UK: Mentor, 1997.

Caldwell, Robert W. *Communion in the Spirit: The Holy Spirit as the Bond of Union in the Theology of Jonathan Edwards.* Studies in Evangelical History and Thought. Eugene, OR: Wipf & Stock, 2007.

Calvin, John. *Calvin's Commentaries*. Edinburgh, UK: Calvin Translation Society, 1844–56; reprint, Grand Rapids: Baker, 2003.

———. *Calvin's New Testament Commentaries*. 12 vols. Edited by David W. Torrance and Thomas F. Torrance. Grand Rapids: Eerdmans, 1959–1972.

———. *Calvin: Theological Treatises*. Translated by J. K. S. Reid. Library of Christian Classics, vol. 22. Philadelphia: Westminster, 1954.

———. *Institutes of the Christian Religion*. 2 vols. Edited by John T. McNeill. Translated by Ford Lewis Battles. Library of Christian Classics, vols. 20–21. Philadelphia: Westminster, 1960.

———. *Tracts and Letters*. 2 vols. Translated and edited by Henry Beveridge. Carlisle, PA: Banner of Truth Trust, 2009.

Campbell, Constantine R. *Paul and Union with Christ: An Exegetical and Theological Study*. Grand Rapids: Zondervan, 2012.

Canlis, Julie. *Calvin's Ladder: A Spiritual Theology of Ascent and Ascension*. Grand Rapids: Eerdmans, 2010.

Carson, D. A. *The Difficult Doctrine of the Love of God*. Wheaton, IL: Crossway, 2000.

———. *The Gospel According to John*. Pillar New Testament Commentary. Grand Rapids: Eerdmans, 1991.

Catechism of the Catholic Church. 2nd edition. Vatican City: Libreria Editrice Vaticana, 1997.

Chan, Simon. *Liturgical Theology: The Church as Worshiping Community*. Downers Grove, IL: IVP, 2006.

Chesterton, G. K. *Orthodoxy*. 1908; reprint, Colorado Springs, CO: Harold Shaw, 2001.

Clark, John C. "Satisfaction, Intercession, Participation: John Calvin on Receiving Christ and Enjoying the Benefits of His Priesthood." In *Between the Lectern and the Pulpit: Essays in Honour of Victor A. Shepherd*. Edited by Rob Clements and Dennis Ngien. Vancouver, BC: Regent College Publishing, 2014.

Cranfield, C. E. B. *The Epistle to the Romans*. ICC. Edinburgh, UK: T&T Clark, 1998.

Crisp, Oliver D. "By His Birth We Are Healed: Our Redemption, It Turns Out, Began Long Before Calvary." *Christianity Today* 56, no. 3 (March 2012): 30–34.

Cross, F. L., and E. A. Livingstone, editors. *The Oxford Dictionary of the Christian Church*. 3rd edition. New York: Oxford University Press, 1997.

Cyril of Alexandria. *On the Unity of Christ*. Translated by John Anthony McGuckin. New York: St. Vladimir's Seminary Press, 1995.

Davis, Thomas J. *This Is My Body: The Presence of Christ in Reformation Thought*. Grand Rapids: Baker, 2008.

Dawson, Gerrit Scott, editor. *An Introduction to Torrance Theology: Discovering the Incarnate Saviour*. London: T&T Clark, 2007.

DeBie, Linden J., editor. *Coena Mystica: Debating Reformed Eucharistic Theology*. Mercersburg Theology Study Series, vol. 2. Eugene, OR: Wipf & Stock, 2013.

Dunn, James D. G. *Romans 9–16*. Word Biblical Commentary. Dallas, TX: Word, 1988.

———. *The Theology of Paul the Apostle*. Grand Rapids: Eerdmans, 1998.

Edwards, Jonathan. *The Works of Jonathan Edwards*. Edited by Thomas A. Schafer. New Haven, CT: Yale University Press, 1994.

Evans, William B. "Twin Sons of Different Mothers: The Remarkable Theological Convergence of John W. Nevin and Thomas F. Torrance." *Haddington House Journal* 11 (2009): 155–73.

Fairbairn, Donald. *Life in the Trinity: An Introduction to Theology with the Help of the Church Fathers*. Downers Grove, IL: IVP, 2009.

Fortman, Edmund J. *The Triune God: A Historical Study of the Doctrine of the Trinity*. Philadelphia: Westminster, 1972.

Gaffin, Richard B. *Resurrection and Redemption: A Study in Paul's Soteriology*. 2nd edition. Phillipsburg, NJ: P&R, 1987.

George, Timothy, editor. *God the Holy Trinity: Reflections on Christian Faith and Practice*. Beeson Divinity Series. Grand Rapids: Baker Academic, 2006.

González, Justo L. *A History of Christian Thought*. 2nd revised edition. 3 vols. Nashville: Abingdon, 1987.

Goroncy, Jason. "The Elusiveness, Loss and Cruciality of Recovered Holiness: Some Biblical and Theological Observations." *IJST* 10, no. 2 (April 2008): 195–209.

Grenz, Stanley J. *The Social God and the Relational Self: A Trinitarian Theology of the Imago Dei*. Louisville, KY: Westminster John Knox, 2001.

———, and Roger E. Olson. *20th-Century Theology: God and the World in a Transitional Age*. Downers Grove, IL: IVP Academic, 1992.

Grounds, Vernon C. "The Postulate of Paradox." *Bulletin of the Evangelical Theological Society* 7, no. 1 (Winter 1964): 3–21.

Grudem, Wayne. *Systematic Theology: An Introduction to Biblical Doctrine*. Grand Rapids: Zondervan, 2000.

Gunton, Colin E. *Act and Being: Towards a Theology of the Divine Attributes*. Grand Rapids: Eerdmans, 2003.

———. *Christ and Creation*. Grand Rapids: Eerdmans, 1992.

Hall, Christopher A., and Steven D. Boyer. *The Mystery of God: Theology for Knowing the Unknowable*. Grand Rapids: Baker, 2012.

Hall, David, editor. *A Theological Guide to Calvin's Institutes: Essays and Analysis*. Phillipsburg, NJ: P&R, 2008.

Hanson, R. P. C. *The Search for the Christian Doctrine of God: The Arian Controversy, 318–381*. London: T&T Clark, 1988.

Harnack, Adolf. *History of Dogma*. Translated by Neil Buchanan. London: Williams & Norgate, 1894.

———. *What Is Christianity?* Translated by Thomas Bailey Saunders. 1902; reprint, Philadelphia: Fortress, 1986.

Hart, Trevor. "Humankind in Christ and Christ in Humankind: Salvation as Participation in Our Substitute in the Theology of John Calvin." *SJT* 42, no. 1 (February 1989): 67–84.

Hawthorne, Gerald F., Ralph P. Martin, and Daniel G. Reid, editors. *Dictionary of Paul and His Letters*. Downers Grove, IL: IVP, 1993.

Hodge, Charles. *Systematic Theology*. Grand Rapids: Eerdmans, 1977.

Hoehner, Harold. *Ephesians: An Exegetical Commentary*. Grand Rapids: Baker Academic, 2002.

Hoekema, Anthony. *Created in God's Image*. Grand Rapids: Eerdmans, 1986.

———. *Saved by Grace*. Grand Rapids: Eerdmans, 1989.

Holmes, Christopher R. J. "The Theological Function of the Doctrine of the Divine Attributes and the Divine Glory, with Special Reference to Karl Barth and His Reading of the Protestant Orthodox." *Scottish Journal of Theology* 61, no. 2 (May 2008): 206–23.

Holmes, Stephen R. "The Attributes of God." In *The Oxford Handbook of Systematic Theology*. Edited by John Webster, Kathryn Tanner, and Iain Torrance, 54–71. New York: Oxford University Press, 2007.

———. "Something Much Too Plain to Say: Towards a Defense of the Doctrine of Divine Simplicity." *Neue Zeitschrift für Systematische Theologie und Religionsphilosophie* 43, no. 1 (January 2001): 137–54.

Hooker, Richard. *Laws of Ecclesiastical Polity*. In *The Works of That Learned and Judicious Divine Mr. Richard Hooker*. Oxford, UK: Clarendon, 1865.

Husbands, Mark, and Daniel J. Treier, editors. *The Community of the Word: Toward an Evangelical Ecclesiology*. Downers Grove, IL: IVP, 2005.

Johnson, Marcus Peter. "Luther and Calvin on Union with Christ." *Fides et Historia* 39, no. 2 (2007): 59–77.

———. *One with Christ: An Evangelical Theology of Salvation*. Wheaton, IL: Crossway, 2013.

Kapic, Kelly M. "Christian Existence and the Incarnation: Humiliation of the Name." Unpublished plenary address. Evangelical Theological Society, November 2011, San Francisco, CA.

———. *A Little Book for New Theologians: Why and How to Study Theology*. Downers Grove, IL: IVP Academic, 2012.

———. "The Son's Assumption of a Human Nature: A Call for Clarity." *IJST* 3, no. 2 (July 2001): 154–66.

Kelly, J. N. D. *Early Christian Doctrines*. London: Adam & Charles Black, 1958.

Kettler, Christian D. *The Vicarious Humanity of Christ and the Reality of Salvation*. Eugene, OR: Wipf & Stock, 2010.

———, and Todd H. Speidell, editors. *Incarnational Ministry: The Presence of Christ in Church, Society, and Family*. 1990; reprint, Eugene, OR: Wipf & Stock, 2009.

Kuyper, Abraham. *The Work of the Holy Spirit*. Translated by Henri De Vries. 1900; reprint, Grand Rapids: Eerdmans, 1941.

Leith, John H. *Basic Christian Doctrine*. Louisville, KY: Westminster John Knox, 1993.

———, editor. *Creeds of the Churches: A Reader in Christian Doctrine from the Bible to the Present*. 3rd edition. Louisville, KY: John Knox, 1982.

Letham, Robert. *The Holy Trinity: In Scripture, History, Theology, and Worship*. Phillipsburg, NJ: P&R, 2004.

Lewis, C. S. *Letters of C. S. Lewis*. Edited by Walter Hooper. 1993; reprint, Orlando: Harvest, 2003.

———. *Miracles*. 1947; reprint, New York: Touchstone, 1996.

———. *The Weight of Glory*. 1949; reprint, New York: HarperCollins, 2001.

Lohse, Bernhard. *Martin Luther's Theology: Its Historical and Systematic Development*. Minneapolis: Fortress, 1999.

Luther, Martin. *Luther's Works*. 55 vols. Edited by Jaroslav Pelikan and Helmut T. Lehmann. St. Louis: Concordia; Philadelphia: Fortress, 1955.

Lutheran Book of Worship, Minister's Desk Edition. Inter-Lutheran Commission on Worship. Minneapolis: Augsburg Fortress, 1978.

Marshall, I. Howard. *Aspects of the Atonement: Cross and Resurrection in the Reconciling of God and Humanity*. Milton Keynes, UK: Paternoster, 2007.

McGrath, Alister E. *Christian Theology: An Introduction*. 2nd edition. Oxford, UK: Blackwell, 1997.

———. *Understanding Doctrine: What It Is—and Why It Matters*. Grand Rapids: Zondervan, 1990.

Meilaender, Gilbert, and William Werpehowski, editors. *Oxford Handbook of Theological Ethics*. Oxford, UK: Oxford University Press, 2005.

Metzger, Paul Louis. "Mystical Union with Christ: An Alternative to Blood Transfusions and Legal Fictions." *Westminster Theological Journal* 65, no. 2 (Fall 2003): 201–13.

Monod, Adolphe. *Adophe Monod's Farewell to His Friends and to His Church*. Translated by Owen Thomas. London: Banner of Truth Trust, 1962.

Moo, Douglas. *The Epistle to the Romans*. New International Commentary on the New Testament. Grand Rapids: Eerdmans, 1996.

Mouw, Richard J., and Douglas A. Sweeney. *The Suffering and Victorious Christ: Toward a More Compassionate Christology*. Grand Rapids: Baker Academic, 2013.

Murray, Andrew. *The Holiest of All*. 1921; reprint, Springdale, PA: Whitaker House, 1996.

Nevin, John Williamson. "Dr. Hodge on the Mystical Presence." *Weekly Messenger of the German Reformed Church* 13, no. 7 (May 24, 1848).

———. *The Mystical Presence: A Vindication of the Reformed or Calvinistic Doctrine of the Holy Eucharist*. 1848; reprint, Philadelphia: J. B. Lippencott, 1846.

Ngien, Dennis. *The Suffering of God According to Martin Luther's Theologia Crucis*. Vancouver, BC: Regent College Publishing, 2005.

Nygren, Anders. *Commentary on Romans*. Translated by Carl C. Rasmussen. Philadelphia: Muhlenberg, 1949.

Packer, J. I. *Keep in Step with the Spirit*. Grand Rapids: Fleming H. Revell, 1984.

———. *Knowing God*. 20th anniversary edition. Downers Grove, IL: IVP, 1993.

Pascal, Blaise. *Pensées*. Translated by A. J. Krailsheimer. New York: Penguin, 1995.

Pelikan, Jaroslav. *The Christian Tradition: A History of the Development of Doctrine*. 5 vols. Chicago: University of Chicago Press, 1975–1991.

Perry, Michael W., editor. *Chesterton Day by Day: The Wit and Wisdom of G. K. Chesterton*. Seattle: Inkling, 2002.

Peterman, Gerald W. *Joy and Tears: The Emotional Life of the Christian*. Chicago: Moody, 2013.

Plantinga, Cornelius. *Not the Way It's Supposed to Be: A Breviary of Sin.* Grand Rapids: Eerdmans, 1995.

Purves, Andrew. *Reconstructing Pastoral Theology: A Christological Foundation.* Louisville, KY: Westminster John Knox, 2004.

———. "Who Is the Incarnate Saviour of the World?" In *An Introduction to Torrance Theology: Discovering the Incarnate Saviour.* Edited by Gerrit Scott Dawson, 21–31. London: T&T Clark, 2007.

Reeves, Michael. *Delighting in the Trinity: An Introduction to the Christian Faith.* Downers Grove, IL: IVP Academic, 2012.

Reno, R. R. *Genesis.* Brazos Theological Commentary on the Bible. Grand Rapids: Brazos, 2010.

Reynolds, Barbara, editor. *The Letters of Dorothy L. Sayers.* Cambridge, UK: Dorothy L. Sayers Society, 1997.

Roberts, Alexander, and James Donaldson, editors. *Ante-Nicene Fathers.* Peabody, MA: Hendrickson, 2004.

Sanders, Fred. *The Deep Things of God: How the Trinity Changes Everything.* Wheaton, IL: Crossway, 2010.

Schaff, Philip, and Henry Wace, editors. *Nicene and Post-Nicene Fathers.* 1890; reprint, Peabody, MA: Hendrickson, 1995.

Schleiermacher, Friedrich. *The Christian Faith.* Edited by H. R. Mackintosh and J. S. Stewart. New York: Harper Torchbooks, 1963.

Schmemann, Alexander. *For the Life of the World: Sacraments and Orthodoxy.* Crestwood, NY: St. Vladimir's Seminary Press, 1973.

Shepherd, Victor A. *Our Evangelical Faith.* Toronto, ON: Clements, 2006.

———. "Thomas F. Torrance and the *Homoousion* of the Holy Spirit." *Participatio: The Journal of the Thomas F. Torrance Theological Fellowship* 3 (2012): 108–24.

Smail, Thomas A. *The Forgotten Father.* Grand Rapids: Eerdmans, 1981.

———. *Like Father, Like Son: The Trinity Imaged in Our Humanity.* Grand Rapids: Eerdmans, 2005.

Smedes, Lewis. *Sex for Christians.* Grand Rapids: Eerdmans, 1994.

Smith, Christian. *The Bible Made Impossible: Why Biblicism Is Not a Truly Evangelical Reading of Scripture.* Grand Rapids: Brazos, 2012.

Stott, John R. W. *The Message of Romans.* Downers Grove, IL: IVP, 1994.

Taylor, Justin. "6 Quotes That Luther Didn't Actually Say." *Gospel Coalition Blog.* February 20, 2014. www.thegospelcoalition.org/blogs/justintaylor/2014/02/20/5-quotes-that-luther-didnt-actually-say.

Thielicke, Helmut. *Between God and Satan.* Translated by C. C. Barber. Grand Rapids: Eerdmans, 1962.

———. *Ethics of Sex.* Translated by John W. Doberstein. New York: Harper & Row, 1964.

Thielman, Frank. *Ephesians.* Baker Exegetical Commentary on the New Testament. Grand Rapids: Baker, 2010.

Thompson, Augustine, editor. *The Anxious Bench, Antichrist and the Sermon Catholic Unity.* Eugene, OR: Wipf & Stock, 2000.

Torrance, James B. "The Vicarious Humanity and Priesthood of Christ in the Theology of John Calvin." In *Calvinus Ecclesiae Doctor*. Edited by W. H. Neuser. Kampen: J. H. Kok, 1979.

―――. *Worship, Community, and the Triune God of Grace*. Downers Grove, IL: IVP Academic, 1996.

Torrance, Thomas F. *Atonement: The Person and Work of Christ*. Edited by Robert T. Walker. Downers Grove, IL: IVP Academic, 2009.

―――. *The Christian Doctrine of God: One Being Three Persons*. Edinburgh, UK: T&T Clark, 1996; reprint, 2006.

―――. *The Christian Doctrine of Marriage*. Edinburgh, UK: Scottish Academic Press, 1989.

―――, editor. *The Incarnation: Ecumenical Studies in the Nicene-Constantinopolitan Creed A.D. 381*. Eugene, OR: Wipf & Stock, 1998.

―――. *Incarnation: The Person and Life of Christ*. Edited by Robert T. Walker. Downers Grove, IL: IVP Academic, 2008.

―――. *The Mediation of Christ*. Revised edition. Colorado Springs, CO: Helmers & Howard, 1992.

―――. *The School of Faith: The Catechisms of the Reformed Church*. New York: Harper, 1959.

―――. *Theology in Reconstruction*. Eugene, OR: Wipf & Stock, 1996.

―――. *The Trinitarian Faith: The Evangelical Theology of the Ancient Catholic Church*. London: T&T Clark, 1991.

Vander Zee, Leonard J. *Christ, Baptism and the Lord's Supper: Recovering the Sacraments for Evangelical Worship*. Downers Grove, IL: IVP Academic, 2004.

Volf, Miroslav. *After Our Likeness: The Church as the Image of the Trinity*. Grand Rapids: Eerdmans, 1998.

Waltke, Bruce. *An Old Testament Theology*. Grand Rapids: Zondervan, 2007.

Webster, John. *Holiness*. Grand Rapids: Eerdmans, 2003.

―――. *Holy Scripture: A Dogmatic Sketch*. Cambridge, UK: Cambridge University Press, 2003.

―――. "Incarnation." In *The Blackwell Companion to Modern Theology*. Edited by Gareth Jones, 204–25. Oxford, UK: Blackwell, 2004.

―――. "Principles of Systematic Theology." *International Journal of Systematic Theology* 11, no. 1 (January 2009): 56–71.

Weinandy, Thomas. *In the Likeness of Sinful Flesh: An Essay on the Humanity of Christ*. Edinburgh, UK: T&T Clark, 1993.

West, Christopher. *Theology of the Body for Beginners*. West Chester, PA: Ascension, 2004.

Young, Frances M. *From Nicaea to Chalcedon: A Guide to the Literature and its Background*. Philadelphia: Fortress, 1983.

Zizioulas, John. *Being as Communion*. Crestwood, NY: St. Vladimir's Seminary Press, 1985.

General Index

Scripture Index

Also Available from Marcus Peter Johnson

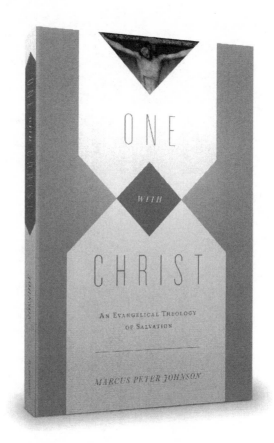

"Johnson does his job outstandingly well, giving us a book that merits careful study."
J. I. PACKER, Board of Governors' Professor of Theology, Regent College

"An excellent discussion of union with Christ."
ROBERT LETHAM, Director of Research and Senior Lecturer in Systematic and Historical Theology, Wales Evangelical School of Theology; author, *Union with Christ*

"This fine book rightly expounds union with Christ as the heart of Scripture's approach to the Christian life."
VICTOR A. SHEPHERD, Professor of Theology, Tyndale University College and Seminary, Toronto

---